The Dysfunctional Politics of the Affordable Care Act

The Dysfunctional Politics of the Affordable Care Act

Greg M. Shaw

 PRAEGER™

An Imprint of ABC-CLIO, LLC

Santa Barbara, California • Denver, Colorado

Library of Congress Cataloging-in-Publication Data

Names: Shaw, Greg M., author.
Title: The dysfunctional politics of the Affordable Care Act / Greg M. Shaw.
Description: Santa Barbara, California : Praeger, [2017] | Includes bibliographical
    references and index.
Identifiers: LCCN 2017006628 (print) | LCCN 2017010062 (ebook) | ISBN
    9781440840029 (alk. paper) | ISBN 9781440840036 (ebook)
Subjects: | MESH: United States. Patient Protection and Affordable Care Act. |
    National Health Insurance, United States—legislation & jurisprudence | Health Care
    Reform—legislation & jurisprudence | Health Policy | Politics | United States
Classification: LCC HG9396 (print) | LCC HG9396 (ebook) | NLM W 32.5 AA1 | DDC
    368.38/200973—dc23
LC record available at https://lccn.loc.gov/2017006628

ISBN: 978-1-4408-4002-9
EISBN: 978-1-4408-4003-6

21 20 19 18 17   1 2 3 4 5

This book is also available as an eBook.

Praeger
An Imprint of ABC-CLIO, LLC

ABC-CLIO, LLC
130 Cremona Drive, P.O. Box 1911
Santa Barbara, California 93116–1911
www.abc-clio.com

This book is printed on acid-free paper ∞

Manufactured in the United States of America

Dedicated to my parents

Contents

Preface

It is difficult to overstate the importance of health care provision and financing to Americans' lives. In 2017, U.S. residents will spend over 17 percent of the nation's gross domestic product on health services and products, making it one of the largest sectors of the economy. More than $1 trillion will pass through the hands of the private health insurance industry, making it a formidable political and economic force. Health services will account for over 27 percent of the federal budget, making it one of the most expensive categories of government spending. Perhaps most importantly, Americans will likely continue to trust their health care providers and distrust their politicians, complicating health policy reforms that could address these problems.

Contemporary American politics has not lent itself to a healthy public discourse about health policy. Just at the moment when informative conversations could help nonspecialists better understand how to match up their values, problems, and possible solutions, American public discourse is instead impoverished to the point that it fosters a lack of a clear defense by recent policy proponents and subterfuge by opponents. Instead of hearing policy talk laden with problem identification and reasoned solutions, the public has been subjected to and encouraged to participate in bumper-sticker conversations that tend to be long on partisan attacks and counterattacks and short on thoughtful debate. This book will not be able to explain fully all of the difficulties and opportunities facing the various actors involved here. However, I hope it will shed significant light on the debate over the Patient Protection and Affordable Care Act. The goal is to challenge and enliven readers' understanding of the most significant piece of health legislation enacted since Medicare and Medicaid were created a half-century ago, in addition to whatever its successor plans might be under Republican efforts to grapple with the issues of health care cost, quality, and access. Since the 2010 passage of the Affordable Care Act, health policy has been and will almost certainly continue to be a moving target. The lessons learned under the ACA have been important. The policy revisions adopted by the 115th Congress and the Trump administration will likely represent a mix of moves that both build on the past and try new experiments, much as the Affordable Care Act did. For policy makers, health service providers, and others, much work still lies ahead. The mass public will need to be a conversation partner—along with politicians, journalists, and others—if our politics is to harmonize Americans' values, needs, and capacities.

One of the goals of this book is to identify the counterproductive ways in which many American politicians over the past several years have chosen to discuss the complicated issues involved in health care reform. Another is to suggest how the public could be better served as it confronts one of the most pressing policy challenges of our time. Because so much is at stake as individuals, employers, medical professionals, and government officials decide how to seek, provide, and finance health services, this book takes a point of view. My abiding belief in the potential collective wisdom of the public leads me to advocate for the clearest and most honest discourse our political institutions can foster. Some readers may accuse me of being optimistic, but if the alternative is to surrender to a politics of cynicism, raw partisan warfare, and sloganeering, I stand guilty as charged.

A considerable amount of evidence shows that the public can make good collective decisions when provided with a reasonable amount of substantially correct information about the problems it faces and the policy choices it might make. By working within this perspective, I stand on the shoulders of a good number of insightful thinkers who have identified the potential strengths and wisdom of the American public.[1] Very briefly, individuals do not require complete information about complex issues to make rational decisions. Modest learning will often suffice, under the right conditions. Further, collective public opinion typically displays desirable characteristics—stability, factual accuracy, and reasonableness of responses to events among them—although these qualities are often lacking at the individual level. Given these insights, if the debate over health policy were conducted differently, public learning could be significantly improved.

Writing a small book on a big topic poses several challenges. First, while I bring to this project what is usually a progressive set of lenses, I am also a policy pragmatist. Keeping one's eyes on the goal of crafting health care financing and delivery systems that work well for the broad population during a time of highly polarized politics is as important as it is difficult. These chapters consider the values that Americans hold about health care provision and the debates surrounding those values, but they also strive to bring to bear a good deal of evidence about how these debates have undermined public understanding, and they suggest more productive ways forward. These are, after all, matters of life and death.

Second, health care policy is in the midst of a rapidly evolving period. This manuscript went to press shortly after Donald Trump was sworn in as our 45th president and began work with a Republican Congress, both determined to turn back many of the policies of the Obama years. As Republicans set about their work to end some of the experiments that were built into the Affordable Care Act, a great many questions remain unanswered. However, when reflecting on whatever replacement plans emerge in 2017 and beyond, readers should bear in mind that just as the ACA was a policy experiment, its provisions were also important steps along a meandering—some would say tortured—path toward improved cost control, insurance coverage, and quality enhancements. Hence, regardless of what the next round of health policy reform looks like, lessons learned from the passage of the ACA will likely inform Americans' perspectives on these matters for a long time to come. For instance, the ACA affirmed that Americans want more consumer protections from insurance company practices. Service providers incorporated greater efficiencies into their practices. State policy makers want more control over their health care expenditures. Employers and market-oriented policy advocates stand emboldened in their desire to see medical patients treated more like selective consumers.

Third, a lot has been written about the ACA. I strive to minimize the overlap between my text and the several superb book-length treatments of this important legislation, including Paul Starr's *Remedy and Reaction*, Stuart Altman and David Schackman's *Power, Politics, and Universal Health Care*, John McDonough's *Inside National Health Reform*, and Stephen Brill's *America's Bitter Pill*. Readers who want to learn more should consult these accounts as well as other books appearing in the Suggested Further Readings section.

Lastly, I have been determined not to engage in too much Monday-morning quarterbacking. Hindsight certainly tempts one to see inevitability where that was not the case, but as this account shows, the policy outcomes that have materialized to date were not in fact inevitable, nor will the future of health policy be.

* * *

The acclaimed short-story writer Alice Munro notes that she often does not read narratives front to back, but rather wanders around the text to find out what happens.[2] These chapters do not entirely progress chronologically, so readers should feel free to wander around. The first two chapters explain why the Democrats crafted the ACA the way they did—with particular attention given to the hugely controversial individual mandate to obtain insurance—and why the Republicans fought the law so fiercely. Chapters 3 and 4 examine the market metaphor that many conservatives apply to health care purchases and explain how a version of this argument helped many Republican state officials to eventually make peace with the ACA's optional expansion of Medicaid despite their you-can't-make-me resistance to this provision during the law's first few years. The ACA was designed not only to focus on access to health services but also to control costs. Chapter 5 examines recent spending patterns and reflects on how limited Congress's tools have been over the past few decades in containing public expenditures. Chapter 6 paints a longitudinal mosaic of public knowledge of the Affordable Care Act's specific provisions, as well as its evaluations of the ACA since 2010. Finally, Chapter 7 considers some of the implications for repealing the policy experiment that was the ACA and its replacement with what will almost certainly be a series of new experiments, in addition to reflecting on some steps Americans might take toward a more constructive public discourse on health care policy.

*   *   *

I have incurred many debts and owe quite a lot of people my gratitude for their help. Jessica Gribble at Praeger has been a source of encouragement and guidance from the beginning of the project, helping me to craft the overall direction as well as many steps along the way. I am grateful for my many conversations with health care professionals who lent valuable insights, including Chereé Johnson, Colleen Kannaday, Aron Klein, Mollie Ward, and Chris Zolnierek at Advocate Health Care; Ann Eckhardt, Vickie Folse, and Brenda Lesson at Illinois Wesleyan University's School of Nursing; and Bridget Wall, who works in the medical device industry. Various participants in the politics of health care also generously shared ideas. Tracy Lytwyn-Fischer and Indiana state senators Brandt Hershman and Patricia Miller helped me better understand Hoosier politics. Representative Mike Callton, Senator Curtis Hertel, Elizabeth Hertel, Representative Andy Schor, Nick Wake, and Amanda West guided me through Medicaid reform in Michigan. Colleagues read drafts, helped locate materials, and lent their time to help me think more carefully about these matters. Among them are Darryl Brown, Irv Epstein, Diego Méndez-Carbajo, William Munro, Patra Noonan, and Karen Schmidt at Illinois Wesleyan University; Timothy Jost at Washington and Lee School of Law; Robert Shapiro at Columbia University; Daniel Béland at the University of Saskatchewan; and Ashley Kirzinger and Jamie Firth at the Kaiser Family Foundation. Several student research assistants at Illinois Wesleyan lent their excellent skills, including Austin Aldag, Amy Gordon, Melissa Guzmán, Sam Kasten, Mike Kistner, Abbey Lee, Siming Peng, Robert Perez, Jordan Prats, and Alani Sweezy. Bob MacGuffie at Right Principles helped me understand some of the opposition to the ACA. Naturally, I am solely responsible for any remaining faults. I gratefully acknowledge financial support from Illinois Wesleyan University.

Of considerable importance have been my supporters at home. Mollie read and commented on many chapter drafts, in addition to being a wonderful backer in so many other ways. Ian and Fiona have tolerated a too-busy dad over the course of this project. Thanks for your patience.

CHAPTER ONE

Designing the Affordable Care Act: Fateful Decisions

When President Obama signed the Patient Protection and Affordable Care Act (ACA) into law on March 23, 2010, the lofty tenor of his comments spoke not only about his party's determination in persevering to this goal but also about how this enactment represented a culmination of a nearly century-long policy struggle. The president's words mingled self-congratulation with a simple but profound assertion about health care as a basic right. On both counts the president couched his message in historical terms about who Americans fundamentally are.

> Today, we are affirming that essential truth—a truth every generation is called to rediscover for itself—that we are not a nation that scales back its aspirations. We are not a nation that falls prey to doubt or mistrust. We don't fall prey to fear. We are not a nation that does what's easy. That's not who we are. That's not how we got here. We are a nation that faces its challenges and accepts its responsibilities . . . we are a nation that does what is hard. What is necessary. What is right. Here, in this country, we shape our own destiny. That is what we do. That is who we are. This is what makes us the United States of America. And we have now just enshrined . . . the core principle that everybody should have some basic security when it comes to health care. And it is an extraordinary achievement.[1]

The brave face President Obama put on this celebration masked the messy complexities, both technical and political, that the president surely understood his administration would have to overcome on its way to implementing the new law. Over the months leading up to this day, the president and Democratic leaders in Congress spoke extensively about the fundamental importance of extending basic health care services to all Americans. They called attention to how excessive U.S. health spending is and the burdens this places on families, employers, and governments.

They extolled the moral value of living in a nation that ensures basic health services to all its citizens. They hoped not only for a moral victory, but a political one as well.

To foster what they hoped would be an electoral success, Democratic leaders strategized about phasing in the ACA over several years. Relatively easy and consumer-friendly provisions came first. Medicare beneficiaries each received a $250 check as a down payment toward closing the prescription drug benefit gap in coverage. States scrutinized insurance premium increases and gained the option to extend Medicaid to more low-income individuals. Young people could remain on their parents' insurance policies until age 26. Insurance companies lost their ability to impose lifetime limits on coverage or to deny policies to children with preexisting medical conditions. Harder provisions would follow, safely on the other side of the 2012 presidential election and far enough into the future that the government would, presumably, enjoy sufficient time to build the required administrative infrastructure. Of course, this last part did not turn out as the law's architects planned.[2] This chapter and the next will discuss these efforts and shortcomings.

In crafting the Affordable Care Act, congressional Democrats, White House policy makers, and Department of Health and Human Services staff strove to accomplish things that had never been attempted on this scale. Copying at the national level what Massachusetts undertook in 2006, with individual and employer mandates for insurance, could be imagined in principle but proved different in practice. In covering the estimated 6 percent of Massachusetts's population that was previously uninsured, officials faced a fairly straightforward task implementing their new law.[3] Accomplishing the same for tens of millions of Americans, many living in states whose political leadership stood opposed to the ACA, proved substantially more difficult. Some of these difficulties were technical: monitoring private insurers, coaxing hospitals into more efficient use of Medicare for in-patients, and guiding ordinary citizens through online insurance purchases. Other problems ran into the buzz-saw of partisan politics. Despite billions of federal dollars on offer, about one-half of the states initially, for transparently political reasons, declined the Medicaid expansion, leaving millions of potentially eligible persons uninsured. To the law's designers, the sweeteners, including virtually comprehensive federal funding for the Medicaid expansion for the first three years and very generous terms after that, were thought to be enough to overcome political resistance. Not only were they wrong about the take-up rate, but they immediately faced lawsuits challenging the legality of the planned expansion.

Democratic leaders expected the public to come along, once millions of Americans fully realized how subsidies would help make insurance affordable. Instead, public resistance to the individual mandate solidified and persisted, with opposition having much more to do with Americans' political ideology and party than their own insurance status. The formula of universal coverage through mandatory private insurance with government subsidies proved insufficient to overcome concerns about big government, partisan politics, and distrust of the insurance industry. What the White House and congressional Democrats granted insufficient credence was just how deep seated the resistance would be. Instead of coming along, the public was drawn into an epic political fight carried on in dysfunctional terms, driven by raw partisanship, and, as these chapters argue, somewhat unlikely to lead to either a satisfactory set of policy outcomes or a truly informative public discourse in the near future.

Why This Book at This Time?

The point of this book is not to argue that somehow Democratic lawmakers should have known better than to write the ACA as they did. Rather, these chapters explain why they pursued the provisions they did and how those choices propelled one of the more protracted, expensive, and frankly uncivil political fights the United States has experienced in recent memory. In response to the Democrats' fateful policy choices but also in opposing comprehensive reform per se, congressional Republicans adopted a course of resistance that led them to essentially become the party of "no" on health care reform, with members spending far more time criticizing the ACA than proposing workable alternatives, at least up through the 2016 elections. In the meantime, the political discourse surrounding the new law caused most ordinary Americans largely to lose sight of the fundamental values at stake and knowledge of good practices in health care quality, service delivery, and financing. As policy makers and health care professionals work to develop and sustain systems that can meet the needs of a national population of some 325 million people in a time of large budget deficits, profound economic inequality, and advancing health technology, the general public needs to be a vital partner. However, the dysfunctional politics surrounding the ACA marginalized citizens at precisely the moment when their participation mattered so greatly to understanding and meaningfully debating the problems facing Americans' health and their wallets. Instead, the debate substantially became one framed by partisan electoral advantage rather than by thoughtful policy advocacy or critique. Both parties erred in approaching these issues, and both sides will come in for some criticism through these chapters.

Why Did the Democrats Come This Way?

Many of the problems confronting America's health care systems were recognized by observers of various political persuasions years prior to the legislation of the Affordable Care Act. Perhaps chief among them was the issue of free-riding, or the pattern of uninsured persons obtaining care at others' expense. Free-riding contributes heavily to the load of uncompensated care that burdens medical providers. A recent and credible estimate of this problem indicates that uncompensated care amounted to approximately $85 billion in 2013. Stated differently, the American Hospital Association reported in 2015 that uncompensated care accounts for approximately 6 percent of services rendered each year.[4]

Second, beyond posing a massive financial problem for America's health care systems, tens of millions of uninsured persons—variously estimated at between 45 and 50 million in 2010[5]—represented a chief failing of the social safety net during the 1990s and 2000s. Observers from across the political spectrum long have lamented America's unique standing as the world's only economically developed nation lacking a universal national health care plan. This lament without much action began to change when a wide range of organized interests—the American Medical Association, the Federation of American Hospitals, America's Health Insurance Plans (AHIP), the Pharmaceutical Research and Manufacturers of America, and other groups—coalesced around the goal of universal coverage in the 2000s.[6] As a direct consequence of this fundamentally changed outlook, the ACA focused heavily on improving access to health insurance and services.

Third, consumer complaints about ill-treatment at the hands of private insurers helped drive calls for greater consumer protections.[7] While the 1990s saw state-level adoption of patients' bills of rights and other regulation of health maintenance organizations, legitimate complaints persisted that insurance companies were more focused on profits than on living up to their promises to pay for their clients' services.[8] This sense that insurers and pharmaceutical manufacturers are overly focused on their bottom lines was addressed in the ACA. The law banned lifetime expenditures, guaranteed issuance of policies to persons with preexisting conditions, heightened scrutiny of premium increases, pressured insurers to spend the lion's share of their revenue on payments on behalf of customers, and took other steps to confront the widely recognized deficiencies of private insurance. While drafting the ACA, Democratic lawmakers blended road-tested practices with proposals that had already won support in diverse quarters to address these problems in ways that were imperfectly

pragmatic while they also tried to navigate Americans' political sensibilities and various points of insistence by players in the health industry. The
passage of the ACA illustrated, if nothing else, the adage that politics is
the art of the possible, not an exercise in perfection.

Naturally, during the run-up to the passage of the Affordable Care Act,
disagreements existed among policy makers and health industry stakeholders regarding preferred solutions. However, broad support had in fact
emerged among experts around several strategies to deal with the problems indicated in the preceding discussion. This partial agreement served
as a basis for drafting the ACA, and legislators generously borrowed from
these ideas and emerging practices. This meant that the intellectual pedi-
gree of the ACA was, while somewhat mixed, certainly not revolutionary.
Most of the major provisions of the law had their geneses in prior practice
or had already been elaborately worked out by policy analysts. The core
ideas derived from existing state practices, national health care programs,
and nuanced academic and medical research on service provision and
consumer behavior. Complementing these experiences was a heightened
political awareness of the needs of such stakeholders as organized medicine, the pharmaceutical industry, and private insurance companies.
Congressional Democrats, beginning in 2008, and later the Obama
administration systematically engaged each of these groups, any one of
which, based on recent historical experience, likely would have derailed
reform. Senator Ted Kennedy's health care working group even polled a
room full of them in the summer of 2008, posing three alternatives:
single-payer, a bundle of incremental changes, or a version of the reforms
enacted in Massachusetts during 2006. Scaling up the Massachusetts
plan handily won, and those few in opposition declined to propose an
alternative, even though their ideas were solicited.[9] The Democrats asked
organized health care interests what they wanted, and then they legislated along those lines.

Law makers had to grapple with numerous issues in creating the ACA,
and a handful of these choices proved decisive to Democrats' ability to
pass significant reform: not creating a broad government-run insurance
option, involving states in the Medicaid expansion, relying heavily on the
private insurance industry, and not pressuring the pharmaceutical industry to face significant price competition. However, in making some of
these choices Democrats substantially failed to generate the kind of positive feedback that would be vital to the ACA's widespread approval by the
general public. Further, some of these choices helped set the terms of
debate and resistance to the legislation. Understanding why the Democrats plotted the course they did between 2008 and 2010 goes a long way

toward decoding the ensuing fierce political resistance. Among these key decisions were the choices to enlist states in creating new insurance markets, to pursue a significant expansion of Medicaid, and, perhaps most importantly, to collaborate with the insurance industry by engaging in a quid pro quo involving insurance reforms and the individual mandate. Each of these decisions was grounded in thinking that, for well-considered reasons, appeared as workable ideas at the time but prone to the whipsawing of national politics during a polarized era and disparate perspectives between experts and ordinary citizens. The following sections consider in turn each of these three choices.

Enlisting States in Building New Insurance Markets

Instead of the government-run insurance option that many House Democrats supported, the final version of the ACA invited state governments to establish their own insurance exchanges, or marketplaces, with enrollments beginning in the fall of 2013 and policies to take effect in January 2014. The House version of the bill would have created a federal exchange operated by a single new agency; the Senate version, which substantially prevailed in the legislative reconciliation, called for the federal-state sharing of this responsibility, the system used since 2013. States declining to create their own exchanges either could collaborate with the federal government or simply refuse to cooperate. In the absence of a state exchange, the law called for the federal government to operate one, accessed via the federal healthcare.gov website. Put simply, this resulted in a mess, as some states moved ahead quickly and capably with their own exchanges, while others, including large sections of the South and Midwest, did not. Some states, such as Georgia, passed laws explicitly prohibiting their public employees or agencies from cooperating with the federal efforts. In these non-cooperating states, residents turned to the federal website, which suffered a highly troubled rollout in the fall of 2013 before finally finding its footing the next year.

The decision to ask states to establish their own health insurance marketplaces, while certainly representing a nod to the tradition of devolved federalism, hindered implementation of the ACA. The failure of the law's text to clarify that federal subsidies were indeed available to all persons who purchased insurance online created another litigation opportunity. These cases, unified under *King v. Burwell*, went to the U.S. Supreme Court and in the spring of 2015 were settled when the Court ruled that federal subsidies would be available to individuals purchasing insurance through the federal exchange. Had the Supreme Court ruled the other way, the new system probably would have collapsed in short order, given that some eight million insured persons would have lost their subsidies. The law's supporters were at this decision, but opponents issued more howls of illegality and excessive judicial activism.

Why did Congress not design a single federal market? States have historically regulated the insurance industry, so states can tailor their regulatory regimes to suit their political preferences. Many insurance companies sell policies in multiple states, but those policies must be tailored on a state-by-state basis in order to conform to varying regulations. States long have had the option to form multistate compacts that would standardize regulatory schemes, but to date they have declined to do so. The ACA invited states to move forward with such compacts.[10]

Expanding Medicaid

A primary goal of the ACA's architects was universal coverage. As indicated earlier, lawmakers placed a great emphasis on the known rather than straying into the land of the unknown. Where workable models of financing were already in place, those programs were augmented. Medicare's coverage of preventative care was expanded. This was administratively feasible, given that Medicare is an entirely federally funded program and Congress can shape the service parameters of the program as it likes. Medicaid, however, presented different challenges, given its federal sponsorship coupled with state implementation and partial funding.

From a perspective of building on the known, expanding Medicaid seemed like a relatively easy move for Democrats intent on assisting more low-income Americans. Various program expansions during the 1980s and 1990s pushed states to cover more poor children and pregnant women, to cover a broader range of services, and gradually to decouple Medicaid eligibility from cash welfare.[11] The 1997 creation of the Children's Health Insurance Program (CHIP) offered federal funds to states desiring to cover children living in low- to moderate-income families that would otherwise be ineligible for Medicaid, and while President George W. Bush vetoed congressional efforts to expand the program, this expansion occurred within a month of President Obama's inauguration. Nearly all of the states adopted CHIP, although they varied considerably in generosity. As of 2016, 46 states covered children in families up to 200 percent of the federal poverty level.[12] The idea of stretching Medicaid a bit further seemed like a reasonable component of a larger strategy to broaden coverage.

However, expanding Medicaid faced serious limits. For the average state, this is the second most expensive program it operates (behind elementary and secondary education), accounting for just over one-quarter of all state expenditures in fiscal year 2014.[13] Even though only one-quarter of Medicaid beneficiaries are elderly or disabled, their services consume nearly 70 percent of the total program expenditures. While the elderly and disabled can more easily garner sympathy than, say, welfare recipients, no matter how one looks at Medicaid, it is a very expensive program. Until the passage of the ACA, most states used the federal poverty thresholds as the eligibility cutoff for Medicaid (excepting children under CHIP). House Democrats, generally more liberal than their Senate counterparts, pushed for an increase to 150 percent of the federal poverty line (FPL), but Democratic senators signaled that there was no way to find 60 votes—the filibuster-proof margin—to expand the program this much. Senators instead indicated a willingness to raise the new coverage level to 138 percent of the FPL.[14] The law provided for this and no more.

Expanding Medicaid without substantial federal assistance would have triggered tremendous resistance by governors and state legislators. To address this, the ACA guaranteed federal funding to cover nearly all additional program expenses under what was, before the Supreme Court intervened, a mandatory extension. During the expansion's first year, 2014, the ACA provided that Congress cover all additional costs, and promised payment for 90 percent of additional costs indefinitely into the future.[15] Democratic lawmakers, however, under-appreciated just how much resistance this idea would generate.

John McDonough, the senior health expert on Senator Ted Kennedy's staff and a person deeply involved in drafting the ACA, later wrote that very little public attention was given to the Medicaid expansion during the legislative drafting.[16] Officials in many conservative states strongly opposed the move. In the spring of 2010, Virginia and Florida, in time joined by 25 other states, sued the federal government, arguing that the mandated Medicaid expansion exceeded Congress's power. In 2012, the U.S. Supreme Court agreed. A powerful partisanship quickly cast a pall over the new law, as Republican political leadership, even in states with high percentages of uninsured residents and large poor populations, decided to leave billions of federal dollars on the table, lest they be tarred with the Obamacare collaborator brush. In the past, governors derided the expansion of certain federal programs they disfavored, but in very few instances they had actually declined the federal money that came with these programs. The Affordable Care Act's Medicaid expansion, like other of the law's provisions, marked a turning point in political warfare. For many of the refusing states, this would mean leaving uncovered between 100,000 and 200,000 potentially Medicaid-eligible persons.[17] For Texas, whose leadership was a leading opponent of the Obama administration, some one million persons would be left uninsured as a result in a state with an uninsured rate of 19 percent as of 2014.[18] For supporters of the ACA, these refusals appeared to be cases of cutting off one's nose to spite one's face. For Republican governors, distancing themselves came to be seen, at least initially, as a political necessity. Through 2014 and 2015, this gradually changed, as many GOP state officials found circuitous ways to accept the Medicaid expansion under cover of modifications that helped mask the big-government support behind this program. Chapter 4 discusses this further.

Looking back, the Democrats' decision to expand Medicaid by mandate involved a couple of missteps from a liberal perspective. First, the move led to a congressional loss in the Supreme Court in 2012. This ruling helped cement the idea that, according to many Republicans, federal attempts to extend health coverage to low-income persons were tainted with the ACA's ideological coloring. Second, in time, the desire to draw down federal Medicaid funds led to waiver-based experiments in many Republican states to remake Medicaid—a program that previously never involved significant cost sharing with its beneficiaries—into a program that explicitly did this. Now that this corner has been rounded, it is entirely possible that Medicaid will never recover its original design to help the most vulnerable of Americans while not charging them payments that many of them cannot readily afford.

Partnering with the Health Insurance Industry: An Awkward Marriage of Convenience

Because past health care reform efforts stalled in the face of highly organized resistance from the health insurance industry—most recently the Clinton plan of the early 1990s—Democrats chose this time around to engage insurers and their lead lobbying organization, America's Health Insurance Plans. The manner in which the ACA accommodated the needs of AHIP and its members, though it later turned into a major liability in the eyes of the public, proved crucial in passing the law. By directing millions of new customers into the arms of private insurers, reformers bought substantial compliance from the insurance industry and tamed what could have been fatal opposition to the law and one of its central tenets: that insurers stop using individual ratings when accepting or rejecting customers. Under the ACA, insurers could not deny coverage based on preexisting conditions and were strictly limited in how highly they could elevate premiums based on individual considerations such as age and tobacco use. These provisions represented significant victories.

One of the basic truths of health politics is that the U.S. insurance industry does over a trillion dollars in business annually.[19] Hence, a frontal assault on this group, such as a move to a single-payer system, would pose political problems almost certainly insuperable. Barack Obama, while still an Illinois state senator in 2003, supported a single-payer system, but he also acknowledged that this was unrealistic in the short term.[20] As president, Obama showed no interest in pursuing a single-payer arrangement, though he did support a government-run insurance option, something widely interpreted as a first step toward a single-payer system. But even here, his commitment collapsed in the face of stiff resistance from noisy town hall gatherings during the August 2009 congressional recess. Tea Party–inspired activists unsettled many Democrats, and some Republicans, with their adamant opposition to any kind of health care reform involving more active government. In this environment, shunting aside the private insurance industry and consequently making yet another enemy simply did not appear politically viable. Insurers would have to be brought on board if Democrats were to pass meaningful reform.

Obama was slow to develop a vision on exactly how to accomplish this partnership. During a 2007 political forum in Las Vegas, he notably failed to articulate his own plan, while fellow Democratic candidates John Edwards and Hillary Clinton virtually talked circles around him with their greater policy knowledge.[21] Both Edwards and Clinton had come to support the idea of an individual health insurance mandate, but Obama remained cool toward it. During a January 2008 candidate debate, Obama rhetorically asked Clinton about individuals subject to a mandate but unable to afford insurance. "If they cannot afford it, then the question is: What are you going to do about it? Are you going to fine them? Are you going to garnish their wages?"[22] The following month, a mass-mailed flier from the Obama campaign challenged Clinton's support for the mandate. "The way Hillary Clinton's healthcare plan covers everyone is to have the government force uninsured people to buy insurance, even if they can't afford it. . . . Punishing families who can't afford health care to begin with just doesn't make sense."[23] Relatively inexperienced at the outset, Obama received an education over the course of the 2008 campaign. Administration insiders differ as to when Obama changed his mind about the individual mandate, but it appears that within a few months of locking up the delegates required to win the Democratic nomination, Obama shifted, likely because of his growing awareness that without a mandate government subsidies alone would probably prove insufficient to lead the uninsured to buy coverage.[24]

Obama's change of position on the mandate was also catalyzed in part by the proactive way in which representatives of the health insurance industry engaged the policy reform movement. After the 2006 adoption of insurance mandates by Massachusetts, AHIP's president, Karen Ignagni, began showing signs of cooperation with reformers intent on expanding access to the uninsured. This new posture stood in striking contrast to the industry's opposition during the 1990s. A couple of forces catalyzed the change. First, through the 1990s and into the 2000s, a number of larger employers began to self-insure, shrinking the for-profit insurance market.[25] Second, following the late 1990s passage of patients' bills of rights and other regulatory efforts in the states, several jurisdictions had considered and New York had adopted more stringent regulations. New York reformed its insurance law to prohibit insurers from discriminating on the basis of preexisting conditions, but the legislature had not included an individual mandate in that new law. The prospect of regulation without the sweetener of the mandate unsettled AHIP, so in June 2008 the organization proposed legislation that would limit exclusions for health conditions and coupled them with an individual mandate. This was essentially the Massachusetts model, and Ignagni saw it as a workable alternative to the changes legislated in New York and potentially elsewhere.[26] In this move, Ignagni showed herself to be a smart pragmatist, positioning her industry to be a partner and beneficiary, rather than a losing antagonist. As the saying goes, it is preferable to have a seat at the table than to be on the menu.[27]

AHIP, from 2008 to 2010, toned down its opposition to increased insurance regulation while not overtly supporting liberal reforms. In the spring of 2008, once Barack Obama emerged as the likely Democratic nominee, Ignagni traveled to Chicago to meet his staffers and to indicate her openness to insurance regulation and a mandatory issue provision if in return the law would include an individual mandate. Clearly, she saw the potential for reform and expressed a willingness to meet Obama half way.[28] In March 2009, Ignagni, along with Scott Serota of the Blue Cross and Blue Shield Corporation, told members of Congress that they would support a must-issue policy if in return they could secure an individual mandate.[29] The quid pro quo was now fully transparent. In October 2009, speaking to a Washington, D.C., gathering of AHIP members to discuss state insurance issues, she insisted that her organization remained committed to seeing through this "massive overhaul of the insurance market" and that it had a "very specific proposal" that would help curtail costs.[30] When in 2009 President Obama publicly criticized health insurers for being obstacles, AHIP weathered the critique largely in silence, at least publicly (though it still spent nearly $9 million on advocacy activities that year[31]). AHIP's members knew that if the individual mandate passed, the

ACA would steer millions of new customers their way, even if some of the association's individual members—including Aetna, CIGNA, Humana, United Healthcare, and WellPoint—surreptitiously funneled over $86 million to the U.S. Chamber of Commerce in order to buy opposition media ads.[32] This awkward marriage concerned both Democrats and AHIP less than some other alternatives they could imagine. As the Senate Finance Committee began work in 2008 on what would become the ACA, Ignagni again affirmed her willingness to cooperate. She offered AHIP's plan, which included coverage for individuals with preexisting conditions, an individual mandate, and enlarged Medicare and Medicaid. All of these ideas were similar to those that Democrats were contemplating at the time.

While this uneasy partnership of sorts between progressive health reformers and the insurance industry was refreshing for those who had fought with AHIP and other reform opponents for years, not everyone was happy with this accommodation. One of the more strident responses to AHIP's newly discovered cooperation came from Republican pollster Frank Luntz. When Luntz met with congressional Republicans in May 2009, he complained that "for ten years we were carrying the water of the insurance companies because they were backing us on health care. . . . Well, they're not anymore. They've sold out."[33] For their part, Republican leaders in Congress had said remarkably little prior to the August 2009 recess about the progress being made in venues such as the Senate Finance Committee. For example, Senate Minority Leader Mitch McConnell could not quite bring himself to confront directly the pending bill when he spoke at a press conference on July 28. When asked, he noted that GOP negotiators were keeping him apprised of developments, but he dodged queries about his support for the bill, commenting blandly that "there's not a plan that I've seen that people can support on a bipartisan basis."[34]

The trade-off between being perceived as a sell-out and being seen as the enemy contributed significantly to AHIP's willingness to play. This tension should be understood in the context of public opinion toward insurance companies. An August 2009 poll asked respondents whom they trusted to protect their access to quality health services. The insurance industry ranked lowest, below congressional Republicans, the president, and even pharmaceutical companies.[35]

In the end, this distrust of the insurance industry worked to advance reform in the short term even if it persisted as a stumbling block over the longer term. Imposing stricter regulation on the industry in 2010 than had ever been accomplished previously allowed the president to claim a significant turning point in Americans' relationships with the insurance companies. The law's authors surely did not anticipate just how profoundly this uneasy partnership would offend Americans' selectively libertarian sensibilities.

The extent to which this agreement made sense in the 2000s depended on a long and curious gestation of the idea among think tank and academic researchers in the late 1980s and politicians of both parties starting in the 1990s. In adopting the individual mandate as a centerpiece of reform, Democrats resorted to a variation on a strategy they had employed in 1965 to launch Medicare and Medicaid. In that instance, they blended a Republican proposal to offer out-patient coverage through voluntary withholding of monthly premiums deducted from Social Security benefits (what would become Medicare Part B) with a Democratic proposal for mandatory withholding for hospital insurance (Part A) and public funding for Medicaid. The famous three-layer cake was not anyone's ideal choice, but it got the legislative job done.[36] In the case of the ACA, blending private insurance with government subsidies and insurance regulation formed a three-legged stool.[37] The development of this particular combination spanned over 20 years, and understanding its development is crucial to comprehending why the Democrats adopted it, as well as why the Republicans, up through 2016, had such difficulty proposing a comprehensive alternative. This central provision is worth considering at length.

A History of the Individual Mandate

No matter how much sense the idea of the individual mandate may have made to health economists and policy makers, solid majorities of the general public have disliked it since it became part of a national conversation in the late 2000s. This provision served as a key catalyst for opposition. Popular opposition turned on several dimensions. First, polls fielded since the passage of the ACA tended to find that large majorities of Americans did not think Congress has the power to require insurance coverage.[38] Most Americans distrust health insurers to play guiding roles in formulating health policy.[39] Further, approximately one-half of Americans are concerned that they would not be able to afford the insurance required by the ACA.[40] An idea that made sense to actuaries, economists, health policy experts, and a good number of politicians simply did not hold much water with the general public.

The Early Conservative Formulation

The idea of mandatory health insurance as a way to combat cost shifting initially grew out of work by conservative thinkers, including the Heritage Foundation's Stuart Butler and the University of Pennsylvania's Mark Pauly in the late 1980s. Various advocates endorsed some version of a minimum coverage requirement between then and its incorporation into the ACA in 2010. Despite the differences among its supporters, a central idea was to instill personal responsibility in health care markets. Experts from diverse fields approached this issue in slightly different ways, but a few common themes emerged to form a consensus around the idea of universal coverage achieved through insurance regulation and government subsidies referred to in the preceding discussion.

In the 1980s, Stuart Butler saw several key problems facing America's health care systems, including high overall costs (11 percent of GNP at the time), tens of millions of uninsured Americans, too much free-riding by these uninsured individuals on the backs of the insured, and over-utilization of services, principally by those with comprehensive insurance coverage for whom the true costs of service consumption were masked. Butler was also concerned that Democrats' calls for an employer mandate or a single-payer system might gain traction, and he wanted to preempt this. Opposition to an employer mandate would be a recurring theme in virtually everything Heritage produced from the late 1980s up to the present. Butler and others characterized pressures on employers to provide insurance as everything from regressive (specifically, depressive of wages) to a violation of private property rights. He also tied an employer mandate to an inequality in how the federal tax code treats employer-provided premiums versus those paid by the self-employed. Butler's 1989 proposal would have provided tax exemptions to the self-employed who purchase their own insurance, with a larger credit for out-of-pocket expenses than for premium payments, encouraging individuals to pay directly for services. Butler's "Heritage Plan" proposed granting individuals a tax break to help them purchase their own insurance. For him, an individual mandate found support in a pair of principles. "First, that health care protection is a responsibility of individuals, not businesses."[41] Further, if a person suffers a catastrophic health crisis, society will care for him or her and that "we don't let people die in the streets," thanks in part to Emergency Medical Treatment and the Active Labor Act, the 1986 federal law that requires hospitals participating in Medicare (virtually all of them) to stabilize patients regardless of their ability to pay.

Butler opposed a single-payer system, insisting that this level of government intrusion is simply inappropriate for the United States. He wanted people to purchase their own insurance, with government subsidies for those in need. The Heritage Plan also proposed decoupling Medicaid from cash welfare or Supplemental Security Income and linking it instead to poverty status, along with a shift to a voucher system for Medicare to prompt recipients to become more cost conscious. The commercial market aspect of the Medicare change has become a mainstay in conservative circles over the past decade, as it fits with the language of consumer-driven health care that has gained traction in recent years. Looking back, this 1989 Heritage document helped establish a set of ideas that enjoyed wide support in conservative circles throughout the mid- to late 2000s: moving toward universal coverage, more clear exposure of consumers to the true costs of their consumption, and an individual mandate supported by government subsidies.

A second line of contemporaneous work closely resembled Butler's thinking. The University of Pennsylvania's Mark Pauly and his colleagues developed an alternative to the Democrats' inclinations toward the single-payer system.[42] While Pauly was not working for the Bush Administration, he wanted to provide the president a market-based alternative. Pauly reasoned that tax credits could ease the purchase of private insurance policies by a large number of Americans but that some other mechanism would be needed to "round up the stragglers who wouldn't be brought in by subsidies" alone.[43]

Because market-driven thinkers fretted considerably about over-insurance, which they argued leads to a wasteful increase in service utilization, Pauly's proposal also targeted policies that extend comprehensive coverage with low levels of cost sharing for beneficiaries. To confront what he saw as the problem of over-insurance, Pauly proposed a federal minimum coverage requirement by which everyone would have to abide. Sensitive to individuals' different willingness to pay for services based on income, his proposal called for higher deductibles for individuals with higher income. In another precursor to the Affordable Care Act, Pauly also wished to tie enforcement of the minimum coverage requirement either to the federal tax system or to welfare payments as a way to minimize administrative expenses.

Pauly's 1991 proposal caught the attention of congressional Republicans, who incorporated some of its ideas into a bill sponsored by Rhode Island Republican Senator John Chaffee in November of that year.[44] While many in the GOP liked the idea, most Democrats, still hoping for a single-payer arrangement, considered it a non-starter.[45] Chaffee's bill, somewhat similar to the Clinton plan, proposed the creation of larger pools of insured individuals to spread risk broadly. Chaffee's bill also would have imposed special taxes on noncompliant individuals, as well as employers who failed to provide insurance to their workers. Vouchers for persons of modest income would have enabled millions of persons to purchase private insurance who otherwise would have found those policies out of reach.[46] As middle of the road as it may have seemed at the time, the Chaffee bill, even with its 21 bipartisan cosponsors (including Senate Minority Leader Bob Dole), never achieved a Senate floor debate, in part due to pressure from conservative fund-raising groups.[47] Republicans splintered. Most approved of an individual mandate but not the employer requirement.[48] Others took a more cautious approach, such as Texas Senator Phil Gramm, who, in aligning himself with more conservative members, proposed a plan that included a mandate that everyone carry a catastrophic coverage plan but not a more conventional health insurance policy.

The conservative approach of requiring catastrophic but not conventional coverage for everyone found support from no less of an eminence than the economist Milton Friedman. In a 1991 *Wall Street Journal* column, Friedman called for a mandate that each family carry a high-deductible policy—he suggested $20,000 per year—and that modest-income families receive a government subsidy to defray costs.[49] Friedman and other conservatives were attracted due to the emphasis they placed on personal responsibility and how advancing in this direction would address the free-riding problem and associated uncompensated care.

Democrats in the early 1990s were aware of the potential advantages of a minimum-coverage requirement, but their sensibilities tended to run toward mandates on employers and leveraging the power of market competition to drive down insurance prices rather than compelling individuals, especially those of low income, to purchase financially burdensome policies. First Lady Hillary Clinton and the task force she chaired during her husband's first administration took a position against an individual mandate in 1993 for this reason. Mrs. Clinton commented to a gathering of Democratic lawmakers that year that "we have looked at that in every way we know how to. . . . That is politically and substantively a much harder sell than the one we've got, a much harder sell."[50] Bill Clinton articulated in a 1993 speech to the National Governors Association that imposing an individual mandate with no pressure on employers to be part of paying the premiums would likely lead to employers dropping coverage. Mr. Clinton rhetorically asked, "If you impose an individual mandate, what is to stop every other employer in America from just dumping [insurance for] his employees or her employees?"[51]

One of the striking continuities across these proposals is their resemblance to the ACA. The heavy reliance on government subsidies to purchase private insurance mandated for virtually everyone had gained a considerable following. For Republicans, the appeal was to utilize competitive markets to the greatest extent possible while minimizing government's role: no single-payer system, no employer mandate. For Democrats, the attraction was achieving universal coverage with significant public sector assistance.

In the wake of the failure of the Clinton plan, Congress took a few incremental steps to enhance access—such as the 1997 establishment of CHIP—but also attempted to address rising health care costs. In 2003, it enacted legislation to enable tax-free, individualized health savings accounts that appealed to market-oriented policy advocates. However, many Democrats felt burned by the failure to enact significant legislation in the early 1990s, and they feared that the public was not ready for another full-court press on health care. Some observers commented that the failure of the Clinton plan catalyzed a rejection of big government, as evidenced by the GOP victories of 1994.[52] The next major act for health reform would take place in Massachusetts under the leadership of a pragmatic governor searching for an accomplishment suitable to launch a presidential bid.

Mitt Romney and the Massachusetts Connector

In Massachusetts in the mid-2000s, the individual mandate turned out to be not a particularly hard sell. Republican Governor Mitt Romney was looking for a policy victory, as he was already contemplating a 2008 presidential run. He had been working on universal health care for a couple of years, and public opinion polls showed that more than 90 percent of Massachusetts residents believed health care to be a right.[53] Romney's ideas closely paralleled those of Milton Friedman and other conservatives at the time, who were concerned about free-riding and uncompensated care. Announcing his proposal for an individual mandate coupled with state subsidies in June 2005, he articulated the logic of requiring personal responsibility through, at minimum, a no-frills, affordable policy with a high deductible. "It's a conservative idea . . . insisting that individuals have responsibility for their own health care. I think it appeals to people on both sides of the aisle: insurance for everyone without a tax increase."[54] Romney pointedly criticized the mentality among uninsured risk takers that leads them to imagine that "if I get sick, I get free health care. . . . We are going to end that."[55]

Romney's push for reform should be understood in practical, not particularly ideological terms. He drew substantial inspiration from Jonathan Gruber, an economist at the Massachusetts Institute of Technology who studies consumer behavior and health insurance. Many health policy thinkers had come to embrace the so-called three-legged stool of consumer protections, the individual mandate, and government subsidies.[56] Gruber had developed models of economic behavior that many considered the best in the business.[57] In 2005, aides to Governor Romney contacted Gruber to learn about his thinking that blended universal coverage with personal responsibility.[58]

Romney found willing partners in Democratic state legislators. Both sides knew that over $1 billion in federal money would be lost if the terms of a federal Medicaid waiver, granted in 2005, were not implemented by the summer of 2006.[59] This, combined with the convergence of ideas on both sides of the aisle, propelled reform.[60] At public appearances, Romney often remarked that compelling a measure of individual accountability was a conservative idea.[61] Democratic House Speaker Salvatore DiMasi echoed Romney's emphasis on individual responsibility.[62] While DiMasi and Romney differed on the employer mandate—something Romney opposed—this did not prevent them from collaborating. Industry leaders in Massachusetts also exhibited a willingness to support reform, though some of them also opposed an employer mandate.

By spring 2006, Romney struck a deal with the legislature to cover some 500,000 previously uninsured persons in Massachusetts, showing himself to be a can-do Republican who could work across the aisle. At the bill signing in April, the governor stood in Boston's historic Faneuil Hall along with Senator Ted Kennedy, the Heritage Foundation's Robert Moffit, MIT's Jonathan Gruber, and others as a sign of the broad thinking that had gone into the new law and the ideological barriers that had fallen on the way to passage.[63] In building the Massachusetts health care Connector, liberals won universal coverage, though not the single-payer system many of them wanted. Conservatives achieved private insurance at the center of the program, though orchestrated by a larger government role, specifically subsidies, than they would have ideally wanted. The broad consensus around the need for universal coverage and tax subsidies, an ideational underpinning that had been percolating for more than a decade, showed itself as a politically successful strategy and one that a broad range of observers believed would work as a technical matter as well. A majority of Massachusetts residents also indicated their support.[64] As for the Heritage Foundation's Moffit, he praised the new state law, saying that "we have retained what is best in American health care while correcting its deficiencies. . . . Too often excessive partisanship corrodes civility. . . . The opposite has happened here."[65] The residents of Massachusetts would have just over one year to purchase insurance.

In taking his victory lap that spring, Romney spoke at the U.S. Chamber of Commerce meeting in Washington, D.C. While his words said the Massachusetts plan was not explicitly designed to apply to all of the states, his language suggested otherwise. He spoke of "Massachusetts . . . leading the way with health insurance for everyone."[66] Further, he remarked that "if we did it here [in Massachusetts], we can do it in other states . . . we have an experiment that the other 49 states can look at and adopt."[67] He defended his approach against conservative critics concerned about individual liberty by again arguing about individual accountability. "Making the individual responsible for his own health coverage is a lot more conservative than a permanent program of government handouts to hospitals," Romney insisted.[68]

Many observers outside Massachusetts saw this model as a way forward. In discussing these ideas with a business reporter in April 2006, the Heritage Foundation's Edmund Haislmaier commented that the mandate was not, in fact, part of a slippery slope toward government-run health care, as staff from the Cato Institute had asserted it to be.[69] Later that summer, Haislmaier authored a working paper stressing the importance of personal responsibility and revealing only a small amount of internal conflict over how, in his words, "unfortunately, the state legislature changed that idea [of an incentive] into a mandate; either buy coverage or pay a fine. This provision is more onerous and philosophically objectionable [than Haislmaier would have preferred], but it is unlikely to prove onerous in practice."[70] He concluded that "other governors and legislators would do well to consider this basic model as a framework for health care reform in their own states."[71] In July 2006, Moffit teamed up with another Heritage colleague to author a working paper that opposed the employer mandate enacted by the Massachusetts legislature over Romney's veto as well as the expansion of the commonwealth's Medicaid program. That paper took no explicit position on the individual mandate but supported the idea of state subsidies to help low-income people to buy insurance on publicly run exchanges.[72]

Other states took note. California's Republican Governor Arnold Schwarzenegger proposed a reform plan in January 2007 that would have used the now-familiar three-legged stool of insurance regulation, an individual mandate, and government subsidies—together with a limited employer mandate—to cover Californians.[73] Pennsylvania's Democratic Governor Ed Rendell advanced a similar idea, though the individual requirement would have applied only to those with incomes above 300 percent of the federal poverty level.[74] The importance of moving toward universal coverage was catching ahold of many policy makers' imaginations across the political spectrum and across the nation.

The practicality of the individual mandate led many Republicans to permit this trade-off with personal liberty since it directly confronted unfair and inefficient cost shifting and preserved a substantial measure of consumer choice across plans.[75] The Heritage Foundation continued churning out material supporting this approach, and as late as the fall of 2008 Moffit still articulated the rationale for what he considered soft coercion—tax credits rather than tax penalties—to encourage Americans to obtain private insurance. (Of course, the distinction between credits and penalties is debatable. People face a marginal loss of utility either way.) Newt Gingrich also supported the mandate, for similar reasons as many of his fellow conservatives, as he clearly indicated in comments on a conference call hosted by Siemens Healthcare during May 2009. He wanted to instill individual responsibility and to end the free-riding problem.[76] After the passage of the ACA and once almost all Republican politicians had turned against the mandate, at a GOP candidate debate Mitt Romney attempted to paint Gingrich, a fellow GOP presidential candidate in the fall of 2011, as an early supporter. Gingrich responded by schooling his Republican primary season opponents, reminding them that "in fighting Hillarycare [in 1993], virtually every conservative saw a mandate as a less dangerous future than the one Hillary was trying to do."[77]

Democrats Adopt the Individual Mandate

Beginning in 2007, some Republicans slowly began distancing themselves from the individual mandate, and many Democrats came to embrace it, including 2008 presidential candidates Hillary Clinton and John Edwards. Barack Obama warmed to this approach only after the 2008 campaign was well under way. Early on, he clearly had expressed that he viewed an individual mandate as akin to robbing people of scarce resources.[78] As of March 2007, Obama expressed his fear that "a mandate would be so politically unpopular as to be unrealistic."[79]

However, over the following months, Obama came to embrace the mandate as part of the three-legged-stool consensus. The exact timing of Obama's conversion remains unclear. In a summer 2008 conversation with Neera Tanden, a Democratic campaign professional, Obama reflected from the comfortable position of having his party's nomination essentially locked up, commenting that "I think maybe Hillary [Clinton] was right about the mandate. . . . I'm not going to talk about it in the campaign, but we may need it."[80] Others point to later dates. In a memoir, former senator and close advisor Tom Daschle wrote of early December 2008 as the turning point.[81] Obama first expressed his new position publicly in a CBS News interview on July 17, 2009, commenting that many people lived without insurance due to the financial burden, not because of any lack of interest in having it. He indicated that he now supported "some sort of individual mandate" as he contemplated subsidies to ease those purchases.[82] Importantly, by late 2008, the individual mandate had become a key part of the Democratic brand of health care reform, and the way in which it mapped onto a big-government versus small-government political discourse made it a prime target for Republican opposition.

In autumn 2008, Heritage's Moffit authored an article in which he acknowledged that the Obama-Clinton debate over the mandate had caught his attention and that this idea bothered him, though he remained on the fence. Moffit offered that there were various reasons to support a mandate: moving toward universal coverage; creating more equal access; reducing adverse selection; eliminating the free-rider problem, uncompensated care, and the consequent cost shifting; relieving emergency room financial stress; and fostering a new social contract surrounding health care.[83] However, he also identified what he thought were some sound reasons to oppose it, based on individual liberty. The net effect was that, in contrast to everything he had produced on health care over the previous decade and a half, Moffit had come to believe that policy should err on the side of individual liberty and that people should not be required to buy insurance. Instead, he held out hope that some type of tax credit could be extended to those wishing to purchase their own insurance on a voluntary basis. Transparency was key for him, and he wrote that a person's decision to decline a tax break

> in effect constitutes its own "penalty." If an individual is offered a $2,500 tax credit . . . to buy insurance and refuses to do so, that person obviously incurs a $2,500 tax penalty that is self-inflicted, not externally imposed. . . . In either case, under [Moffit's proposal] . . . the law would impose a tax penalty just as it would under an individual mandate.[84]

Moffit seemed to be arguing that he approved of a self-imposed penalty (voluntarily passing up a tax credit) but not with the externally imposed one (an extra tax), despite explicitly acknowledging their essential equivalence.

Conservatives Turn against the Mandate

The story of how conservatives turned against the individual mandate between 2007 and 2009 is complex, and it is one that involved a good deal of bottom-up leadership and that saw many prominent Republican officials caught off-guard by the ground-level resistance among constituents. In a sense, this movement stands in opposition to much of the recent literature on elite leadership of public opinion.[85] The philosophical conviction that Romney, his supporters at Heritage, and conservatives elsewhere had in the individual mandate turned out not to be as solidly reflected among Republicans in the general population as these would-be opinion leaders imagined. Beginning in 2007, Republican presidential candidates John McCain, Rudy Giuliani, and Fred Thompson began to equate the mandate with too-intrusive government.[86] For his part, Romney vacillated or simply avoided talking about his accomplishment in Massachusetts. At the February 2007 Conservative Political Action Committee convention in Washington, D.C., he chose to not mention what he had earlier called his crowning achievement.[87]

Meanwhile, in late 2007 and early 2008, the fractured talk among Republicans over the individual mandate catalyzed a subtle but unmistakable shift in the minds of Republican identifiers in the general public. Pollsters asked about the mandate in the 1990s and resumed doing so in 2006. Polls compared it to auto insurance. They asked if people would support this as a general strategy for universal coverage. They queried if Congress should have the authority to require insurance policies. After 2010, they asked about its constitutionality. While all of these surveys, regardless of question wording, showed Republicans to be less supportive of the individual mandate than Democrats, the cross-party gap remained relatively small until the autumn of 2007. At that time, however, partisans in the general population dramatically went their separate ways. To illustrate this crucial partisan divide, Figure 1.1 shows the difference between Democratic and Republican identifiers from 1994 to 2012 on questions about the individual mandate. Figure 1.2, showing the actual support figures by party, appears at the end of this chapter.

Because question wording varied considerably across these 35 polls, Figure 1.1 isolates the cross-party gap rather than showing levels of support for specific phrasing among partisans.[88] Two polls from the 1990s show gaps of 12 and 14 percentage points between Democrats and Republicans. While these are significant differences, they pale compared to the spread in the late 2000s. The trend shows a distinct turn starting in November 2007. Up to this point, the cross-party gap had never been

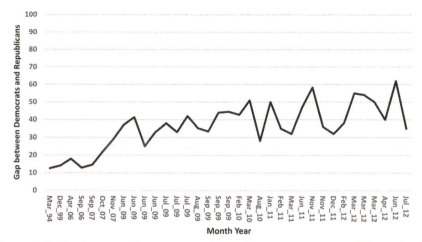

Figure 1.1 Gap between Democrats and Republicans in Support of the Individual Mandate, 1994–2012

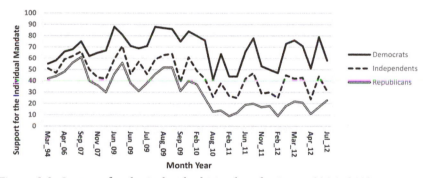

Figure 1.2 Support for the Individual Mandate, by Party, 1994–2012

more than 18 percentage points. However, commencing with this probing of the public, a 22-percentage-point gap emerged and continued to grow: 29 percent the next month, and by mid-2009, fully 37 percent. Only twice following this did the gap amount to less than 30 percentage points. By June 2012, it reached an astounding 62 points. Whereas this issue did not dramatically separate Americans based on partisanship prior to the gearing up of the 2007–2008 presidential campaign, this period caused Democrats to increase their support and Republicans to move away from an idea that between 42 and 61 percent of them had previously supported.

This sharp division of the public raises at least two questions. First, why did Republicans in the general population abandon their earlier position in support of the individual mandate? Second, why were so many congressional Republicans slow to perceive the ground shifting under their feet on what was about to become a key issue of partisan division? Perhaps one of the most tardy to realize this, Republican Senator Chuck Grassley, the ranking minority member on the Finance Committee, appeared on Fox News as late as June 14, 2009, and stated "when it comes to states requiring it for auto insurance, the principle then ought to lie the same way for health insurance, because everybody has some health insurance costs, and if you aren't insured, there's no free lunch. Somebody else is paying for it. So I think individual mandates are more apt to be accepted by a vast majority of people in Congress."[89] Grassley was arguably right at the time, but within two months constituents chastised congressional Republicans about adopting a different tack.

Republicans in the general public had multiple reasons to turn away from comprehensive health policy reform between about 2008 and 2010: opposition to government involvement, partisan competitiveness, and fear of unintended consequences flowing from comprehensive policy reform, among others. The health policy summit Prepare to Launch, organized by senators Max Baucus and Charles Grassley in June 2008, brought together some 250 House and Senate members and staff who coalesced around an understanding that doing nothing simply was no longer tenable. Moving toward broader coverage and finding ways to attack rising costs were of primary importance in the minds of many in attendance.[90] However, by this point Americans who identified as Republicans had distinctly moved in opposition to a key provision of this reform strategy. According to numerous accounts, most members of Congress were surprised by the uproar at their August 2009 town hall gatherings with constituents. In these normally routine meetings, Tea Party–inspired protesters, many of whom were probably as upset over the 2008 bank bailouts and the early 2009 stimulus package as they were about pending health care reform, confronted their representatives with shouting, physical intimidation, and wild distortions of what the developing health legislation aimed to accomplish. The protests seemed to become much more about thwarting Barack Obama's presidency than about discussion of health care policy. A handful of conservative opinion leaders had emerged to oppose the individual mandate beginning in the spring of 2009, but these efforts occurred only after the opinion shift among Republicans in the broader public.

Belatedly getting on board to oppose the mandate was the Republican pollster, Frank Luntz. In April 2009, he issued a strategy memo with talking points to use when discussing health care. He urged them not to seem antireform, given the widespread sense that the policy status quo is untenable. He wrote:

> You simply MUST be vocally and passionately on the side of reform. The status quo is no longer acceptable. If the dynamic becomes "President Obama is on the side of reform and Republicans are against it," then the battle is lost and every word in this document is useless. Republicans must be for the right kind of reform that protects the quality of health care for all Americans. And you must establish your support of reform early in your presentation.[91]

By the time DeMint and Luntz issued their challenges, members of Congress were about to discover something that many Republican constituents back home had already begun to sense: comprehensive health policy restructuring in a Democratic mold was simply intolerable. It appears that many congressional Republicans took Luntz's advice on not seeming antireform too seriously.

Stoking this popular upset were several conservative mobilizing groups using heated rhetoric. FreedomWorks, organized by former U.S. House Majority Leader Dick Armey and funded by Philip Morris and the conservative Scaife family, agitated conservatives with a message on its website instructing those who were planning on attending August town hall meetings, "If you're going to go ugly, go ugly early," borrowing a crude phrase popular among young, sex-seeking males resigned to the reality that they are unlikely to take home any of the unusually attractive women in the bar and that they might as well go ahead and hook up with the less glamorous ones.[92]

To enhance the effectiveness of going ugly early, a Connecticut-based Tea Party blogger, Robert MacGuffie, authored an online guide in early June 2009 titled "Rocking the Town Halls: Best Practices." Among his advice was to watch for early opportunities in the meeting to yell out challenges to the representative. "The goal is to rattle him."[93] MacGuffie shared this document with the Tea Party Patriots, who posted it on their website. Although health care was a significant issue for MacGuffie's group—Right Principles, which he had helped launch as a political action committee in early 2009—frustration over government spending and the stimulus act initially provided the catalyst for his anger at liberal

Democrats in Congress. He later noted that he was very pleased at the reactions the town hall meetings generated, even if they were marked by much personal vitriol.[94] Across the nation, local media coverage strongly focused on these fights. A North Carolina journalist hoping to have his account of a town hall meeting with Democratic Representative David Price published was told by his editor that "your meeting doesn't get covered unless it blows up."[95] Behind these local efforts stood Charles and David Koch, the conservative businessmen-cum-political activists, and their group Americans for Prosperity, which launched a group in June 2009 called Patients First, which organized bus tours to mobilize opposition to reform around the country.[96] By mid-August, their efforts paid off, as the president announced that the creation of a public insurance option was no longer a necessity for him and as congressional Democrats pulled the plug on the provision that would have allowed Medicare to pay doctors to share end-of-life care conversations with patients who desired those, something Sarah Palin, Charles Grassley, and other critics had recently characterized as "pulling the plug on grandma."[97]

Given these events, the conservative turn away from the individual mandate was felt in many places by mid-2009. Back at the Heritage Foundation, health care thinkers were no longer straddling the fence, as Robert Moffit had done as late as late 2008. In the wake of the summer rage over Obamacare, other Heritage writers published a legal memorandum in December 2009 arguing unambiguously that the federal government lacks the constitutional power to require individuals to purchase private insurance.[98] They further asserted that surely the U.S. Supreme Court would find that the individual mandate is not supported under Congress's taxing power or under the Commerce Clause. While they would turn out to be wrong (in 2012[99]) about the Court's reading of the taxation power, this marked a fundamental turning point for the nation's leading conservative think tank.

In a 2012 retrospective in the *National Journal*, conservative commentator Ramesh Ponnuru argued that Heritage had been an "outlier" in its earlier support for the mandate.[100] This is a difficult claim to substantiate, depending on how one defines the term "outlier." In May 2008, the American Enterprise Institute published a lengthy and glowing assessment of Singapore's mandatory health savings plan, a plan that augments personalized health spending accounts with government contributions. Singapore's arrangement bears more than a passing resemblance to the ACA's individual mandate.[101] Senator John McCain criticized the mandate during his 2008 campaign for president, though he supported government vouchers to subsidize insurance purchases.[102] Ponnuru was correct that conservatives did not uniformly support the mandate, but he was mostly wrong on the larger point that the Heritage Foundation was a solo outlier. Regarding Cato, it is true that the organization opposed the mandate, as one would expect of staunch libertarians. In fact, at a celebratory dinner in 1994, Cato president Edward Crane awkwardly attempted humor at Stuart Butler's expense by pointing him out among the attendees and commenting, "At first Stuart didn't want to come. So we decided to mandate that he appear." No one laughed.[103]

Aside from the rift between Heritage and Cato, it is difficult to find organized conservative opposition to the idea of the individual mandate in the 1990s, even if in retrospect some of them attempted to disavow their earlier positions. Butler himself took to the pages of *USA Today* in early 2012 to insist—in what was surely an exercise in hair splitting—that his late-1980s proposal was different from a mandate because of its supposed intentions.[104] He insisted that his earlier rationalization of the mandate was a way to protect others rather than to ensure one's own good. Further, he said he had characterized the enforcement mechanism differently than other conservatives, insisting he had favored tax breaks in the form of carrots rather than sticks; that is, tax breaks were actually an "incentive" rather than a "mandate."[105] Perhaps. But he was quite clear back in 1989, for he titled section 2 of The Heritage Plan to read "Mandate All Households to Obtain Adequate Insurance." He continued (in 2012) writing that in the late 1980s neither the federal nor state governments "require[d] all households to protect themselves from the potentially catastrophic costs of a serious accident or illness. Under the Heritage plan, there would be such a requirement." It is difficult to see how by this he meant something other than the requirement that all families purchase insurance for their own protection.[106] Butler acknowledged this awkwardness in a 2012 column, admitting that he had changed his thinking over the years. He left Heritage in the summer of 2014 for a position at the Brookings Institution, where he continues to work on health care, among other issues. In an interview with the *Wall Street Journal*, Butler noted that he, as the reporter put it, was "attracted to Brookings by the idea of working at a place that is not monolithic in its approach to public policy." As for the switch on the mandate, Butler said that "changing one's mind about the best policy to pursue, but not one's principles, is part of being a researcher at a major think tank."[107]

Explaining the Conservative Shift

As with political attitude formation generally, several factors likely played roles in explaining the turn away from the individual mandate by Republican identifiers. However, none of them provides as compelling an explanation as partisan motivation, given how this particular issue mapped onto cross-party conflict, catalyzed by gradually emerging dissent among a modest number of Republican cue givers, including some presidential candidates. Those few seeds of doubt germinated during 2007 and 2008, growing into a full-blown partisan divide.

As for the alternative explanations, consider first the lack of trust Americans tend to exhibit toward health insurance companies. This conceivably might have led Republicans to resent how the mandate required unwanted transactions with distrusted corporations. The problem with this explanation is that in surveys conducted around the time of the ACA's passage, Democrats distrusted insurance companies somewhat *more* than did Republicans, exactly the opposite of what this explanation would suppose.[108] Second, Republicans might have come to resent government more than Democrats during the late 2000s. The shortcoming of this explanation is that Republicans expressed *greater* confidence in the federal government than did Democrats from 2001 up through the final months of the George W. Bush presidency.[109] (A large part of this almost certainly had to do with the Bush Administration's war on terror and the resulting rally-around-the-president effect.) Hence, the Republican turn away from the individual mandate occurred at a time when Republicans' confidence in government significantly exceeded that expressed by Democrats. A third possible explanation is that the change in White House control from Bush to Obama in January 2009 turned off Republicans from the idea of health care reform. Here again, the timing is wrong, as the change in the presidency occurred only well after the shift in opinion on the individual mandate among rank-and-file Republicans during 2007.

A better explanation is that during 2007 a relatively small number of Republicans—including presidential candidates John McCain, Rudy Giuliani, and Fred Thompson—spoke out against the mandate, and the summer 2007 rift between candidates Clinton and Obama highlighted this as a contentious issue of partisan import. During that year, Republican identifiers came to understand this as an emerging partisan division point and one that was covered extensively in the news media. Press coverage of this issue expanded during 2007, as the Associated Press generated an average of 2.4 stories per week in 2007, compared to only 1.4 stories per week in 2006.[110] Republican identifiers in the general population appear to have picked up on this partisan mapping and the growing salience of the issue, and their responses to public opinion surveys recorded this growing rift.

For their part, the tardiness of most congressional Republicans to recognize how deeply unpopular the individual mandate had become among rank-and-file conservatives appears to have been driven by their two-decade-long quest to bring greater efficiency and personal responsibility to health care financing. Their nonexpert constituents simply saw things differently. The consensus among stakeholders—medical providers, insurers, and drug makers—regarding coverage and cost appears to have been lost on a large swath of ordinary, conservative-leaning Americans who, starting in 2007, expressed more concern about the symbolic issue of government involvement than with plausible solutions. Oddly, this was despite a February 2011 poll by the Kaiser Family Foundation finding that most opponents of the ACA surveyed approved of most of the provisions in the law, including tax credits to small businesses, eliminating Medicare's doughnut hole, subsidies to low-income Americans, and guaranteeing the issuance of health insurance policies to all.[111]

One of the interesting features of Republican opposition to the ACA is that most of those who disliked the law did so for partisan rather than personal-interest reasons. Dissecting polling data on the individual mandate reveals that economic self-interest did not seem to play much of a role in opposing the law. Specifically, one's insurance status only modestly correlates with support for the Affordable Care Act.[112] Evidence on this comes from a monthly tracking poll by the Kaiser Family Foundation, beginning in the spring of 2010.[113] In most months, respondents with insurance were closely divided—within 5 percentage points—on their approval and disapproval of the ACA. The pattern of approval and disapproval among uninsured respondents was somewhat more dynamic over time, with the long-term trend seeing a growth in disapproval, though here too this group was closely divided—within 10 percentage points—in most months, and the uninsured did not display any long-term trend of becoming any more or less divided. Drawing on other polling data from 2009, subjective concerns over losing one's health insurance did not systematically vary with support for the mandate in a poll by NBC News and the *Wall Street Journal*. Among those who were "very concerned" about losing their insurance, 66 percent supported the mandate, compared to a similar 61 percent of those who were "not concerned."[114] A June 2009 poll by NBC News and the *Wall Street Journal* similarly found that concern over potentially losing one's insurance did not significantly correlate with responses about whether "Obama's healthcare plan . . . is a good idea or a bad idea."[115]

In contrast, political party identification correlates very strongly with approval of the ACA. In fact, party identification correlates more strongly with approval of the law than any other factor that the monthly Kaiser poll included from 2010 to 2016, such as gender, ethnicity, age, insurance status, and income. Clearly, Americans used their party identification as a perceptual screen to evaluate the ACA, much as they do when evaluating presidential candidates.[116] This is what we would expect of people when they initially confront a complex issue and seek a heuristic to help them come to judgment. Ordinary Americans cannot be expected to read the hundreds of pages of legislation. However, over time we might expect them to sort through evidence of the law's performance. They could consider the millions of new individuals with health insurance, or the cost of those premiums, or the ability of insurers to rescind policies or place lifetime limits on payment, or the ability of young people to remain on their parents' insurance, or any number of other objective indicators. Clearly, large numbers of Americans placed party success over policy success or failure.

A Case of Dysfunctional Politics

It may be tempting to blame the general public for rather uncritically viewing the ACA in strongly partisan terms. However, this book argues that many of our politicians have short-circuited our national discourse on health care and that as a consequence the bulk of ordinary citizens defaulted to a partisan lens on the ACA rather than evaluating it on the merits. The name-calling, platitudes, and radical oversimplification of complex matters that has characterized our political discourse on health care since 2009 has actively interfered with citizens learning what they need to know.[117] Health care is a sprawling area that encompasses tens of millions of jobs and multiple industries and that implicates nothing short of the vibrancy and productivity of the entire population. Reforming a sector of our economy that has experienced steeper inflation over the past half-century than have consumer prices generally, that leads us to spend more as a percentage of our gross domestic product than any other nation, and that leaves Americans with worse health outcomes than most other developed economies will be supremely complicated.[118] This complexity requires more focused political leadership than Americans have seen on this issue. Such leadership has been absent.

The tragedy of the ACA is that neither party demonstrated great competence in formulating long-term workable solutions. In crafting this law, Democrats sought consensus by building on foundations that were problematic. The marriage of convenience with private health insurers is perhaps paramount here, but it is not the only fateful step that congressional Democrats took. Expecting young and healthy people to purchase insurance that effectively subsidizes the policies of older and less healthy people should have been recognized as a recipe for adverse selection problems.

Relying on states to build and promote online marketplaces was a weak mechanism. Similarly, expanding Medicaid—a program that while familiar is also fairly widely despised by state officials—indicated trouble. For their part, congressional Republicans showed little evidence of serious, constructive engagement of the issues from 2010 through the elections of 2016. This pattern of dysfunctional politics left large swaths of the general public unsure as to how to evaluate the law though any lens other than that of ham-fisted partisanship. Given the complexity of the issues involved here, partisanship is a woefully inadequate cue for Americans to use when trying to address problems in one of the more important policy areas facing our nation. The following chapters assess this resistance, critique the major alternative to government-subsidized health care (i.e., consumer-driven health care plans), evaluate how many but not all Republican state officials learned to live with parts of the ACA, examine likely policy directions for the Trump Administration, and begin a discussion about how the general public might be better integrated in one of the more important conversations Americans are likely to have over the coming years.

CHAPTER TWO

Fighting Obamacare

Legal challenges to the Affordable Care Act (ACA) began piling up before the ink could dry on the new legislation. Literally within minutes of President Obama signing the bill into law, Virginia's Attorney General Ken Cuccinelli filed a law suit in federal district court arguing that Congress lacked the authority to compel Virginians to obtain health insurance. Virginia's legislature—as well as Idaho's—had recently passed laws prohibiting their residents from being required to purchase health insurance. Lawmakers in at least 30 other states introduced similar measures, following a piece of model legislation created by the conservative American Legislative Exchange Council.[1] Given Virginia's stance, Cuccinelli argued that the individual mandate was unconstitutional.[2] Thirteen other state attorneys general jointly filed a separate suit in federal district court in Florida on the ACA's first day. In the U.S. Supreme Court's 2011 term, this litigation, along with others, would be consolidated as *National Federation of Independent Business et al. vs. Kathleen Sebelius*, then secretary of the U.S. Department of Health and Human Services (HHS). These legal challenges to the new legislation formed one major prong of the conservative attack on Obamacare. The refusal by many states to cooperate with the unfolding federal effort and, following the 2012 elections in which the GOP retained congressional control, dozens of efforts to repeal the law would form two other fronts of attack. For many Republican office holders, the implementation of the ACA portended a new level of government intrusion into one of the largest sectors of the economy, and the prospects of this new status quo gaining a broad constituency unhinged them with fear and anger.

Fighting the new law to prevent it from gaining a toe hold was quickly framed as a matter of partisan survival. The fateful decisions made by congressional Democrats during 2009 and 2010, particularly the choices to rely on the individual mandate and Medicaid expansion in the states, provided battlegrounds for stiff political resistance at both the federal and state levels. Opposition to the law in Congress and a willingness (or not) of state officials to cooperate with the law came to separate what many ideological activists on the political right would define as true conservatives versus collaborators with the enemy. Presidential candidate Donald Trump, even though his own conservative credentials came under quite a lot of scrutiny from within his own party, made repealing the ACA a key plank of his campaign platform in 2016.

This chapter describes the opposition to the Affordable Care Act during its first six years, from litigation, to attempted repeal, to state resistance. This deep conflict arose in large part due to the already polarized state of American politics. It was also driven by the decisions made by Democrats to fashion the law as they did, as described in Chapter 1, and by the hostility exhibited by Republicans to prioritize fighting a Democratic policy victory over efforts to address seriously a mounting crisis in America's health systems. The chief tragedy of this reform episode is that Americans have been largely deprived of meaningful discussions that move beyond slogans about possible responses to the nation's mediocre public health statistics and world-record-setting health care expenditures.

The great extent to which the general public was largely stable and closely divided in its approval and disapproval of the law since its passage provides one sign of an unproductive public discourse over health care reform efforts. Despite ample opportunities for Americans, particularly political independents, to evolve in their assessments of the law, evidence suggests that only a very small segment of the public budged in its views. Some of the best evidence for this comes from the Kaiser Family Foundation's monthly Health Tracking Poll, conducted since the spring of 2010. Measuring overall approval and disapproval of the law, this long trend showed slightly more opposition than support, with the gap between those who generally approved of the law and those who disapproved averaging just 5.5 percentage points from April 2010 to October 2016.[3] Aside from a few moments when opposition peaked—such as during the bungled launch of the healthcare.gov website in October 2013—the public remained closely divided on this landmark legislation. The gap between approval and disapproval showed considerable stability, exceeding 10 percentage points in only 8 of these 75 polls. Democrats strongly approved of the law (typically between 60 and 70 percent) and Republicans strongly disapproved (typically between 70 and 80 percent). Among political independents, an average of 48 percent expressed disapproval, compared to an average of 36 percent who approved.

This is a remarkable story of public opinion stability, given the many developments that could, and arguably should, have changed citizens' minds.[4] These include three Supreme Court decisions on various aspects of the law (with mixed outcomes), the troubled rollout of the healthcare. gov website, some 20 million individuals gaining new coverage either by Medicaid or by private insurance, Medicare enhancements, rising private insurance premiums, added consumer protections, initial refusal by approximately half of the states to cooperate, and innovative cost-cutting measures developed by providers. When pollsters asked Americans to assess various parts of the ACA, the large majority of those provisions enjoyed majority bipartisan support. However, the law as an entire package still did not win the approval of a majority of Americans.[5] Despite ample opportunities for public opinion to evolve on the ACA, as it did toward the Social Security Act through the 1940s and Medicare in the 1960s, that evolution never occurred.[6] This was a recipe for continued partisan posturing and little in the way of policy solutions.

The fights over the ACA took various forms. Some of these acts of defiance were expressed as state refusals to adopt the Medicaid expansion. Others were more dramatic. Various advocacy and opposition organizations—Americans for Prosperity, The Cato Institute, Freedom-Works, The Club for Growth, The Senate Conservatives Fund, and others—spent hundreds of millions of dollars to turn the public away from the ACA without proposing anything that could be considered a well-developed alternative. From 2013 through 2016, the Republican-controlled U.S. House of Representatives voted more than 50 times to repeal the law, in whole or in part, knowing such legislation stood no chance of getting past President Obama.[7] The common theme across these efforts is that they helped to frame the debate as one about government power rather than how to address coverage gaps and rising costs. For their part, Democrats largely failed to convince the public of the law's usefulness. This dysfunctional discourse represents not only a low point in cooperation in U.S. national politics but more importantly a failure of national policy leadership.

Congressional Politics: Repeal and More Repeal

From late 2009 through 2016, nearly all of the congressional Republican rhetoric and legislative effort on health policy focused on repealing the ACA. Republican presidential nominee Donald Trump echoed this line of attack. As one conservative commentator wrote in 2015 describing his own party, "ever since President Obama signed [the ACA] . . . into law . . . the elusive goal of repealing the legislation has been the driving force behind Republican politics."[8] This determination to repeal Obama's signature legislation led House Republicans to pass symbolic bills that would not have replaced the ACA or even contemplated the details of how the law should be undone. Illustrating this was the January 2011 passage of House Resolution 2, titled the Repealing the Job-Killing Health Care Law Act. It included no discussion whatsoever about how the executive branch was supposed to unwind the numerous provisions of the ACA. The text of the operative section 2 of this bill read that "effective as of the enactment of Public Law 111–148 [the ACA], such Act is repealed, and the provisions of law amended or repealed by such Act are restored or revived as if such Act had not been enacted."[9] Had this become law, it would have granted the executive branch complete autonomy in implementation and would have offered no guidance on how to recalculate the ACA's reduction in Medicare payments, to reclaim the $250 checks sent to more than 30 million Medicare recipients in 2010 to defray their prescription drug expenses, to undo the ban on insurance companies excluding children with preexisting medical conditions, or to handle any of the other provisions. Serious lawmakers would not have wanted this bill to become law, as the results would have been chaotic. In a pair of reports in 2013 and 2015 by the Congressional Budget Office and the Republican-controlled Joint Committee on Taxation, congressional staffers and members themselves acknowledged as much.[10] The Democratically controlled Senate ignored the bill.

Despite the absence of an elaborated alternative from critics, this debate raged, sustained by several factors. First, arguments over health care financing map onto party divisions particularly well because of the way they tap disagreement over the size and scope of government. Second, a health care provision is highly personal for people because it relates to their sense of wellness and relationships with medical providers. Third, health spending consumes approximately one-quarter of the federal budget (27 percent in 2015) and has accounted for approximately 15 percent of state funds spent over recent years.[11] Given these factors, health care arguments make for a highly effective electoral-wedge issue.

The wedge nature of this debate means that lacking an alternative plan did not stop opponents of health reform from doggedly pursuing the repeal of the ACA for political advantage far more than with any problem-solving goal in mind. Typical of this was a 2008 essay by Michael Cannon of the Cato Institute titled "Blocking Obama's Health Plan Is Key to GOP's Survival. Ditto Baucus' Health Plan. And Kennedy's. And Wyden's." Writing shortly after Obama's first election, Cannon argued that the adoption of a single-payer system would likely shape party loyalties. Citing the

British example, he wrote: "After the Labor Party established the National Health Service after World War II, supposedly conservative workers and low-income people under religious and other influences who tended to support the Conservatives were much more likely to vote for the Labor Party . . . Republicans might want to take note." Cannon's warning was that to allow the Democratic comprehensive reform would swing conservative voters in their direction.[12]

Cannon was not alone in this focus on party strategy over policy solutions. Similar language came from James Pethokoukis of the American Enterprise Institute—an organization usually known as a thoughtful policy incubator—just weeks after Obama's election in an essay titled "How Tom Daschle Might Kill Conservatism." Pethokoukis approvingly quoted an unnamed GOP strategist ominously intoning, "If Democrats take the White House and pass a big-government healthcare plan, that's it. Game over." Pethokoukis continued, contrasting Obama supporters to the more worthy "investor class" of society and complaining that if the Democrats achieved major health care reform it would enduringly "pull America to the left."[13]

Several other conservative organizations also emphasized strategy over policy solutions. In February 2013, FreedomWorks posted a document on its website reading, in part: "On January 1, 2014, new money from Washington will begin flowing to states and individuals, all but ensuring that these new entitlements will become a permanent fixture of life in America. The window of opportunity to stop the implementation of these massive new subsidies is closing."[14] The leftward pull feared by some of these commentators did not materialize. For instance, the overall Republican vote percentage in U.S. House elections stood at just over 43 percent in 2008 but rose significantly to nearly 52 percent in the autumn of 2010. While this figure retreated slightly to 48 percent in 2012, it rose again to 53 percent in 2014.[15] Republican office seekers benefitted from the debate over the ACA. This conservative tide extended to state governments. Between 2009 and 2015, Democrats lost a net 919 state legislative seats and two governorships, in addition to suffering the loss of both congressional chambers.[16] All this, of course, was capped by the Republican victories in 2016, which ensured that repeal efforts would finally gain serious traction. However, prior to 2016, frustrated that their electoral successes did not allow them to repeal the law, Republicans dedicated themselves to accomplishing the next best thing: stoking skepticism of the ACA to undermine the law and to win campaigns. This effort began before the ACA became law, launched in Congress during January 2010 when the conservative Club for Growth appealed to Tea Party members, including

Senator Jim DeMint and Representative Michelle Bachmann, circulating a pledge for Congress members and candidates to sign promising to work to overturn the ACA.[17] While the GOP still awaited the outcome of primary elections in several states, many Republican candidates pledged to "sponsor and support legislation to repeal any federal health care takeover passed in 2010, and replace it with real reforms that lower health care costs without growing government." By March 2010, 37 House and Senate members plus 163 congressional candidates—all of them Republicans—had signed the pledge.[18]

At this early stage, some Democrats also saw this fight as politically useful. In 2010, the Democratic Senatorial Campaign Committee called on its candidates to urge their GOP opponents take a stand on the pledge, something that some, but not all, Democratic campaign professionals viewed as a liability. Democratic pollsters Pat Caddell and Doug Schoen expressed concern that Democrats would "be punished severely" in the fall of 2010 unless they turned around the negative perceptions these pollsters detected as early as March 2010.[19] Caddell and Schoen were largely correct, given the 63 House seats Democrats lost in the 2010 election, the largest mid-term seat loss for the president's party since 1938. Democrats also lost in state legislatures in 2010, with the number of seats controlled by Republicans rising 8 percent, from 3,282 to 3,890.[20]

Using the ACA as an election issue successfully in 2010 was not enough for the law's opponents. Conservative advocacy groups persisted with calls for repeal, and the large majority of them did so without any pretense of an alternative.[21] Not until October 2013 did The Heritage Foundation, arguably the political right's most well-developed policy shop, publish the sketch of a replacement plan, but even this document was limited to broad principles.[22] Jim DeMint, Heritage's new president as of the spring of 2013, decried Obamacare and insisted that conservatives always have had better ideas about health reform. In asking for public support, he insisted that "we can move ahead, taking the best health care system in the world and making it better."[23] This was clearly a decision neither to acknowledge the serious problems with America's systems nor to offer a substantive alternative. Presidential candidate Donald Trump similarly called for repealing the ACA without articulating how he would replace it, beyond a short list of general directions posted on his campaign website.

A number of other conservative groups continued to treat health care as an ideological football far more than as a serious policy problem. Americans for Prosperity, The Senate Conservatives Fund, The Club for Growth, and even the Cato Institute did not provide templates for reform.

This heavy focus on strategy over substance was echoed by members of Congress. Iowa Republican Steve King, in an e-mail to GOP colleagues during the summer of 2010, wrote that members should "resist the urge to fill a policy void" and to "let the Democrats stew in their own mess . . . Let the people vote. We need to fix the problems with the next Congress and the next president." King indicated that the Republicans, once in control, would "not push through a broad, comprehensive [replacement] package. That's what they [the Democrats] did; we won't do that."[24]

Representative King got his way. Once in control of the House, and after the 2014 elections the Senate too, Republicans did not attempt to advance a comprehensive alternative. Part of this inaction appeared attributable to their reluctance to legislate in sweeping fashion for fear that to do so would look like activist government, something they wanted to avoid. Divisions over what a replacement would involve also played a major role. House Speaker John Boehner found himself caught between mainstream Republicans and his caucus's 70-some Tea Party–inspired members who were willing to shut down the government in order to defeat the ACA. When Boehner publicly stated after the president's 2012 reelection that "Obamacare is the law of the land," seeming to signal a truce, he revealed the significant gap between his agenda and that of many in his party.[25] This intra-party conflict came to one of several crisis points during the fall 2013 budget negotiations. The episode revealed Speaker Boehner not to be truly in control of his caucus, a tension that culminated in his autumn 2015 resignation from Congress.[26]

Careening Over the Budget Cliff

For most critics, Barack Obama's 2012 reelection was, to say the least, an unsettling disappointment. These opponents had envisioned a change in White House control as their chance to reverse if not altogether halt the ACA's implementation. Not only did Obama win reelection, the GOP lost eight House seats and two in the Senate. Conservative leaders became desperate to stop the ACA. Shortly after the November election, a group of some 30 conservative political organizations led by former attorney general Ed Meese gathered to strategize. They concluded that their core of conservative Congress members could leverage change via the 2013 budget negotiations. They would attempt to force the repeal or at least the defunding of the Affordable Care Act in exchange for passing the coming year's budget and for the increase in the nation's borrowing authority that the budget would require. Michael Needham, director of Heritage Action for America, The Heritage Foundation's political arm, said "we felt strongly at the start of this year that the House needed to use the power of the purse . . . this was a fight we were going to pick."[27] The group created a tool kit of talking points for Congress members to use when discussing a possible government shutdown. Conservative groups, including the Freedom Partners Chamber of Commerce (not to be confused with the more temperate U.S. Chamber of Commerce), Americans for Prosperity, FreedomWorks, and the Club for Growth, funded by the millions each year by Charles and David Koch, purchased advertisements, funded Tea Party–affiliated politicians, and organized events—such as the nine-city tour of Heritage Action's Defund Obamacare Town Hall Tour—designed to shift public opinion against the Affordable Care Act.[28] For these groups, this was a full-court press. Their willingness to go to the mat over funding the ACA would occur simultaneously with the rollout of the online insurance marketplaces during October 2013. The Obama administration's lack of preparedness for this new element of the law, when combined with the mass furloughs of federal employees that same month due to a partial government shutdown, created a difficult season for the ACA's supporters and for the public's opportunity to learn about this new way to shop for health insurance.

In early 2013, positions within the Republican Party ranged widely from those who did not particularly want this fight, to those who were willing to withhold spending authority from parts of the government in order to defund the law, to those who were quite willing not only to hobble the government but also to withhold interest payments on the national debt, that is, to prompt a government default. Approximately in this order were House Speaker Boehner and his reluctant recognition of the ACA as "the law of the land" (even if at other times he referred to the ACA as a "train wreck"[29]), Texas Senator John Cornyn, who commented in January 2013 that "it may be necessary to partially shut down the government in order to secure the long-term fiscal well-being of our country,"[30] and Texas Senator (and later presidential candidate) Ted Cruz who filibustered the federal budget for over 20 hours in October 2013. Broadly speaking, the strongest resistance came in the House, where Tea Party–affiliated members welcomed a government shutdown in order to try to force the president's hand. Members who had lived through the budget crises of the 1990s warned these less experienced but passionate conservatives that the public might blame the Republicans more than the Democrats for this, as they had in the 1990s (and would again), but Speaker Boehner gave these newer members their chance to stake out their position. This episode was ultimately unsuccessful, but it provided the strongest opponents of the law their opportunity to make their point, posturing for their constituents.

Along the way to making that point, a small group of GOP senators in July circulated a letter warning that they would not approve any government spending "if it devotes a penny" to Obamacare. The signatories included senators Mike Lee, Ted Cruz, Rand Paul, John Cornyn, John Thune, and Marco Rubio.[31] Following up on this in August, 80 members of the House Republican caucus signed a letter to Republican leaders "demanding that any spending bill that reaches the House floor be free of funds to implement or enforce the president's healthcare reform law."[32] For some of these Republicans, this represented an effort to stave off Tea Party challenges during the primary election season of 2014 by burnishing their conservative credentials.

With these various positions staked out, House conservatives later insisted on advancing a budget in September with provisions to defund the ACA. Uncomfortable with this strategy, the House leadership delayed for a week a budget vote. Speaker Boehner explicitly wanted to avoid both a shutdown and default on the national debt, which would have occurred by mid-October. The Republican Study Group proposed an increase in the debt ceiling in order to avoid a default but also insisted on a one-year delay on the implementation of the ACA. House GOP leaders, principally Speaker Boehner and Majority Leader Eric Cantor, called for a short-term budget approval at current spending levels until December 15. Dozens of members of Boehner's caucus opposed a short-term deal.[33] By mid-September, then-former member Jim DeMint (who had moved to the Heritage Foundation) spoke out about the need to force a shuttering of government if necessary, and he wanted to see the GOP send Obama a bill in order to prompt a veto. Boehner was in a tough spot, and Cantor's support for the short-term deal would work against him in a stunning primary election defeat by free-market conservative Dave Brat in 2014.[34]

Congressional Democrats and the president eschewed compromise, confident the Republicans would blink. Faced with a choice of bringing a bill to the House floor that represented a compromise with Democrats versus one supported by his Tea Party members, Speaker Boehner decided on September 18 to stick with his conservative wing instead of pursuing Cantor's strategy of calling for an implementation pause. The bill offered for a vote would have defunded key parts of the law and imposed a one-year moratorium on any further implementation. The measure succeeded in the House, but the Senate stripped out the ACA defunding and passed the remainder. Beyond Senators Lee and Cruz, very few proved willing to sustain a filibuster long enough to close the government. Senate GOP leaders, including Minority Leader Mitch McConnell and his deputy John Cornyn, announced they would not join the small group of senators pushing for a government shutdown.[35] When the Senate version arrived back in the House, members stubbornly reinserted the defunding provisions and passed this on September 29. On October 1, major portions of the federal government ran out of spending authority.

By October 10, it became clear to many congressional Republicans that the public was losing confidence in them more than in the Democrats. At this point, Boehner, along with Cantor and Budget Committee Chair Paul Ryan, spoke publicly about the possibility of solving the budget problem without mentioning health care. They were willing to discuss a settlement that did not insist on defunding the ACA. Even Grover Norquist, leader of the antitax group Americans for Tax Reform, and Tim Philips, the director of Americans for Prosperity, lamented the insistence on tying the ACA to the budget and debt payment.[36]

Finally, on October 16, Majority Leader Reid and Minority Leader McConnell agreed on a short-term funding arrangement that authorized an increase in the debt limit, funded the government into February 2014, and did not defund the ACA. The measure passed the Senate 81–18 and hours later the House by 285–144. Senators Cruz, Lee, Rubio, and Paul all voted against the measure. Speaker Boehner told a Cincinnati radio station, "We've been locked in a fight over here, trying to bring government down to size, trying to do our best to stop Obamacare. We fought the good fight. We just didn't win."[37]

What constitutes winning varies considerably, depending on one's perspective. For the Obama White House, preserving the law, even if that meant not offering a full-throated public defense, appeared sufficient. For Tea Party or Freedom Caucus Republicans who truly believed that the ACA represented a Washington takeover, nothing short of full repeal would do. House Speaker Boehner and other mainstream Republicans were clearly conflicted. They wanted to avoid a reputation-damaging shutdown, but at the same time hammering away at the ACA served them remarkably well as an electoral strategy. This approach did not require drafting new and presumably complex legislation that itself would likely involve shortcomings. In this sense, keeping the ACA around as a whipping boy, as opposed to actually repealing it and then facing some pressure and technical challenges to replace it, provided an effective campaign tool.

The contours of public opinion surrounding the withholding of government funding changed somewhat from the 1990s to late 2016. During a pair of such episodes in the mid-1990s and again in 2013, three-quarters of the public considered the shutdowns "a bad thing" (74 percent in 1996 and 75 percent in 2013), and more people blamed the Republicans than the Democrats. However, one of the products of increased ideological polarization among the general public is that both self-identified Democrats and Republicans more strongly blamed the other party for the breakdown in 2013 than was the case in 1996, when the public exhibited frustration in somewhat more even-handed fashion.[38] This shift suggests that as Congress members consider shutdowns during budget fights, they can increasingly dismiss broad public preferences and instead focus on their partisan bases. For Republicans, the added incentive toward brinksmanship is that shuttering the government substantially conforms to what their most conservative cue givers espouse. Consider Grover Norquist's quip that his "goal is to cut government in half in twenty-five years . . . to get it down to the size where we can drown it in the bathtub."[39] With this being the tenor of elite discourse about how to run the government in general and how to address the nation's health care needs in particular, the near-term future for productive collaboration on policy reform seems dismal.

Self-Inflicted Wounds

The implementation of the Affordable Care Act was hindered by numerous exercises in litigation and legislative grandstanding, but it was also tarnished by a series of hitches, some of which were self-inflicted wounds induced by the Obama administration. Insurance rate increases (despite provisions in the law to limit those), cancellations of insurance policies that fell short of the law's minimum coverage provisions (despite the president's assurance that "if you like your insurance you can keep it"), and the substantially failed rollout of the healthcare.gov website during the autumn of 2013 all caused serious headaches for the ACA's supporters. More importantly, they damaged the law's credibility in the eyes of the general public precisely at a time when addressing problems of health care access and cost mattered so much. Here I address some avoidable problems that undermined public approval of the ACA and poisoned the politics of health care reform.

Healthcare.gov's Failure to Launch

Aside from the critics' attacks undermining public confidence in the ACA, the Obama administration itself made a couple of significant mistakes in the early years of implementation, and these almost certainly added to the public's skepticism toward the law. Chief among them was the incompetent rollout of the website that was supposed to simplify the task of comparison shopping for a health insurance policy. Given Americans' growing comfort with purchasing goods and services online, building a web-based health insurance marketplace should have been a fairly straightforward step in the phased implementation of the ACA. As it turned out, this was anything but straightforward. The website initially proved so slow that people found it tedious or impossible to navigate, and while the administration fixed the problems within a few months, the lasting reputational damage done was significant enough that nearly two years passed before the portion of the public expressing disapproval of the law settled back down to the pre-web-debacle level.[40]

Healthcare.gov needed to include pricing information from numerous insurance plans, sort those based on individuals' states of residence and demographics, determine the amount of the federal tax credit a person would be eligible for, and do this quickly and accurately. The experience of many millions of people who attempted to shop for insurance during the fall of 2013 painfully revealed the inadequacies of the initial version of the site. Instead of a smooth shopping experience that people expect at any number of online retailers, the website instructed shoppers to engage in convoluted site navigation, unnecessarily repeated steps, and unreasonably long wait times and sometimes forced them to endure outright crashes. Despite millions of website visits within the first few days (seven million within the first 48 hours), very few people were able to enroll. By the beginning of the second day, the HHS confirmed 6 enrollments and by the end of that second day 100. By the morning of October 4, 248 had managed to sign up.[41] This story became a monumental embarrassment for the administration and tainted the Affordable Care Act with an image of gross inefficiency. The critics' message was that if you like long waits to speak to grumpy clerks at the department of motor vehicles, you'll love healthcare.gov.

Briefly, several factors contributed to this highly troubled launch.[42] Two of them stand out. First, intentional delays in issuing administrative regulations during 2011 and 2012 meant that private insurance companies could not submit pricing data that then would need to be built into the website. Second, design features selected by the site builders were unnecessarily complicated and virtually closed to scrutiny by senior administration figures, meaning that when problems first appeared to those relatively few individuals tasked with monitoring its development, they were able to minimize oversight by others. There existed no effective way for the work to be checked by the White House. Only very late in the process did White House officials gain a clear indication that the website had serious problems and would not be easily fixed. The troubles provided critics ample opportunity to indict the entire law along with this one major implementation headache. Compounding the problems with the October 2013 rollout was that autumn's budget impasse, which meant that large numbers of HHS employees were furloughed on the federal marketplace's opening day. Of course, by then, the damage of administrative delays had already been done.

The delay in issuing regulations about the details of insurance policies that could be marketed online was driven primarily by fears that promulgating regulations would raise troubling issues during the presidential election campaign. While proposed regulations appeared in the Federal Register as early as August 17, 2011, the vast majority of them were stalled until after the 2012 election.[43] As journalist and health policy expert Steven Brill writes in *America's Bitter Pill*, the slowdown was deliberate. A pair of officials at the Center for Medicare and Medicaid Services (CMS), the agency tasked to run the federal marketplace, later stated that "beginning in January 2012 they were told by their superiors that the already-slow rule-making process had to be slowed still more. They could take their time sending drafts to the White House for approval . . . because the White House was only going to stall before sending . . . the rule over to [the Office of Management and Budget], which would stall even more. They did not want to make any waves before the election."[44] Brill quoted a senior official at CMS as saying "we were told by the White House to do nothing, not even circulate drafts of regulations, because they might leak out if lobbyists got ahold of them."[45]

The other chief problem with the website development was a lack of skilled designers assigned to the work. In an e-mail exchange between CMS officials during July 2013, less than three months before the scheduled launch, they noted that the

> build appears to be way off track and getting worse. We also were finally told that there are only 10 developers total working on the build for all functionality. Only one of these developers is at a high enough skill level to handle complex issue resolution. . . . We are one week out from production deployment, and we are being told already that it doesn't work.[46]

This news of trouble and the need for more money to hire skilled staff does not seem to have reached beyond the agency.[47] Later in July, both the office director Henry Chao and CMS administrator Marilyn Tavenner testified to a congressional committee, and when asked if the fixes for the shortfalls in readiness that had been briefly touched on were "going to be 100 percent complete on October 1," Chao responded "Correct" and Tavenner responded "yes sir . . . we will start on October 1, and we will certainly have hiccups along the way, and we are prepared to deal with this."[48] Chao and Tavenner's boss, Secretary Sebelius, had assured Montana Senator Max Baucus—a chief architect of the law—earlier that spring by pointing to her plan to have thousands of navigators to sit with people to help them enroll. Baucus had expressed his concern that small business people did not know what to expect and that the HHS simply was not disseminating enough information in the run-up to the opening of the marketplaces. Indeed, Baucus described what he saw as a looming "train wreck."[49]

CMS's secrecy surrounding the development problems was complete enough that the news media did not pick up on the story prior to the week of the October launch. Neither *The Washington Post* nor *The New York Times* ran a story about the unpreparedness of the website prior to October 2.[50] Whereas the CMS staff could have asked the White House for more resources in a timely way, it did not. When combined with the intentional foot dragging by the White House, the incompetent web design made the launch far more problematic than it had to be. Once the problems became obvious to anyone attempting to sign up for insurance at healthcare.gov, media coverage exploded, not only highlighting the design failures but also reinforcing the notion of government incompetence generally. When opinion pollsters asked in mid-October whether the site failure was an isolated incident or a sign of broader problems in implementing the law, fully 56 percent of respondents connected it with broader problems. In line with the high level of partisanship discussed in Chapter 1, Democrats and Republicans strongly clustered in the expected directions, with 62 percent of Democrats seeing this as an isolated incident and a whopping 82 percent of Republicans considering this failure as part of a larger pattern.[51] In a more general assessment of the law, Americans became somewhat more negative, with the percentage disapproving moving from 43 percent in September to 50 percent by January 2014 in the Kaiser Family Foundation's monthly tracking poll.[52]

To the extent the narrative during the closing months of 2013 became about the failed website, this framing may have helped the ACA's supporters compartmentalize the public's frustration with the law. So long as the complaint was about the website, that was a fixable problem. And it was fixed. By April 1, 2014, over five million Americans signed up for insurance through healthcare.gov (plus nearly another three million on state-operated exchanges). The federal number exceeded 8.6 million in April 2015.[53] Critics certainly made political hay out of this episode, harshly critiquing administration officials and trying to paint one failure—albeit a very consequential one—as emblematic of the entire statue. However, over the past few years, enrollment figures show that many millions of people came to rely on this federal marketplace for health insurance.

The Minimum Coverage Provision: "If You Like Your Insurance You Can Keep It"

From the beginning of Obama's push for health reform, he sought to assure Americans that if they were happy with their insurance and medical providers, they could keep them under his plan. The president and other senior White House officials, as well as congressional Democrats, said so.[54] The repeated promise was aimed at defusing the concern over government interference with the doctor-patient relationship. Obama went to great lengths to convince the public that comprehensive reform need not entail bureaucratic control over how, when, and where people obtain health care services. The problem with this promise was that the ACA set minimum coverage requirements on health insurance policies. In crafting the law, Congress wanted not only to ensure that people got insurance coverage but that this coverage was meaningful, including a range of basic services with no lifetime limits. Policies sold on the exchanges would need to cover out-patient and in-patient care; emergency room services; pre- and post-natal care; mental health and substance use disorder services; prescription drugs; services designed to help recover from injuries, disabilities, and chronic conditions; laboratory services; preventative services such as counseling, screenings, and vaccines; and pediatric services. It turned out that many existing policies did not offer this breadth of coverage.

Insurance industry leaders were anxious about this provision and said so within a few months of the law's passage. The administration, realizing that tens of millions of Americans could be affected, responded with a regulation allowing these noncompliant policies to be grandfathered until 2015 (later extended to 2017). The impact was feared to be potentially tremendous. Various studies projected that between one-half and two-thirds of all policies could be determined to be substandard.[55] The grandfathering took the form of a rule issued on June 17, 2010. This regulation indicated that in order to be grandfathered, policies had to have been in force on the day the law was signed, and in order to maintain their grandfather status they could not reduce benefits significantly or raise prices or co-pays beyond simple cost-of-service adjustments accounting for medical inflation.[56] Going forward, these grandfathered plans could only continue to cover their previous enrollees, not enroll new ones. In short, the administration envisioned a long downward taper in the portion of the population carrying these noncompliant policies. This approach split the difference between forcing cheap policies out of the market and effectively making good on Obama's promise that people could maintain their policies.

Despite this effort to create a pressure-relief valve via grandfathering, the move only defused the unpopularity of the minimum coverage requirement so much. The president's rhetoric stood at odds with the language of the law because the grandfathering was tailored narrowly enough that many harbored legitimate concerns that even small changes might negate the policies' continuation. News accounts said as much, revealing that the president's own staff had known of this problem back in 2010, yet the president had continued with his promise.[57] Throughout the fall of 2013, as the effective date for the minimum coverage provision approached, this issue came to a head. During October 2013, thousands of subscribers suffered the frustration of notices of imminent cancellation from their insurers. Initial concerns of a large minority or even most of the policy holders turned out to be overstated. The Urban Institute produced a study in the fall of 2013 showing that only a very small percentage of people would actually lose their coverage.[58]

Caught in this uncomfortable situation, Obama apologized in an NBC News interview in early November: "I am sorry that [Americans] are finding themselves in this situation based on assurances they got from me, [the president said] . . . We've got to work hard to make sure that they know we hear them and that we're going to do everything we can to deal with folks who find themselves in a tough position as a consequence of this."[59] Obama's apology did little to quell the criticism. Opponents dwelled on the president's broken promise. The administration announced in December 2013 that anyone whose policy was cancelled would be exempt from the individual mandate throughout 2014. In March 2014, the administration extended to 2017 the duration of the grandfathering option.[60] The consequent vagueness of this administrative limbo left many Americans uncertain of their health insurance coverage, which was precisely the outcome the ACA sought to combat.

The ACA in Court

Beyond the friction in Congress over the ACA throughout this period, organized opponents also worked assiduously in the courts to block the legislation. In the states, Republican officials filed multiple suits challenging the law on two important fronts. First, they argued that the required Medicaid expansion was unconstitutional. For numerous states, such an expansion would involve covering hundreds of thousands of new enrollees. Acquiescing to such a major move was repulsive to many GOP state officials because of how it represented an endorsement of Obamacare. (This outlook later changed; see Chapter 4.) Additionally, beyond the first three years, the Medicaid expansion would cost states a small percentage of program costs, and it became a standard Republican complaint that this percentage might grow in the future, even though the law specified that the federal government would provide the overwhelming majority of these funds.

Second, numerous state attorneys general challenged the individual mandate in court, arguing that Congress lacked the authority to require their states' residents to purchase insurance and that the attempt trampled states' rights. Virginia's attorney general, Ken Cuccinelli, led in this respect. Cuccinelli, elected attorney general in 2009 and by spring 2010 already contemplating a run for governor, had earned a reputation as highly ideologically driven and acknowledged his image in some quarters as a politician who was "off his rocker."[61] As a newly inaugurated attorney general in the spring of 2010, he argued that state attorneys general are the last line of defense of the Constitution against excesses by the federal government and that his suit was as much about protecting citizens' fundamental liberties as it was about the financial implications of the ACA for Virginians.[62] Cuccinelli was determined to defend Virginia's new law barring residents of the commonwealth from being required to purchase health insurance.[63] In time, 13 additional states and the National Federation of Independent Businesses joined in this litigation. The legal arguments focused mainly on the scope of the U.S. Constitution's interstate commerce clause. As it turned out, the Supreme Court majority supported the law based not on the commerce clause but instead on Congress's taxing power. More on this follows.

From the beginning, this litigation was a highly partisan affair. The map of opposing states closely came to resemble recent maps of presidential election outcomes, with the vast majority of red states refusing to cooperate with the ACA and the vast majority of the blue ones moving forward to help implement it, either by developing plans to expand Medicaid or to create a state health care exchange or by both. The uncertainty over these two key provisions of the ACA would cause many states to delay their preparations for the launch of some important components of the law, meaning many states found themselves rushing to be prepared for the implementation of various parts of the law during the first few years following its 2010 passage.

In December 2010, Federal District Court Judge Henry Hudson, a George W. Bush appointee, became the first federal judge to declare the ACA unconstitutional based on his interpretation of the interstate commerce clause. He wrote, in part, that "neither the Supreme Court nor any federal circuit court of appeals has extended commerce clause powers to compel an individual to involuntarily enter the stream of commerce by purchasing a commodity in the private market. In doing so, [the health-care law's individual mandate] exceeds the commerce clause powers vested in Congress."[64]

Within a few weeks, the multistate suit over the individual mandate was heard in the federal district court for northern Florida. In the course of hearings, Judge Roger Vinson, a Reagan appointee, quipped that if Congress could compel Americans to purchase health insurance, it could probably also force them to eat broccoli. This comparison trivialized the economic stakes of a system that had left tens of millions of uninsured persons living in the United States, but the sentiment certainly bolstered the argument from supporters of smaller government.

Vinson's ruling, if upheld, would have rendered the entire ACA unconstitutional. This sweeping decision flowed from Vinson's conclusion that the commerce clause could not justify the individual health insurance mandate and that this provision was not severable from the rest of the act, reflecting his judgment that the interlocking pieces of the ACA could not function as intended without the large boost in insurance coverage that the mandate would create. On appeal, the circuit court agreed in part and disagreed in part with Vinson's ruling, noting that while Congress lacked the power to impose an individual mandate—either under the commerce clause or as a taxing power—this provision was severable from the rest of the law, meaning the remainder of the ACA was allowed to stand for the time being. Other federal courts, including those in Virginia and Michigan, also heard challenges, resulting in a half-dozen lower court rulings in all. These rulings were mixed, setting up the issue as one ripe for the Supreme Court to hear.

As this case moved through the federal courts, the Democrats flip-flopped on their argument about the individual mandate. During the legislative process, Democrats, especially those in the administration, insisted that the financial sanction for violating the individual mandate was not a tax but rather a penalty. As awkward as this was, this language squared with then-candidate Barack Obama's 2008 campaign pledge not to support increased taxes on anyone with an annual personal income below $250,000.[65] The administration considered several ways to justify the mandate. Relying on the Constitution's general welfare clause seemed vague. The commerce clause appeared more promising, as it had already enjoyed some support in the lower federal courts. Once in the Supreme Court, and sensing the justices' skepticism about the reach of the commerce clause, the administration's attorney suggested it was instead a tax. Justice Samuel Alito pointed out the inconsistency during oral argument when he commented: Solicitor "General Verrilli, today you are arguing that the penalty is not a tax. Tomorrow are you going to be back, arguing that the penalty is a tax?"[66]

In the end, Chief Justice Roberts sided with the Court's four liberals to craft what many observers lambasted as a convoluted argument. Roberts ruled that the penalty attached to the individual mandate was permissible as a tax but not justifiable as a regulation of interstate commerce, nor under the Constitution's necessary and proper or general welfare clauses. Along the way to this outcome, Roberts accomplished a couple of other objectives. First, he worked around an argument that would have sidelined the courts. Roberts wrote that the federal Anti-Injunction Act, which normally precludes the federal courts from hearing challenges to congressionally enacted taxes, did not apply in this case. In the view of the chief justice, the individual mandate is not a tax for the purposes of the Anti-Injunction Act since Congress did not appear to *intend* this provision to operate as a tax. However, once this issue was disposed of, Roberts continued by writing that it is permissible to think of what the ACA called a "shared responsibility payment" as *operating* as a tax, thus properly under Congress's power. He wrote that "the federal government does not have the power to order people to buy health insurance. . . . Section 5000A would therefore be unconstitutional if read as a command. [However,] the federal government does have the power to impose a tax on those without health insurance. Section 5000A is therefore constitutional because it can reasonably be read as a tax."[67]

Appearing to anticipate how this ruling would disappoint many fellow Republicans, Roberts took the opportunity in his ruling to strongly suggest that the ACA was imprudent and that the question of expanding health care reform should be put to the electorate. At several points in his opinion, including his opening paragraph, Roberts wrote that "we do not consider whether the Act embodies sound policies. That judgment is entrusted to the Nation's elected leaders. We ask only whether Congress has the power under the Constitution to enact the challenged provisions."[68] Later he wrote that "we [the Court] possess neither the expertise nor the prerogative to make policy judgments. Those decisions are entrusted to our Nation's elected leaders, who can be thrown out of office if the people disagree with them. It is not our job to protect the people from the consequences of their political choices."[69]

As much as the chief justice seemed to hold out hope that the congressional elections of 2012 would provide a policy corrective, his fellow conservatives experienced little comfort in this. They howled. The range of responses ran from confusion, to anger, to redoubled determination to kill the ACA. Typical of the conservative response was an essay posted on the website of the National Federation of Independent Businesses, which noted in apocalyptic terms that "today marks a sad day in the history of America. With this decision, Americans have lost the right to be left alone, which Justice William O. Douglas once called 'the beginning of all freedom.'"[70] While it might have been awkward for a conservative organization to cite one of the Supreme Court's strongest liberals of the twentieth century, the sentiment—with all its dramatic reference to bedrock principles and supremely high stakes—was echoed in others' rhetoric right on up through the 2012 congressional elections and beyond.

If conservatives could take any satisfaction from Roberts's ruling and his unexpected alliance with the Court's liberal wing, it was that his opinion limited the scope of the commerce clause, at least for the near future. This is a logical trade-off, given that his ruling allowed him to chalk up a win for the conservatives on an issue of government power that is larger than simply the ACA. Of course, only time will tell if this ruling remains precedent setting.

The other major question in this case dealt with Congress's effort to mandate that states expand their Medicaid programs to cover individuals living in families with income up to 135 percent of the federal poverty level. In Roberts's view, by threatening to take away current Medicaid funding for those states refusing to broaden the program, Congress was setting up a structure that "runs counter to this Nation's system of federalism."[71] These federal funds were highly significant, amounting to approximately 12 percent of the average state's budget. To threaten their withdrawal was to dragoon states into a level of program implementation that was inappropriately coercive, Roberts opined. Such a withdrawal of funds would not be "relatively mild encouragement" but rather "a gun to the head."[72] In the wake of this ruling, states could expand their Medicaid programs but would do so on a voluntary basis.

In the months following the June 2012 ruling, the public stood closely divided in its assessments of the Court's decision. Several public opinion polls fielded during the spring and summer found only a few percentage points between the approving and disapproving shares.[73] Given the Court's recent decline in public approval—from 49 percent in 1997 to only 30 percent in mid-2015—Americans seem more willing now than in the recent past to criticize the U.S. Supreme Court, both in a general sense and regarding particular decisions.[74] Their highly mixed assessment of the 2012 ACA ruling is a case in point.

Mandating Contraception Coverage: The Hobby Lobby Case

In pursuit of one of the primary goals of the Affordable Care Act—to expand access to basic health services for all Americans—the act pushed employers and insurance plans to include a range of contraceptive options. Congress did not specify exactly how contraceptive coverage would work, leaving this instead to the HSS to work out through administrative regulation. Sensitive to how this type of coverage might clash with religious beliefs, the HHS carved out an exception to the contraceptive coverage requirement for churches and other explicitly religious organizations. Unfortunately, the definition of an explicitly religious organization was left fuzzy. Into this ambiguity stepped the Green Family of Oklahoma City, members of which own Hobby Lobby Stores, and Mardel, a chain of Christian bookstores. Based on their conservative Christian beliefs, the Greens did not want to provide four specific kinds of contraceptives or devices that interfere with the development of a fertilized egg. Believing these four products to be abortifacients (and yes, there is political debate about this[75]), the Green Family, together with Conestoga Wood Specialties, sued the HHS over its regulation requiring this broad contraceptive coverage.[76] The Supreme Court had to decide if Hobby Lobby and the others could be exempted from this insurance requirement under the Religious Freedom Restoration Act, a federal law that requires governments to demonstrate a compelling interest before issuing a rule that interferes with religious expression and to use the least restrictive means possible when crafting such a rule.

The Green Family indicated that they had no opposition to most forms of birth control, except those that interfere with attachment of a fertilized egg to the uterine wall. Given this, the family opposed four forms of birth control and was determined not to offer them under the health insurance it provides to its workers. Under the ACA, Hobby Lobby would face an annual fine of $475 million.[77]

As this case progressed to the Supreme Court, debate ensued along what were, perhaps, predictable lines. The Greens argued that as a family business they are entitled to project their deeply held religious values into their corporate practices. They also pointed out that the company still provided for a wide variety of contraceptives and that its objection was limited to four products.[78] Hobby Lobby's critics, including New Hampshire Senator Jeanne Shaheen, argued that Hobby Lobby's refusal to cover these contraceptives stands in for a much larger pattern of gender-based discrimination and that to allow employers to skirt the ACA's contraception coverage requirements jeopardized basic health care coverage for countless women.[79] At issue as well was the matter of whether the HHS had used the least restrictive means available to accomplish the legislative goal, that is, that the regulation interfered as little as possible with the religious beliefs of company owners.

Hobby Lobby won. The Court's majority ruled that the HHS had not used the least restrictive means possible to achieve the law's broad goals and that in the instances of these small, privately held companies, decisions about employee benefits were merely those owners' ways of doing business. On the matter of the scope of the religious organization exception, Justice Samuel Alito, writing for the majority, distinguished between small and "closely held" companies operated on religious principles versus larger corporations whose directors may or may not be motived by religious principles. Alito went out of his way to portray this ruling as narrow and not one that would cover other forms of differential treatment by small employers, such as declining to pay for blood transfusions or vaccinations. He noted that larger corporations would not likely qualify for religious recognition and thus the majority was trying to say that this ruling for Hobby Lobby would not be the entering wedge for numerous suits by larger, publicly traded companies seeking to exempt themselves from the ACA's insurance requirement.

This, however, has become the source of significant concern among defenders of broad access to contraception. If any small company—and most Americans work for small companies—can claim a religious exception to the contraception coverage rule, the rule potentially had only modest effects. Religious organizations, including Little Sisters of the Poor, a Catholic religious order that operates nursing homes for the poor and elderly, as well as several church-related universities, further challenged the scope of the ACA's accommodation of religious groups.

Federal Subsidies on Healthcare.gov: *King v. Burwell*

Challenging Obamacare in court has continued to offer opponents a potentially productive venue in light of their failure to stop the law legislatively. In 2015, the Supreme Court ruled for a third time on a significant provision of the ACA, this one regarding tax credits to individuals who purchase health insurance on the federally operated healthcare.gov exchange. Owing to a legislative drafting glitch, section 18031 of the law, although it stated that credits would be available to those purchasing insurance on a state-operated exchange, inadvertently omitted mention of credits for purchases on the federal marketplace. This problem resulted from a copy-and-paste error amending the Senate version of the bill, which was passed early in the morning on Christmas Eve, 2010.[80] The error set up a conflict between the overall and rather clear intent of the law to make subsidies available to eligible individuals on either a state or the federal exchange, on one hand, and the specific language of section 18031, which seemed to limit the availability of the subsidy, on the other. The Internal Revenue Service (IRS), responsible for approving federal tax credits, interpreted the legislative language as permitting subsidies for purchases made on either type of exchange. The Court had to decide whether the drafting error in this particular section would trump the overall intent of the law. The affordability of health insurance for an estimated six million Americans living in 34 states would rely upon the Court's decision. Without these federal subsidies, millions of persons likely would have dropped their insurance, adversely impacting health insurance markets. Like the 2012 case over the individual mandate, this 2015 case was a very high-stakes moment for the Affordable Care Act.

This litigation was initiated by four individuals living in Virginia who did not want to purchase health insurance. Because Virginia chose not to establish an exchange, these persons read the law to mean that they were not eligible for the federal subsidy. Being ineligible for the subsidy meant that they would have to spend more than 8 percent of their income to cover the premium, an expense that would excuse them from the requirement to obtain health insurance. If instead they received the subsidy, their premiums would fall below the 8 percent threshold, exposing them to the insurance mandate. These petitioners argued that because section 18031 of the ACA defines individuals as eligible for subsidies in "an exchange established by the state," they were not eligible.[81]

Two significant ways of interpreting statues involve either a holistic reading of the text to discern legislative intent or a passage-by-passage more literal reading.[82] The difference in these interpretational approaches divided various federal courts in this case. For some, close adherence to the text must prevail over broader thinking about the supposed intent of a law. For them, this provided a highly compelling judicial strategy. However, for others, the clear overall intent of the law led them toward a different reading. Several passages in the text of the ACA indicate the authority of the HHS to create a federal exchange where states decline to do so. These passages would have been rendered nonsensical if primacy were given to section 18031 and its clumsily crafted language about "an exchange established by the state." For instance, section 1321 of the law read that if a state did not establish a marketplace, the HHS "shall . . . establish and operate such Exchange within the State," with "such exchange" suggesting an equivalent function across both state and federal marketplaces.[83] Further, section 18031 required all exchanges to operate outreach programs to "distribute fair and impartial information concerning . . . the availability of premium tax credits under section 36B" of the law.[84] Such promotions make no sense if these same tax credits available on state exchanges were not also available to persons purchasing insurance on the federal exchange. Given this, only a very narrow reading of the passage about subsidies and state exchanges, ignoring the various other parts of the law that clearly refer to the federal marketplace, could lead one to construe the law in the way the litigants did. In defending a broader reading, the administration argued that the intent of the law was clear and that even if one passage is ambiguous, the federal courts should defer to the IRS interpretation.

A Federal District Court in Virginia,[85] and later the 4th Circuit Court of Appeals, found the administration's interpretation of the law permissible. In opposition, the Circuit Court of Appeals for the District of Columbia supported the plaintiffs' case. This conflict among the appeals courts, together with the inherent gravity of the case, made it an interesting one for the Supreme Court, which agreed to hear in November 2014. For the justices, this case represented another opportunity not only to uphold or overturn the ACA but also to engage in statutory interpretation that was indicative of their jurisprudential styles. For Associate Justice Antonin Scalia, this case presented a clear instance of following the text of the law, not Congress's purported intent. For him, the phrase "exchange established by the state" meant exactly what it said, not what the larger context of the statute implied. However, for pragmatists, such as Justices Anthony Kennedy and John Roberts, considering the larger meaning of the law was crucial. For them, one must consider the overall intent of the law, not isolated passages, and how the subsidies constitute one of the legs of the three-legged stool discussed in Chapter 1. In fact, near the beginning of his majority opinion, Chief Justice Roberts explicitly tied the tax subsidy provision to Massachusetts's 2006 insurance reforms, and he exhibited no trouble agreeing with the idea that Congress intended the federal tax credit to be available to purchasers of insurance on either state or federal exchanges. For Roberts, the individual mandate together with the guaranteed issue provisions and the tax subsidies embodied in the ACA were "closely intertwined" elements "that made the Massachusetts system successful," and thus they make most sense when understood as working together.[86] Roberts gently chided Congress for several instances of what he called "inartful drafting" and pointed out that "the Act does not reflect the type of care and deliberation that one might expect of such significant legislation."[87] In particular, he critiqued Congress for its reliance on the budget reconciliation process to pass the bill through the Senate while side stepping a filibuster, a technique that resulted in the language of the act not being comprehensively and carefully integrated from start to finish. In the end, however, six of the justices, including Roberts and Kennedy as well as the four more liberal members, ruled that the federal tax credits should be available on either federal or state exchanges.

Associate justices Alito, Thomas, and Scalia strenuously disagreed, characterizing the majority's reasoning as "absurd," to read the five words in section 18031—"Exchange established by the state"—to mean an exchange established by either the federal government or by states.[88] True to his textualist approach, Scalia, a declared foe of the ACA, focused sharply on this phrase and accused the majority of bending over backward to support the law, no matter the violence that this required to a plain meaning of the text in the much-debated section 18031.[89] In closing, Scalia linked this ruling to the earlier decision in *National Federation of Independent Businesses v. Sebelius* and accused the majority of doing whatever was necessary to preserve the law. He acerbically noted that perhaps "we should start calling this law SCOTUScare."[90]

In crafting a decision on this case, the Court was operating in the context of a deep concern over the consequences for its ruling. Had the tax credits not survived judicial scrutiny, millions of individuals would have exited the health care market, unable to afford their newly purchased insurance policies. Various experts, including some who authored amicus curiae briefs in this case, argued that the withdrawal of the subsidy and the resulting loss of policy subscriptions would have led to a so-called death spiral in the insurance market, forcing up prices for the remaining subscribers and in turn leading still more of them to exit the market. Chief Justice Roberts explicitly acknowledged this concern in his opinion.[91] Policy makers in numerous states also took a keen interest in the outcome with this particular concern in mind. In fact, 23 states signed onto amicus briefs supporting the IRS, compared to only 7 supporting briefs in opposition.[92] The supporters represented a mixture of Republican- and Democratically controlled states. The opponents all hailed from GOP strongholds.

The responses to the Court's decision ranged from anger, to relief, to incredulity. For its part, a solid majority—63 percent in a June CNN poll—of the general public approved of the decision.[93] However, conservative commentators belittled the majority's broad reading of the law and expressed dismay at the decision to dismiss what critics saw as the plain meaning of the text. Texas Senator and presidential candidate Ted Cruz characterized as insufficient the frustration expressed by other GOP presidential candidates, insisting that they were feigning their opposition to the ruling and too willing to consider the ACA the law of the land. Cruz insisted that "one day of faux outrage from the Washington Cartel won't fool the millions of courageous conservatives across our country. They know the Republican leadership in Washington is quietly celebrating the Court's decision."[94] Other opponents took pragmatic turns, laying out strategies for moving forward and reforming Obamacare by way of waivers that were to be available to states beginning in 2017 under section 1332 of the law.[95] Given the significant track record of section 1115 waivers under Medicaid over several decades, this avenue for reform appealed to those intent on turning parts of the ACA into more market-oriented and state-tailored policies.

Fighting the Affordable Care Act in federal court, while certainly a legitimate strategy, provided the public a less clear—and less democratic—way to sort out the finer points of this landmark act compared to working out these issues among the elected branches. The courts provide venues for raging ideological conflicts on a regular basis, and while historically they may have been able to minimize the overt politicking that characterizes the elected branches, the Supreme Court has paid a price in recent years for its penchant for fully engaging the partisan combat that has spilled out over the entire political landscape since about the 1980s. While the Supreme Court historically has been and continues to be the most approved of branch of the federal government, since 2009 a substantially increased portion of Americans have voiced their disapproval to pollsters, and following its 2012 *NFIB vs. Sebelius* ruling, fully 4 in 10 Americans came to see the Court as too liberal, up from one-third just before the decision. As of 2015, only about 45 percent of Americans approved of the way the justices handle their jobs, down from the 60 percent range in the early 2000s.[96] Regardless of how much—or little—importance one attaches to the job performance ratings of the courts, it is clear that making key decisions about health care policy reform by way of the judicial branch deprives the general public of the opportunity to lobby, pressure, or even understand the reasoning behind these decisions. And while the legislative process is often far from transparent, at least that conveyor belt for public preferences lends itself to pluralistic pressures far beyond those that might enter into the work of an exceedingly small number of jurists. To the extent scholars think of courts as protectors of individual rights with the courage to take positions that elected legislators will not—for example, standing up against racially segregated schools, discriminatory marriage laws, or defending unpopular cases of free speech—we can relish courts' partial independence from day-to-day politics. However, given their insularity from pluralistic politics, they make a suboptimal venue for law making on more routine matters.

Where Are the Critics to Go Next?

The take-no-prisoners politics that developed around the ACA made it virtually impossible for the Obama administration to return to Congress to ask for technical corrections to the law that could remedy the issue of noncompliant insurance policies, the drafting glitch that led to the *King v. Burwell* case, and other uncertainties. A broad swath of congressional Republicans signaled that they had no interest in seeking solutions to the law's shortcomings. This extreme uncooperativeness was on full display during the two-week-long government shutdown in the autumn of 2013 and the response to the failed website launch. On the other side, purposeful administrative delay in issuing regulations to guide insurance companies during 2011 and 2012 contributed significantly to lagging development of the federal marketplace. This in its own way marked a failure of cooperation with important players in the reform process.

The public substantially followed the polarized leads offered by national politicians. In numerous opinion polls, party identification divided Americans more sharply than other characteristics, including objective factors that, arguably, should weigh more heavily, such as insurance coverage and income. For instance, party identification drove assessments of subjective matters such as confidence in the president's handling of the law. Here Democrats and Republicans divided sharply, with two-thirds of Democrats approving during January 2014, despite the failed website launch a few months earlier, and 87 percent of Republicans disapproving.[97] Party identification also strongly affected what people said they knew about factual aspects of the law. In December 2014, fully half of Republicans (compared to one-third of Democrats) mistakenly reported that the ACA established "a government panel to make decisions about end of life care for people on Medicare."[98] Over half of Republicans (56 percent, compared to 31 percent of Democrats) were also mistaken in this same poll about whether undocumented immigrants could receive tax subsidies to purchase health insurance.[99] Rage against the law from the political right appears to have led large portions of the population not only to despise the law but factually to misunderstand it. This is not a recipe for constructively addressing one of the chief policy challenges of our times.

Lastly, the congressional GOP's calls for repeal through this period rang so hollow that even their own supporters pointed this out. Ramesh Ponnuru, the conservative commentator for the *National Review*, wrote in

June 2013 that "Republicans' confidence that Obamacare will collapse has contributed to their lassitude in coming up with an alternative. It is a perverse complacency. . . . Congressional Republicans have not reached agreement on what should replace Obamacare, let alone a strategy for enacting that replacement."[100] When in early 2015 the House of Representatives voted yet again to repeal the ACA fully and Senator Orrin Hatch, together with two Republican colleagues, introduced an alternative that bore more than a passing resemblance to the ACA (but this one without the individual or employer mandate or the goal of universal coverage), Speaker John Boehner commented that this proposal would be only one part of the conversation about replacing Obamacare.[101] Others, such Michael Cannon at the Cato Institute, dismissed this proposal as "Obamacare lite."[102] As Philip Klein, a conservative columnist at the *Washington Examiner* explained in book-length fashion, Republicans through this period were deeply conflicted about whether to reform, replace, or restart with health policy.

Following Donald Trump's election, they will have this opportunity. Over the next election cycle, and perhaps beyond that, they will face multiple challenges in addressing health care costs, quality, and access issues. By all appearances, they have gravitated toward market-driven strategies that purport to control cost and enhance quality outcomes. As it turns out, the evidence is more complicated than meets the eye. Explaining what we know about health care markets and consumer behavior in these settings is undertaken in Chapter 3.

CHAPTER THREE

Will Markets Save Us?

The failure of congressional Republicans to rally behind a coherent alternative to the Affordable Care Act (ACA) caused no small amount of consternation, both within and without the party during the first several years after the act's passage.[1] Instead of advancing a comprehensive replacement strategy, Republicans tinkered with various ideas of limited scope, such as repealing of the law's medical device tax and the excise tax on expensive employer policies or equalizing the tax code's treatment of individual- versus employer-purchased insurance.[2] By the summer of 2015, House Republicans had voted 54 times to repeal the law either in part or entirely.[3] The Hatch-Upton-Burr proposal of early 2015 perhaps came closest to offering a well-developed alternative to the ACA, but that, as of autumn 2016, had failed to garner significant support in the House or Senate, as Republicans remained divided over substantive policies and political strategies.

Divided as they have been on many issues, Republicans tend to gravitate toward the individual rather than the collective end of the spectrum of ideas on health care financing. They have sought to shift how Americans think about access to health services, away from a citizenship right and toward treating it more like any other market commodity. Broadly speaking, the principles of price transparency, individual accountability, and competition became key Republican talking points on health care financing since the 1990s. To the extent medical patients can be thought of as shoppers, a consumer-driven approach to health care could make a good deal of sense. This chapter examines a broad range of evidence to scrutinize this analogy.[4] These studies in consumer behavior range from the widely cited RAND Corporation Health Insurance Experiment of the 1970s and 1980s, to recent work by the non-partisan Employee Benefit Research

Institute, to analyses conducted by university- and think tank–based scholars examining corporate, military, and other government data.

Regardless of how one assesses the data on consumer-driven health plans, such arrangements have undeniably become popular across the private industry and, to some degree, in states' Medicaid plans (more on this in Chapter 4). What turns out to be mixed evidence for the effectiveness of consumer-driven health care (CDHC) has not kept its supporters from touting its virtues, often in glowing terms. Conservative-minded health care economists, advocates, and business consultants praise this as the only sensible way to rein in costs and boost quality. As with other such big ideas, when all one has in one's ideological toolbox is a hammer and one is desperate for a remedy, a lot of policy problems come to look like nails.[5]

The Logic of Consumer-Driven Health Care

The intellectual justification for treating patients like shoppers is currently driven by the work of thinkers such as Regina Herzlinger and Joseph Newhouse at Harvard University, Mark Pauly of the University of Pennsylvania, John Goodman and Devon Herrick of the National Center for Policy Analysis, Michael Tanner at the CATO Institute, and Christopher Conover at the American Enterprise Institute. Many of these thinkers advance this approach as though it offers a comprehensive solution to our worst health-financing problems. This consumer-driven health care group is not homogenous. Less strident advocates, such as Michael Morrisey at Texas A&M University and Paul Fronstin at the Employee Benefit Research Institute, freely acknowledge some of the limits of the logic of and evidence on consumer-driven plans. Most of these policy advocates situate themselves on the demand side of the problem, advancing proposals to expose consumers to more of the true costs of the goods and services they consume. Others also consider the supply side, such as advocating limitations on out-of-pocket maximums to make care more affordable.[6] Staking out the staunch libertarian position is Richard Epstein, a research fellow at Stanford University's Hoover Institution. Epstein views access to medical services as a market commodity; if one cannot afford them, one cannot access them. Period. The logical extension of Epstein's marketize-everything perspective calls for legalization of the sale of babies and spare kidneys.[7] Perhaps not surprisingly, Epstein does not often receive invitations to coauthor with other mainstream CDHC advocates.

A key point of departure for CDHC advocates is the moral hazard that economists tend to see amidst the consumption of health care goods and services. In this view, over-insurance via one-size-fits-all policies commonly leads to over-consumption.[8] Third-party payers, such as private or government insurance programs, incentivize enrollees to consume with little or no mind paid to the costs of those services. From the CDHC perspective, when individuals must pay more out of pocket, they shop more selectively, focus their expenditures on the most effective treatments, and take better care of their health.[9] In a nation where a sizable minority of medical services are deemed nontherapeutic (defensive medicine, inappropriate antibiotic use, etc.) and where 35 percent of adults are obese, this argument has some appeal. The cost implications of this lead many CDHC advocates to focus more on what they see as the problem of over-insurance rather than the tens of millions who lack health insurance.

CDHC closely links over-insurance and over-consumption with price transparency. Herrick and Goodman write that "the biggest obstacle to transparency is a tax system that favors third-party insurance over individual self-insurance. . . . This has encouraged consumers to use third-party bureaucracies to pay every medical bill."[10] As it turns out, this is highly debatable. More on this follows.[11] In any case, this is a call for more individualized payment and less collective accountability. Instead of masking the costs of goods and services, CDHC supporters privilege transparent freedom of choice. From this perspective that stresses transparency and individual accountability, persons most clearly express their preferences in the ways they spend their money, meaning that framing health expenditures as instances of consumer choice is key to understanding what people truly value most.[12] An emphasis on consumer choice not only enhances efficiency in service selection, but it also stands as morally aesthetic and politically virtuous. This language of "patient centered" and "consumer centered" has become a significant trope in Republican discussions of health care reform in recent years, particularly since the passage of the ACA.[13]

Just as clear financial stakes are thought to motivate consumers to choose more wisely, the argument is that economic competition should lead to more competitive pricing of goods and services.[14] To the great extent third-party billing—that is, insurance—covers most Americans' medical bills, individuals do not have to care much about what services cost, at least not in the short run. CDHC argues that when patients act like shoppers, providers will compete for their business on both quality and price. Many observers, not only those on the political right, lament the lack of transparency or even logic of pricing of medical goods and services. Steven Brill's essay in *Time* magazine in the spring of 2014, for instance, laid bare the almost complete disconnect between the cost of delivering services and providers' charges for those services.[15] Catalyzing providers to list their prices will require a significant cultural shift, as this approach has been explicitly discouraged by leaders in organized medicine for more than a century.[16]

Of key importance to consumer-driven thinkers is the rejection of the idea of a *need* for health services. Owing to varying levels of pain tolerance, health status, values, and financial priorities, health care economists long have recognized that there is no objective optimal level of service provision for any given individual. Although economics Nobel laureate Kenneth Arrow arrived at this conclusion in the 1960s, this logic can be troublesome.[17] It posits that any particular level of medical service consumption reflects nothing more than personal taste. For example, some people run to the doctor at the first sign of a sniffle, while others self-medicate and endure significant pain, hoping one's body will solve the problems on its own. For instance, when the General Social Survey asked in 2000 how likely people were to seek medical care if problems with their physical health prevented them from performing daily activities, fully 29 percent said they would either "probably not" or "definitely not" go to a doctor (as opposed to the 71 percent of respondents who said they would "probably" or "definitely" go).[18] Granted, while preferences on care seeking vary quite widely, to push this logic very far leads one to conclude that no one can be said to *need* any particular level of health care. It is instead a *want*. Of course, when thinking about trauma injuries, complicated pregnancies, cancer, or any number of other conditions, this perspective of health care as a *want* comes to seem rather preposterous. For the non-suicidal, fighting a curable cancer by seeking professional help is not simply a preference. An alternative conclusion is that we might do better by referencing from some sense of an adequate range of services, albeit one-size-fits-all in nature, when setting a minimal level of service provision, rather than tying provision levels to what people are able to afford or choose to spend.

Another important underlying assumption to CDHC is that there are no inherent limits on demand for care.[19] By this way of thinking, if individuals do not face a financial consequence for their consumption, the only limit will be the practical constraints of time and inconvenience. Thus, according to this logic, as curious as it will seem to most serious economists, Americans will eventually spend nearly all of their resources on health care.[20] This line of thinking seems to assume that people actually enjoy seeking medical services and that they will consume as much as they can afford. Counter to this, while Americans' trust of doctors runs high,[21] evidence indicates that one's subjective sense of life satisfaction acts as an important determinant of the frequency of doctor visits. In a recent study of older Americans, upward movement by one step on a six-point life satisfaction scale corresponded to an 11 percent decrease in the frequency of doctor visits. This relationship remained significant, though reduced, even after controlling for a wide variety of factors, including baseline health status.[22] In other words, those with higher life satisfaction voluntarily limit their doctor visits because they feel better about their lives, regardless of their ability to pay (95 percent of the study subjects had health insurance). Other studies also show that a subjective sense of well-being and personality type correspond to reduced service use.[23]

More generally, the assumption that price will consistently provide a meaningful explanation for consumption faces nontrivial empirical exceptions. Various goods defy this. Americans do not eat nearly as much chocolate as they could afford (9.5 pounds per person in the United States during 2014, less than half of Swiss per capita consumption[24]). The easy availability of free Internet pornography does not mean people spend all their time viewing it (though consumption is high). Given this and the evidence from studies discussed later, the fear that making access to health services more affordable will lead people to endlessly increase their use of those services limited only by time and inconvenience is simply not defensible. As health policy scholar Timothy Jost writes, "a common trope in the consumer-driven literature is to liken first-dollar health insurance coverage to first-dollar coverage for car maintenance, housing costs, or restaurant dining, which, they argue, would lead to wanton abuse. . . . This analogy ignores, of course, the fact that health care is usually time-consuming, inconvenient, unpleasant, uncomfortable, and sometimes just plain painful. A few people do pathologically pursue health care services, but most of us have better things to do."[25]

Another line of argument in the CDHC arsenal posits that well-insured persons tend to engage in risky behaviors—smoking, drinking, over-eating—more than do individuals who face more direct costs for their health care.[26] Here, the problem is portrayed as too many people having too much insurance, enough to provoke risky behaviors in the knowledge that injuries and illnesses can be fixed. As discussed in subsequent passages, this assumption rests on inconsistent evidence.

Despite the mixed empirical support for CDHC, employers have applied these principles to their insurance plans over the past decade or so. Many firms have moved to higher-deductible policies and more cost sharing for workers. Payments toward deductibles by workers at large employers rose 256 percent between 2004 and 2014 (despite wages rising only 32 percent over this period).[27] Individualized accounts for health care spending have flourished both because this helps employers limit their financial liability that might otherwise be unpredictable and high and because funds in health savings accounts (HSAs) can be carried into retirement as tax-sheltered deposits, making them popular with workers who can afford to use such investments.

Contemporary health savings accounts had their genesis in the 1990s in medical savings accounts and were available to the self-employed and to employees at firms with fewer than 50 workers. These accounts provided a tax shelter for funds deposited for future use to pay for qualifying health services. The idea caught on, and in 2003 the health savings account became the new vehicle for a broader class of workers under the Medicare Prescription Drug, Improvement, and Modernization Act. HSA deposits offer a three-way tax benefit: sheltering payroll withholdings and the investment growth of these accounts and designating the funds as tax free upon withdrawal. Unused portions of HSA deposits can be rolled over year to year and into retirement, when withdrawal limitations loosen.[28] In order to qualify for an HSA, a person's insurance policy must have an individual deductible of at least $1,250 or a family deductible of $2,500 per year.[29]

Critics see consumer-driven health care plans as problematic in several ways. First, modest-income people lack the funds to pay substantial out-of-pocket expenses inherent in consumer-driven plans. For those with little disposable income, the prospect of facing higher—perhaps much higher—out-of-pocket expenses simply is not viable. Second, critics wonder if by exposing people directly to more of the costs of their services they will indeed curtail consumption and that they will do so in a way that involves reducing not only less effective but also more effective services. Third, placing the onus of reduction on relatively less informed consumers—that is, on the demand side of the relationship—rather than incentivizing relatively more informed service providers—on the supply side—is, arguably, not the most promising strategy. The next section considers several lines of evidence on these questions.

What Does the Evidence Say about Consumer Behavior in Health Care?

The question of whether medical patients can effectively act like savvy shoppers has attracted vast attention over the past two decades.[30] Studies have examined single firms transitioning from traditional insurance to cost-sharing plans, they have examined subscriber behavior across employers, and they have tracked service usage among particular populations, including Medicaid recipients and members of the U.S. military.

Regrettably, much of this literature examines the volume of purchases rather than expenditures. Overall, the results of these studies are mixed but tend to show modest levels of demand elasticity on the part of consumers. However, to the extent this body of evidence shows any price sensitivity at all, it has provided support for employers intent on limiting their financial liability for employee benefits. It also gives market-oriented politicians a way to pivot away from the paradigm of government-provided health benefits for poor and vulnerable populations as well as to counter liberal urges toward a single-payer system.

The most widely cited study on consumer behavior in health care was conducted by the RAND Corporation during the 1970s and 1980s.[31] Despite the passage of years, this is still considered the gold standard by many experts who write about consumer-driven plans.[32] The RAND study examined the behavior of 2,000 non-elderly individuals living in six areas of the country to determine the extent to which different levels of cost sharing affects consumption of health goods and services and health outcomes. Random assignment of participants to different co-payment levels—ranging from 0, to 25 percent, to 50 percent, to 95 percent—allowed researchers to analyze consumer behavior across cost-sharing conditions. All participants were protected from catastrophic costs by a $1,000 out-of-pocket limit (lower for low-income participants). As expenses accumulated, participants were ultimately reimbursed so that no one ended the experiment financially worse off than he or she started. However, in the short term, some participants experienced high levels of financial liability. The different co-payment levels exerted a significant influence on service use but not always in ways that fit neatly with the contemporary rhetoric about consumer-like behavior. At the extreme, those in the zero co-payment (free care) condition used between 25 and 30 percent more services than did those in the 95 percent co-pay condition. Hence, a 95 percentage point difference in premium was associated with approximately a 25 percent difference in consumption. Differences across smaller ranges of the co-payment continuum were associated with much smaller differences in service consumption, more or less in line with more recent research involving marginally increased cost sharing.

Beyond changes in financial behavior, the RAND study also monitored participants' health outcomes. For the average participant, variation in co-payment condition did not particularly correspond to differences in health outcomes. However, several significant differences emerged across levels of cost sharing, especially for low-income participants. Individuals with tooth decay, serious injuries, and high blood pressure tended to end the study in better condition when placed in the free care group than when faced with a high co-payment. Of particular note, the 6 percent or so of people who were both poor and sick benefitted when placed in the free care condition. Blood pressure fell for this group compared to that of the co-pay participants, and importantly the mortality rate fell by 10 percent for the free care participants, whereas this did not happen for the participants facing co-payments.[33] The study's lead investigator, Joseph Newhouse, acknowledged but downplayed these differences, pointing out that these individuals comprised only a small portion of the sample and noting that "we can virtually rule out any substantial adverse effect among the group subject to increased initial cost sharing."[34] The families of those who died during the experiment who would not have died so soon had they been placed in the zero co-payment condition presumably would disagree.

The RAND study recommendations included broadened cost sharing in an effort to incentivize more judicious consumption of health services. As the study's results began to be published, several corporations adopted higher co-payments for their workers. These included the Xerox Corporation, which in 1983 raised its employees' co-payments from the previous yearly deductible of $100 per individual or $200 per family upward to 1 percent of earnings per family. It also adjusted its co-insurance from 0 to 20 percent.[35]

Over the intervening years, America's health care systems have changed in ways that potentially limit the applicability of the RAND findings. Technology has improved, expectations for treatment and access to services have changed, managed care has spread, and prices have increased. Hence, more contemporary studies of consumer behavior and price sensitivity have attempted to determine consumers' price sensitivity under current conditions. These studies have tended to examine individuals situated in natural experiments of one sort or another, often employees of firms transitioning from traditional insurance plans to high-deductible ones. Some studies have monitored a single population—workers at a particular firm—over time as their insurance coverage changed. A problem with this approach is that variation in the health care inflation rate during the years under study introduces a potential confounding variable. Other studies have compared a group of employees at one firm undergoing an insurance transition with a separate group of workers at a different employer not undergoing such changes conterminously. These studies then compare simultaneous consumption changes over time across different insurance conditions. Such difference of differences studies have been numerous and produce the best evidence we currently have on the impacts of CDHC plans.

An example of this type of research is a 2009 report by the American Academy of Actuaries that reviewed several studies conducted in the 2000s. The researchers examined three studies by insurers (CIGNA, Aetna, and Uniprise) involving workers across a range of situations. They found that high co-payments generated savings via reduced service usage but that those savings occurred mainly in the first year of the plans' introduction, not during the second and subsequent years. First-year savings tended to be in the range of 4 to 15 percent, relative to the pre-transition year, compared to savings of 3 to 5 percent in the later years.[36] The explanation seems to be that people initially respond to the cost sharing and become more selective about their usage, perhaps putting off elective or non-critical services. However, after a year or two of conservation, they return to something like their prior consumption habits, though at a slightly reduced rate compared to their pre-program level of usage. This is to say that when asked to share in the cost of their services, workers indeed tend to respond, but they do not tend to change their behavior in dramatic or enduring ways. Clearly, fundamental life changes are difficult, thus atypical. Other studies have also found similar patterns of initially curtailed consumption followed by a substantial return to previous usage patterns.[37]

Several studies of employee behavior come from the Employee Benefit Research Institute, a non-partisan but market-inclined organization. These studies vary in the particulars of their structure and findings. Most show price sensitivity at a noticeable but modest margin. In one such study, Paul Fronstin and Christopher Roebuck examined service use by employees of a large Midwestern employer that adopted a consumer-driven health plan at the beginning of 2007 for all of its nearly 19,000 active workers and their dependents.[38] Another firm provided a comparable control group of approximately 82,000 employees and dependents. Under the new plan, workers selected from two options: one offered a lower deductible of $1,250 per person and the other a higher deductible of $2,500 for individuals. Approximately 90 percent of the workers selected the high-deductible plan with an HSA option, since it involved no mandatory employee contribution. (The other plan required a $300 annual payment per worker.) The study examined 11 annual measures of service use during 2006, including well-child visits, adult chronic-disease-monitoring measures, cancer screenings, diabetes care, and overuse measures, such as rapid resort to antibiotics. Only a few statistically significant differences emerged across the two firms. Findings from the first year (2006) for most of the indicators showed no statistically significant differences in spending or frequency of use. The high-deductible group had slightly fewer hospital admissions than the control group (34 per 1,000 persons, compared to 38 per 1,000 for the control group). Also, employees in the high-deductible plan used fewer in-patient hospital days (105 per 1,000 persons, compared to 131 per 1,000 for control group). Other than these two differences, none of the comparisons showed statistically significant differences in the first year. Watching participants over the following four years (through 2010) revealed a few cross-group differences, but overall the results were inconsistent with CDHC thinking, either because of a lack of cross-group differences or, in the case of a few indicators, because the differences pointed in the unexpected direction. For instance, the high-deductible group did a poorer job of avoiding ineffective imaging of lower back pain and early use of antibiotics than did the control group (the opposite of what CDHC predicts), and the high-deductible group participated in less monitoring of medications in each of the latter years than did the control group. In the end, the authors acknowledged that the results were mixed.

In a 2010 analysis, Stephen Parente and colleagues looked at four large firms that transitioned away from their traditional plans to high-deductible policies during the 2000s. None of the four firms showed a statistically significant decrease (one actually experienced a significant increase) in total medical expenditures from the pre-CDHC plan implementation to the first year of the new plan, but one of them managed to shift from what had a been a 6 percent increase the year before to a 1.28 percent increase the year after.[39] The other three firms could not show such inflation reductions once their high-deductible plans took effect.

Another study examined individuals' out-of-pocket spending as a function of employer contributions to HSA accounts.[40] As employers increased their deposits, employees spent more, slightly in excess of their employers' contributions. For each additional dollar employers deposited to an account, total spending rose by $1.20, with virtually all of this going toward prescription drugs and out-patient services. The use of preventative services did not systematically vary across traditional insurance versus CDHC plans. Further, people showed some signs of shifting to less expensive generic drugs, but a nontrivial number of participants stopped taking their drugs under CDHC plans. In describing these findings, EBRI's Fronstin wrote that "there are many unanswered questions" about consumer behavior under cost-sharing plans.[41]

In a large-scale study in Tennessee involving two diverse groups— including an experimental and a control group—researchers found that people enrolled in a high-deductible plan slightly decreased their use of primary care physicians and emergency departments (EDs) but that they also slightly boosted their use of prescriptions and specialty physicians.

Across the range of services and individuals, the authors found no systematic difference in dollar expenditures across cost-sharing conditions. They noted that "most important, in our data, no patient subgroup showed a significant fall in overall healthcare expenditure upon conversion to a [high-deductible health plan]."[42]

Preventative services have been an area of special concern, as health experts have pointed out that low-income people might inappropriately curtail their use of preventative services, only to undermine their health, potentially requiring more expensive services later. The RAND health insurance experiment found that people in higher co-pay categories significantly reduced their use of preventative services. In light of this, in the 2000s some plans moved to shield preventative services from cost sharing, and the Affordable Care Act prohibits cost sharing for certain preventative services. Even prior to this legislative mandate, there was evidence that consumers could distinguish between those services that triggered cost sharing versus those that did not, though not consistently.[43]

A potentially important qualifier on this minimal-effects argument is that people show a good deal of price sensitivity when selecting insurance plans. Up-front costs loom large. Studies find that changing the out-of-pocket payment level causes many employees to move from one plan to another. Fronstin and Roebuck, examining plan changes in the late 2000s, discovered that raising one plan's monthly premium by $5 relative to another employer-sponsored plan was associated with some three-quarters of employees leaving the more expensive plan. Others' research corroborates this finding.[44] Morissey found similar tendencies at other firms, though he pointed out that elevated insurance premiums seem to do little to dampen the take-up rate, or the percentage of employees who subscribe to insurance, at any given employer.[45]

These findings of modest impacts of cost sharing are echoed in numerous studies. Parente and colleagues found that a 2001 adoption of a CDHC plan at one large employer produced lower overall expenditures after the adoption but that, digging a little deeper, hospital costs, admission rates, and physician expenditures were significantly higher for the CDHC enrollees relative to those in either a Health Maintenance Organization or a Preferred Provider Organization plan.[46] Burke and Pipich's 2008 article reported a mere 1.5 percent decrease in health spending under HSAs compared to traditional insurance plans. Another study of employees at a firm that began offering a CDHC plan in 2004 found a few cross-group differences, but these were slight. The authors concluded that "there were no significant differences between plans in the proportion of enrollees who reported initiating appropriate cost-saving behavior in 2004."[47]

Morrisey, in a 2005 meta-analysis, noted that investigators continue to find only marginal price sensitivity. He wrote that health care service demand elasticity tends to be approximately –0.1, meaning that for every dollar increase in direct cost, consumers reduce their use only 10 cents. Compare this to studies of price sensitivity for gasoline (–0.5) and for new cars (–0.12).[48] In another meta-analysis, Singel and colleagues at the RAND Corporation produced a study for the U.S. Department of Defense, examining the literature on demand elasticity. They concluded that studies generally find that demand elasticity in health care is somewhat higher than Morrisey's figure but still under –0.2 (meaning 20-cent reductions in use for every dollar increase in price). Summarizing their findings, they noted that "despite a wide variety of empirical methods and data sources, the demand for health care is consistently found to be price inelastic . . . it tends to center on –.17, meaning that a 1 percent increase in the price of health care will lead to a 0.17 percent reduction in health care expenditures."[49] Despite these somewhat varying estimates, health care appears to be an area in which individuals are less price sensitive than they are regarding many other market commodities.

At the macro level, other studies have concluded that price elasticity can account for only a tiny fraction of overall growth in health care costs.[50] This, however, has not dampened the enthusiasm for CDHC advocates to combat what they see as moral hazard.

Hospital Emergency Department Use

According to the Centers for Disease Control and Prevention, in 2013 Americans made 136 million visits to one or more of the nation's approximately 5,000 emergency departments and that an estimated $18 billion could have been saved had the persons with non-emergent conditions sought care in a simpler setting.[51] Because of the expense of obtaining care in an emergency department—on average $969 in 2010—inappropriate use of EDs has become a target for would-be cost cutters.[52] Given this, co-payments have become common for non-emergent ED use. Co-payments of between $50 and $150 are typical.

The RAND Corporation's health insurance experiment found that participants were somewhat price sensitive in their emergency department use; they also found that once in a hospital, the relationship between co-payment level and service consumption disappeared.[53] Apparently, people can judge for themselves whether or not to visit a medical provider, but once in that person's office the patient largely ceases to be in control of service consumption. Other research has largely confirmed this tendency. A 1996 study appearing in the *New England Journal of Medicine* analyzed ED use by members of a Kaiser Permanente HMO in California who experienced a new co-payment requirement of $25 to $35 from 1992 to 1993 and compared these individuals to members in a pair of comparable control groups that did not experience this new requirement. The comparison found that the introduction of a co-payment for ED use was associated with a 14 percent reduction in ED visits compared to the control groups.[54]

Wharam and colleagues studied ED use as a function of high-deductible plans. Leveraging the power of large samples (8,724 in the experimental group that moved from a traditional to a high-deductible plan, and 59,557 persons in the control group), they found that the high-deductible group reduced their ED visits from 197 per 1,000 members to 178 after moving to a plan that imposed a $100 charge for non-emergent ED use.[55] The control group maintained its rate at approximately 220, a statistically significant difference from the other group. An interesting twist is that this cross-group difference was entirely attributable to changes in second and subsequent ED visits, not in the number of initial visits.

Sabik and Gandhi, using 2001–2009 data, also examined the impact of co-payments on ED use on adult Medicaid enrollees. Medicaid enrollees tend to use emergency departments at more than twice the rate of privately insured individuals, making this population financially important for state governments.[56] While only 13 percent of the nearly 34,000 ED visits in this study were for non-emergent reasons, the authors found an increase of between 5 and 6 percent in the likelihood that a condition would be urgent when a co-payment was assessed.[57] This finding remained essentially unchanged when statistically controlling for the age and race of the patients.

Not all studies of ED use find price sensitivity. For example, in an analysis of cross-state data (2001–2006) on Medicaid enrollees' ED visits in states that increased their ED co-payments versus those that did not, no statistically significant differences emerged, whether the ED visit related to an emergency or not.[58]

These studies have some limitations inasmuch as it can be difficult for laypeople to determine with precision what medical conditions are truly urgent and which are not. Given this, policy makers should exercise great care in designing cost-sharing provisions that might discourage individuals from seeking truly necessary care. Further, as in studies examining price sensitivity generally, decreases in service use attributable to cost sharing occur at a fairly narrow margin. While saving 5 or 6 percent of expenditures is certainly a fine goal, co-payments will hardly address the overall expense of the program in a major way. Similar concerns apply to co-payments attached to prescription drug use, the topic to which we now turn.

Prescription Drug Consumption

Concerns about medication adherence as a function of drug costs has given rise to a significant body of research, with a particular focus on economically vulnerable populations. As with studies of medical service consumption in other areas, the findings here tend to be mixed. Several studies indicate reduced adherence under cost sharing, often expressed as not filling prescriptions or taking a reduced dosage. None of the evidence indicates that most people are appropriately discriminating in deciding which medications to defer and which to prioritize.

A 2001 study in the *Journal of the American Medical Association* analyzed prescription drug use among tens of thousands of elderly people and welfare recipients in Québec, Canada. In the months following the 1996 introduction of 25 percent co-insurance for prescription drugs by the province of Québec, the use of essential drugs fell by 9.1 percent among the elderly and by 14.4 percent among those on welfare. Unfortunately, serious adverse health effects associated with decreased prescription drug use more than doubled, from 5.8 percent of Québec's elderly population prior to the imposition of cost sharing to 12.6 percent in the months afterward and comparably from 14.7 percent to 27.6 percent among welfare recipients.[59] Not only did the rate of adverse health events rise with reductions of prescription drug use, but emergency department visits did as well. The rate of ED visits associated with the reduction of essential prescriptions increased by 14.2 percent among the elderly and by a whopping 54.2 percent among welfare recipients. While this study did not involve a control group as comparison, the authors note that there was no other plausible explanation for the abrupt change in habits and that their findings comport with those of others.[60] Clearly, when people skip their important medications, serious and expensive repercussions tend to follow.

Parente and colleagues examined prescription drug use among enrollees in a high-deductible plan during the early 2000s and found lower use overall among CDHC enrollees compared to those in a traditional insurance plan. However, these reductions in use were uneven in a couple of ways. First, reductions achieved during the first and second year under the CDHC plan did not continue into the third year, in line with findings on overall service use described previously. As the authors write, "these reductions did not persist into the third year, suggesting that CDHP enrollees subsequently updated their prescription use patterns."[61] Second, CDHC enrollees with chronic illnesses who had reached their deductible curtailed their prescription use despite facing no further cost-sharing requirements. This paints a picture of uneven consumer adjustment to direct costs.

More recently, Dixon and colleagues examined the drug-purchasing patterns among workers in a single firm that offered three different plans starting in 2004: a high-deductible CDHC plan, a lower-deductible CDHC plan, and a PPO plan. In the first year, enrollees engaged in what the authors characterized as "risky behaviors," such as putting off going to the doctor when they thought they should, or taking a lower dose or not filling a prescription. For example, 6.5 percent of enrollees in the high-deductible CDHC plan deferred a doctor visit compared to only 1.9 percent of those enrolled in the PPO plan, and 4.3 percent of those in the high-deductible plan decided against filling a prescription compared to 1.6 percent of the PPO enrollees. These were the largest two cross-group differences across five categories examined, four of which showed statistically significant cross-group differences. However, in the second year under the new CDHC plans, all of these cross-group differences disappeared, as those in the CDHC enrollees came to closely resemble those in the PPO plan.[62] Once again, the initial modest impacts of a new individual responsibility faded over a couple of years.

In a review of five other studies of prescription drug adherence, EBRI's Fronstin summarized them as producing distinctively mixed results, ranging from no difference in adherence across cost-sharing levels to adherence being significantly lower among CDHP enrollees. He concludes by noting that moving to a CDHC plan "does not automatically produce more cost-effective behavior."[63]

How Well Do Consumers Understand Their Own Health?

One of the challenges to health care providers and policy makers is the uneven knowledge levels held by many Americans about their own health. Among the nonmedically trained, ability to critically evaluate treatment options tends to be poor. Further, many people seem to hold flawed estimations of their own health. For instance, when the Gallup poll asks people about their weight, about 35 percent of respondents say they are "somewhat overweight" and another 5 percent "very overweight." Depending on how one defines "somewhat overweight," these figures do not square with the CDC's reporting that 35 percent of adults in the United

States are obese, that is, with a body mass index of 30 or more.[64] When asked in 2007 by a CBS/*New York Times* survey, fully 40 percent of respondents said they do not keep track of their blood pressure.[65] When EBRI has asked Americans whether increased medical costs have prompted them to talk to their doctors more carefully about their own health, just over 40 percent in multiple recent surveys said they have not.[66]

Given this and other evidence that many people lack reliable self-knowledge about health, experts have attempted to determine best practices for increasing patient engagement.[67] Briefly, there are a couple of schools of thought on this. One stresses the importance of activities such as health education and coaching to encourage people to engage in healthier behaviors—fitness, medication adherence, weight management, smoking cessation, and so on—and to become more involved in decision making about medical procedures.[68] A substantial body of evidence shows that patients who play more active roles in their own health care experience better outcomes at lower cost.[69] However, recognizing the limits of coaching, another school of thought focuses on the decision-making contexts in which patients find themselves, or what decision researchers call *choice architecture*.[70] This approach places a great deal of importance on, for example, known patterns of program engagement. For instance, automatic enrollment in health savings plans leads to higher levels of participation than do opt-in enrollment procedures that require an action on the part of workers. This approach is not necessarily at odds with outreach efforts; rather it focuses on the limits of teaching and learning strategies.

Quick learners might be able to engage their medical providers, eliciting good information that can help in making treatment decisions. However, for most, optimizing one's own decision making remains a challenge. Of course, this is why people hire skilled practitioners to assist them with medical decisions. The problem with this is the potential conflict of interest such practitioners face. As patients and doctors choose which technology to employ (the expensive MRI or the cheaper X-ray?), doctors are both consultants and service vendors. Naturally, in these contexts, patients should seek information. However, when asked in a 2009 survey how often their doctors discuss reasons for recommending a particular treatment, 60 percent said "often," while a significant 40 percent said "sometimes," "rarely," or "never."[71] Other evidence corroborates this finding that such information-sharing behavior varies widely but tends toward the low end.[72] Work by EBRI's Fronstin shows that large percentages of workers enrolled in consumer-driven plans poorly understand where cost sharing applies and where it does not. In this study, fully 57 percent of CDHC enrollees mistakenly believed their deductible applied to all medical services, when in fact it did not apply to preventative services. The general pattern of these findings was that employee knowledge decreases as plan complexity grows.[73]

Another study compared behavior across plans (at a single firm), predicated on the idea that information seeking will rise along with cost sharing. When enrollees in a traditional PPO were compared to those in a low-deductible CDHC plan and others in a high-deductible CDHC plan, the enrollees in the CDHC plans indeed sought more information than those in the PPO. However, among enrollees in the CDHC plans, those with lower deductibles actually sought information at higher rates than did those in the higher-deductible condition, contrary to expectations.[74]

Certain kinds of medical information are difficult to obtain, and prices can be particularly elusive, making it nearly impossible for patients to act like smart shoppers. As surgeon and health policy writer Atul Gawande notes, insurers operate "in a tumultuous market that regards prices as trade secrets."[75] Prices lack transparency for two related reasons. First, charges and payments for medical services are fundamentally ambiguous.[76] For example, an obstetrician providing prenatal care and attending a routine vaginal delivery in central Illinois, where I live, would receive $924.45 if Medicaid paid the bill.[77] In contrast, the obstetrician who attended the delivery of my two children would charge $8,600 for a patient paying out of pocket.[78] That same service would earn this physician between $6,020 and $7,740 (based on either a 30 percent or a 10 percent discount negotiated by an insurance plan). Of course, any hospital that wants to participate in Medicare (virtually all of them) would have to deliver the baby for any woman showing up in active labor regardless of her ability to pay, per the 1986 Emergency Medical Treatment and Active Labor Act, and the hospital might receive zero dollars for this if she were uninsured.

The second reason behind this difficulty has to do with medical providers' reluctance to publish their prices. Part of this has to do with their need to shift revenue to cover uncompensated care. A doctor's office is, perhaps, understandably reluctant to publicly fix its prices in a way that complicates the accounting shuffle that goes on after the fact to cover bad debt. Furthermore, doctors historically have tried to frame their relationships with patients as entirely focused on quality care rather than as economic exchanges.[79] Patients have tended to adopt this framing, and most of them report not liking to discuss pricing with their clinicians.[80] When in 2008 the Kaiser Family Foundation asked people if they "usually talk to [their doctors] about the cost [they] will have to pay for a new medication," 55 percent said "no."[81] Similarly, when the American Association of

Retired Persons in 2004 asked adults over 50 years how often they shop around for the best price on prescriptions, 19 percent said "always," 6 percent "often," 16 percent "sometimes," but fully 58 percent said "never."[82] When a CBS/*New York Times* survey asked people in 2006 whether individuals should be able to shop around for the best insurance price, if employers should do this, or if the government should regulate insurance prices, 34 percent pointed to individuals and another 34 percent to government. Only 23 percent saw this as a job for to employers, who are, after all, the entities who pay the premiums for the majority of Americans who obtain their insurance through a workplace.[83]

Getting to a point where consumers can readily comparison shop will require a significant culture shift by both providers and patients. As health researcher Howard Stein noted years ago, doctors are "loathe to affix a price tag to services at the time of the transaction or as an official precondition to 'delivering' them. Somehow it would be immoral to do so."[84] More recently, when Gawande spoke with a group of doctors in 2009 for what became a widely read *New Yorker* article, he asked them to imagine a negotiation over price. The conversation went like this:

> A cardiologist tells an elderly woman that she needs bypass surgery and had Dr. Dyke see her. They discuss the blockages in her heart, the operation, the risks. And now they're supposed to haggle over the price as if he were selling a rug in a souk? "I'll do three vessels for thirty thousand, but if you take four I'll throw in an extra night in the I.C.U."—that sort of thing? Dyke shook his head. "Who comes up with this stuff?" he asked. "Any plan that relies on the sheep to negotiate with the wolves is doomed to failure."[85]

One other insight on health care expenses deserves attention. Consumer-driven health plans seek to lower overall expenditures by asking individuals to pay more directly for their services. This strategy turns out to be something of a blunt instrument, given that the large majority of health care dollars are accounted for by a small portion of the population. This means that behavior changes by most of us do not contribute much to the nation's total health care bill. As of 2010, the top 1 percent of the U.S. population, ranked by their health care expenses, accounted for 21 percent of total health care expenditures. This group of intensive users racked up an annual per capita mean expenditure of $87,570. The top 5 percent of the population, ranked by their expenditures, accounted for 50 percent of overall expenditures. The least consumptive half of the population is responsible for less than 3 percent of total health spending.[86] Sure, we can ask everyone to pay a larger share of her or his medical costs in the hope this causes many people to curtail their expenditures. However, evidence from numerous studies shows that the savings are likely to occur at a modest margin and in ways that defy CDHC expectations. Further, most of the problem of spiraling costs lies with a relatively few intensive users, not with the broader population.

A fairly clear picture emerges from this discussion indicating that proponents of CDHC are more interested in opposing the advancement of a progressive political agenda than they are in saving money. This perspective informs the following section on how CDHC has gone far beyond employers' decisions about cost sharing with their workers and has become a common theme in conservative political strategy and rhetoric on health care.

How the Consumer-Driven Movement Works in Politics

Despite the mixed evidence about consumer-driven plans, these ideas have gained considerable political purchase in recent years. In 2003, under the Medicare Modernization Act, medical savings accounts (initially a pilot project) became health savings accounts (a permanent fixture), and the number of their subscribers grew into the millions, as employers adopted higher-deductible insurance plans that made more people eligible for these arrangements. By 2014, an estimated 10.6 million HSAs held $22 billion, with an average account balance of just over $2,000.[87]

This shift encouraged market-oriented advocates to adopt the language of "patient-centered" medicine as cheaper and better. The phrase "patient-centered" was borrowed from the authors of a 2001 report from the Institute of Medicine, *Crossing the Quality Chasm*, who used it to emphasize the importance of patients being informed about and engaged in their own care, mainly for the sake of improved health outcomes. However, in the intervening years, CDHC advocates attempted to co-opt the term to refer to patients paying more of their own way in medicine.[88] In contemporary conservative rhetoric, "patient-centered" typically stands in opposition to "government-centered," as in a health care system that has been "taken over" by Washington bureaucrats. For example, the conservative American Legislative Exchange Council advises state legislators to repeal the ACA, noting that "the best health care is patient- and market-driven, not government-driven—and Obamacare embodies neither of these qualities."[89] In similar fashion, when Senator Orrin Hatch spoke on the five-year anniversary of the ACA, he framed his comments in terms of Republican ideas for reform being "patient-centered" as opposed to "government-centered." He said the pending bill he had co-sponsored in early 2014 was a

> legislative blueprint that repeals and replaces Obamacare with common-sense, patient-focused reforms that reduce health care costs and increases access to affordable, high-quality care. In contrast with Obamacare and its government-centered mandates and regulations, this proposal empowers the American people to make the best health care choices for themselves and their families.[90]

This framing of health care financing emphasizes individual choices, in contrast to choices by some government bureaucrat. This language is the new incarnation of the "socialized medicine" critique that stood opposed to progressive reform from the 19-teens well into the 1990s: symbolically effective while broad enough to not invite listeners to wade into important policy details. However, this framing ignores, for instance, fee-for-service payment systems that encourage overutilization, and, of course, any sense of collective provision of health care as a public good.

While Senator Hatch's very general language enjoys broad appeal across a range of conservative schools of thought on health care, moving from these abstractions to particular strategies and legislative provisions largely eluded congressional Republicans for the first six years of the ACA's life. At least two obstacles stood in the way. First, as a matter of political strategy, congressional Republicans were divided about how much energy to spend fighting the law, given that it had survived two Supreme Court challenges and several election cycles and that continuing to pass repeal bills came to be seen as overly theatrical by many observers. Second, conservatives were divided over how to craft any legislative alternative. On this latter point, broadly speaking, they fell into three camps.[91]

In the first group were those who either had not taken the time to develop their own ideas on health financing or declined to join any of the emerging alternatives. These repealers succeeded in having the House of Representatives vote dozens of times (more than 60 by the beginning of 2016) to overthrow parts or all of the Affordable Care Act since the Republicans took control in January 2011. These efforts worked well enough for members who felt an electoral need to stake out anti-Obama positions. Even members who were unsure of the consequences of repealing the law without replacing it with something else could take comfort in the knowledge that no such repeal effort would overcome Obama's veto.

Second, others took a more discerning look at the ACA and sought to repeal only parts of it, shearing off what they saw as the most egregious provisions ("job killing" was a favorite denunciation). Into this category fell components such as the individual mandate, the Medicaid expansion, the medical device and tanning parlor tax, and the requirement that all insurance policies meet federally prescribed minimum standards. In the autumn of 2015, the House passed yet another partial repeal bill, this one of limited scope so that all of its provisions could get through the Senate's budget reconciliation procedure that allows passage in that chamber with a simple majority. House members also attached a one-year pause in Planned Parenthood funding, a conservative cause du jour.[92] A few hard-line senators, including 2016 presidential candidates Ted Cruz and Marco Rubio, threatened to oppose the bill because it would not have repealed the entire act (both ended up voting yes).[93] These sorts of bills did not seek to build anything new in place of the ACA. This bill passed the Senate but was vetoed by the president in January 2016.

Third, there were those who would have repealed parts of the ACA and replaced them with market-oriented provisions, such as modified (read *less generous*) tax credits to assist people to purchase health insurance. A great deal of disagreement played out among this group, meaning that no alternative got much traction with a critical mass of congressional Republicans. At a high level, some of these disagreements turned on whether the more onerous problem with the ACA was its generous tax subsidies or its reliance on federal government regulation of the health insurance industry.[94] Subsidies have been part of the health care landscape since World War II and appeal to a broad range of politicians, both liberal and conservative. The split occurs over how generous those subsidies should be and how to target them: to the poor or the middle-class. Critics argue that to reduce the price of insurance significantly risks an over-insurance and moral hazard situation. Supporters see subsidies as a way to spread out wealth in a targeted way that helps people purchase needed coverage. The matter of regulation also divided conservatives, with some supportive of this but only at the state level, while others pushed deregulation in the expectation of fostering more affordable insurance products.

Within this third camp were those such as Senator Orrin Hatch and colleagues who would have preserved many elements of the ACA, but in revised fashion. Although their GOP critics derisively referred to these plans as "Obamacare Lite," there was a certain political practicality to these proposals.[95] For supporters of these alternative plans—several emerged during 2014 and 2015—the general idea of government subsidies to help people buy insurance was very appealing. Along with this came the idea of modest regulation of insurers, particularly surrounding the hot-button issue of denials of coverage due to preexisting conditions. As attractive or practical as such legislation might have been, these compromise bills failed to gain much traction in a Congress whose agenda was largely held hostage by far right members opposed to anything like compromise.

Just as congressional Republicans were divided over how to respond, conservative pundits also splintered. The Heritage Foundation continued to advocate repeal and to urge unspecified "patient-centered" free-market reforms.[96] Others have offered specific proposals. The conservative *Weekly Standard* praised the Hatch, Burr, and Upton plan in a long column in September 2014.[97] The Brookings Institution's Stuart Butler responded to the revised version in early 2015 in generally approving terms.[98] These commentators emphasized both the financial efficiencies and the reduction in federal regulation embodied in the bill.[99] Even while conservatives struggled to coalesce around a specific plan, they widely agreed on broad notions of greater individual responsibility, a position that fits with their development of the individual mandate back in the late 1980s. Paying for what one uses is, after all, a conservative notion.[100] How to arrive at a system that embodies this principle, as of late 2016, proved, for both technical and political reasons, elusive.

Advancing the Market Metaphor

Portraying health care purchases as analogous to other consumer purchases while appealing to market-oriented thinkers faces several significant problems. First, health care purchases are conceptually different in their nature from most other purchases. Unlike buying a sweater, obtaining medical services often poses high stakes for personal well-being, even if accessing those services does not involve a question of imminent mortality. Further, evaluating a physician or a surgical procedure involves information demands that usually far exceed the abilities of nonmedically trained persons. Sometimes, such information is simply unavailable. There is a great deal of trust involved in obtaining medical treatments from the person who will benefit financially from the purchase of that treatment. Second, while consumer-driven plans appeal to policy makers largely because of their promise to lower costs (after all, if the United States did not spend 17 percent of its gross domestic product on health care last year, you would probably not be reading this book), the bulk of health care spending goes toward a relatively small portion of the population. Thus, while we may wring marginal savings out of a large number of people, a relatively small portion of the population will still consume a large portion of our medical resources. Given how cost sharing encourages deferred care, by hanging our hopes for savings on a broad but shallow intervention, we are simultaneously risking the well-being of many. Third, numerous studies of consumer behavior under a wide range of cost-sharing plans provide modest and uneven evidence that simply does not match the enthusiastic claims of CDHC advocates. While these studies typically show savings in the 5 percent range, such savings do not consistently result, and a pattern emerges across many of these analyses indicating that initial reductions often do not endure. Fourth, the political push toward market mechanisms in health care represents not only the advocacy of an economic perspective but also a statement of political principles. To argue, for instance, for government policies that encourage employers to buy their workers insurance that only covers catastrophic illnesses or injuries while depositing modest amounts (if any at all) into employees' health savings accounts clearly represents an effort to shift financial liability from employers to workers. In an age of defined-contribution employee retirement plans, this fits a larger pattern, though it does little to save individuals money or to improve their health.

But here's the twist: despite the modest evidence in support of CDHC, and despite the strength of congressional Republicans' opposition to the Affordable Care Act, Republican leaders in a large number of states found ways to live with both the ACA—which they indeed availed themselves of—and market-oriented arguments about consumer behavior. They rebranded Obamacare and its Medicaid expansion as state creations. A growing sense that the ACA, for better or worse, had indeed become the law of the land also led a number of congressional Republicans to reconcile themselves to the act in significant ways through 2014 and 2015. While these adaptors were criticized for advocating Obamacare Lite, they too found ideological ways to live with the enemy.

CHAPTER FOUR

Learning to Live with the Enemy

During 2013 and 2014, the strong opposition to the Affordable Care Act (ACA) exhibited through its first few years began colliding with the practicality of accepting certain provisions of the law. On the part of many opponents at the state level, this grudging acceptance marked the limits of ideological resistance in the face of powerful financial considerations. For states to continue to refuse the Medicaid expansion, made optional in the 2012 Supreme Court ruling in *National Federation of Independent Businesses vs. Sebelius*, began to look like a case of cutting off one's nose to spite one's face. With hundreds of millions of dollars at stake annually, and, in the cases of many states, hundreds of thousands of individuals left uninsured, dollars gradually outweighed ideology. These cracks in the wall of opposition occurred first in early 2013 and progressed significantly from then. By mid-2016, most Republican-controlled states either had adopted the expansion or were in serious discussions about doing so.

As of late 2016, it remained uncertain what would become of the Medicaid program under the Trump administration. House Speaker Paul Ryan, in his 2016 sketch of health policy ideas, called for the program to shift away from the long-standing, open-ended entitlement funding to a fixed block grant, under which states could, presumably, reimburse services across whatever scope and clientele they like, impose work requirements, or even time-limit eligibility. Trump also called for block grant funding on his campaign website, as did the Heritage Foundation in an October 2014 report.[1] Such a program conversion would encounter resistance from service providers, but Medicaid's very large price tag would also continue to attract Congress members' attention until strong cost-control measures are instituted. Medicaid reform may turn into a multiyear conversation that pits the practicalities of covering at least some of the health costs of low-income persons against the calls for sweeping entitlement reform advocated by many congressional Republicans.

As the earlier chapters in this book have indicated, practicality argu-ably has been in short supply regarding the politics of health care reform through recent years. However, the experiences of many conservative states from 2013 forward highlighted the possibilities for bridging politi-cal chasms that otherwise seemed impossible to bridge. Republican lead-ers in numerous states, despite their ferocious opposition to the ACA, found ways to expand their Medicaid programs. The road to working within the framework of the ACA was, no doubt, a rocky one for Republi-can state officials, but many of them found ways to live with an initiative many of them saw as the enemy while at the same time increasing insur-ance coverage for their states' residents. The amount of federal money available for these expansions played a vitally important role. Sates wish-ing to expand their Medicaid programs had to invest significantly, but in return they were able to draw down vast numbers of federal dollars. The extent to which the Trump administration may learn to live with parts of the ACA that have engrained themselves into the nation's health care practices between 2010 and 2016 remains an open question as of this writing. However, the pragmatism described in this chapter suggests that even a presidential candidate who repeatedly called for repealing and replacing the ACA may himself find ways to live, in part, with the enemy.

This chapter examines the important evolution of thought among pre-viously implacable foes of the ACA. By closely examining decisions made by officials in two Republican-controlled Midwestern states—Indiana and Michigan—we see how many Republicans learned to make the Med-icaid expansion work for them, if not exactly making complete peace with it. When faced with the practical considerations of lagging public health statistics, mounting uncompensated care costs, and large uninsured pop-ulations, state officials exhibited considerable pride of authorship over their innovative Medicaid reforms. Both of these early-leader states found ways to cover the Medicaid expansion with a layer of individual financial accountability, creating enough political cover to permit an expansion of a big-government program with Republican branding. Hundreds of thou-sands of individuals were made newly eligible as a result, and doctors and hospitals were assured of at least a modicum of payment to defray a mounting burden of uncompensated care. These two states' approaches to Medicaid expansion were replicated by many other Republican states, and some of those stories appear next.[2]

The Medicaid reforms in Indiana and Michigan reflect part of a larger phenomenon that political scientist Suzanne Mettler calls the "submerged state."[3] In Mettler's formulation, opponents of government programs have found it useful to continue delivering big-government services, such as Medicaid and Medicare, while masking their big-government nature. While she focuses substantially on how this masking of government benefits assists the wealthy—such as with the home mortgage interest deduction—other activities benefit diverse recipients. In the case of the Medicaid expansion, low-income families receive many of the services they need while doctors and hospitals receive a modicum of payment for their work. As Mettler puts it, the "hallmark [of such masked programs] is the way they obscure government's role from the view of the general public, including those who number among their beneficiaries. Even when people think about these policies, many perceive only a freely functioning market system at work."[4] In this vein, many states found ways to wrap Medicaid in a veneer of private market health insurance in ways that give conservative politicians the political cover they needed to implement these programs while simultaneously criticizing the Affordable Care Act. Michigan State Representative Mike Shirkey, a leading champion of his state's Medicaid expansion, stated in 2013: "I hate Obamacare. I hope at the end of the day Obamacare is a miserable failure. But it is the law of the land."[5] Despite his enmity toward the ACA, Shirkey was instrumental in shepherding the Medicaid expansion through the legislature. However, he also positioned himself to have it both ways: that is, to help Michigan draw down the federal dollars while also condemning Obamacare. Examining the evolution of these efforts helps explain how one-time opponents of the ACA came to live with the enemy—and to benefit considerably from it.

State Medicaid Policies

Because of the way Congress wrote the ACA, various important provisions relied on states for implementation. Among these was the expectation that states would expand their Medicaid programs to raise their upper eligibility threshold—typically the federal poverty level—to 138 percent of that level, the point at which a person could purchase insurance with federal subsidies on state or federally operated exchanges. More than half of the states initially refused this Medicaid expansion. These refusals left individuals with income levels between the federal poverty threshold and 138 percent of that threshold without an affordable insurance option, unless their employer provided it.

State decisions about expanding Medicaid immediately assumed a partisan pattern. The large majority of Democratically controlled states readily expanded, while nearly all Republican states did not. Reinforcing this was rhetoric from congressional Republicans and conservative opinion leaders opposing the expansion and targeting for particular criticism those few states with Republican leadership that did expand. The imperative to find a way to cover these uninsured persons reached a level that caused several Republican-led states to reconsider their initial reluctance to expand Medicaid, particularly under pressure from chambers of commerce, local governments, and medical providers facing expenditures running to millions of dollars annually through uncompensated care.[6] By the summer of 2015, several conservative states moved toward expansion. Governors tended to take the lead, either cajoling their legislatures to adopt the enhanced program formally or resorting to unilateral measures, as John Kasich in Ohio and Bill Walker in Alaska did. Governor Walker's arguments for what he called Medicaid "reform and expansion" in Alaska were typical of the larger movement.[7] Walker argued that someone has to pay the bill when uninsured people receive medical care and that millions of dollars, paid by Alaskans in federal income tax, were available but would not return to Alaska without this expansion. He insisted that providing for more individuals' health needs was the right thing to do. Walker's argument was mostly one from pragmatism, not partisanship.

Republican supporters of expansion in other states, however, layered market-oriented ideological arguments atop pragmatic calls for change. Whereas federal law has allowed nominal co-payments for Medicaid since 1982, only since the passage of the ACA have states sought to amplify these to create a more consumer-driven feel for the program. Indiana and Michigan provide two early examples of this approach executed through the full legislative process, affording a vista on how former ACA opponents accommodated themselves to one very important provision of the law—the Medicaid expansion—claiming quite a lot of pride for doing so and opening themselves for criticism from ideologues further to the political right.

The Healthy Michigan Plan

Michigan stands out as a state that took an early lead in rebranding its Medicaid program to make it palatable to conservative opponents of the Affordable Care Act. Throughout the spring and summer of 2013, a handful of Republican legislators worked with the governor and the staff of what was then the Department of Community Health (later renamed the Department of Health and Human Services [HHS]) to craft a cost-sharing arrangement involving a modest premium for enrollment. This offered adult Medicaid recipients an incentive to perform health assessments and monitoring in consultation with medical providers. Dubbed the Healthy Michigan Plan, this program initially charged participants 2 percent of their monthly income to enroll in Medicaid. The expansion of the program meant that persons in households with income up to 138 percent of the federal poverty level could receive coverage, compared to the earlier 100 percent threshold. Healthy Michigan continued the modest co-payments permissible for years under federal Medicaid law. By developing and following through with a personal health assessment in collaboration with their health care provider, recipients reduced the required premium by half during the first year and eliminated it entirely during the second and subsequent years. At its core, the policy aimed to involve recipients in thinking more deliberately about their health and to help stakeholders experience what Michigan policy makers refer to as skin in the game. For market-oriented opponents of big government, this rebranding, involving an element, however thin, of personal accountability, was enough to justify an expansion of Medicaid in the face of persistent opposition from many Republican legislators and political activists.

The Healthy Michigan Plan, legislated during 2013 and implemented in April 2014, began as a series of conversations between state legislators and Republican Governor Rick Snyder's staff. Aware that his state often ranks poorly in public health statistics, and that Michigan was missing out on hundreds of millions of federal dollars each year by not expanding Medicaid, the governor spoke about his support for Medicaid expansion as early as February 2013, two years into his first term.[8] Two months later, when asked by a journalist whether beneficiaries should experience more of a financial stake in their health, the governor spoke in generalities about cost sharing and wellness programs, two ideas that would become important components of the new program.[9] Under the leadership of Republican Representatives Matt Lori, Al Pscholka, and Mike Shirkey, the Michigan House considered House Bill 4714 during May and June of 2013.

Representative Shirkey initially opposed the expansion but reversed himself. For him, the towering burden of uncompensated care costs for Michigan's medical providers together with the opportunity to access what he saw as the state's share of federal Medicaid dollars justified this engagement with the ACA. In Shirkey's vision, a chief element of reform involved cost sharing for program recipients. Although the co-payment amounts would continue at their prior levels, the 2 percent premium and its incentives for health assessments and improvement lent this new approach to Medicaid enough of a conservative sheen to justify allowing an initially estimated 322,000 new persons onto the rolls. This figure quickly grew to over a half million.[10] Although Representative Shirkey was certainly persuaded, he could not convince a majority of his Republican colleagues of the wisdom of this expansion due to their intransigent opposition to further government involvement. However, with strong Democratic support, the bill passed committee on a 9–5 vote on June 12. All of the opponents were Republicans.

The next day, the House speaker, with encouragement from the governor, brought the bill up for a vote, even though he understood that most in his party opposed it. However, thanks again to Democratic support, the measure passed by a margin of 76–31.[11] The bill moved to the Senate, but members in the upper chamber initially declined to pass it. Frustrated, Governor Snyder returned home from a trade mission abroad and scolded the Senate, imploring members to "take a vote, not a vacation" and to move the bill forward.[12] After some legislative jockeying, the bill came up for a vote on August 27 and narrowly passed the Senate 20–18, garnering the votes of only eight of the chamber's Republicans. All 12 of the chamber's Democrats voted yes. Governor Snyder endured considerable criticism from within his own party over this measure. At the bill-signing ceremony, he almost sounded like a Democrat. With U.S. representative and longtime progressive health reform advocate John Dingell at his side, Snyder pleaded, "For the sweet love of God, let's understand that we have to work together to make our government work. . . . We are all in this together."[13]

Several elements played crucial roles in securing the passage of the Healthy Michigan Plan. Michigan's organized medical providers lent important support. A representative from the Michigan Health and Hospital Association testified before a House committee in May supporting the expansion. The association noted that while Medicaid reimburses less than the cost of service delivery, hospitals urgently need to rein in the staggering amount of uncompensated care they deliver. With an expansion, funds would cover an estimated 90 percent of the $880 million in uncompensated care that Michigan's hospitals provided in 2013. Pragmatically, the association observed that "using Medicaid to achieve coverage is a flawed tool, but it is the tool we have."[14] Uncompensated care also weighed greatly for Kenneth Elmassian, the president of the Michigan State Medical Society. He noted during the campaign for passage that "as physicians, we know that those without insurance frequently delay their care and they end up sicker. Prevention, early detection, and treatment are far better prescriptions."[15] Not all medical providers supported this, however. Dr. Richard Armstrong, a surgeon in Newberry and CEO of the antireform group Docs4PatientCare, called the governor's expansion "a colossal mistake."[16]

Within state government, several actors advocated for this change. The governor strong-armed legislators and toured the state in 2013 trying to change minds. Lieutenant Governor Brian Calley advocated for the change and worked to persuade legislators, so much so that Tea Party–affiliated members of his own party tried, albeit unsuccessfully, to derail his re-election in 2014.[17] House Representative Shirkey also confronted significant trouble with his fellow Republicans. Staunch ACA opponents pressed him to explain his support for a core component of Obamacare. In a lengthy June 2013 interview with a conservative talk-radio host, Shirkey attempted to reframe the expansion as reform of a long-standing program that pre-dated the ACA instead of as an endorsement of the Obama initiative.[18] His rhetoric blended the practicality of addressing the high costs of not expanding with criticism of the Affordable Care Act more generally. Shirkey and other GOP supporters adopted the language of "reform" rather than "expansion" in referring to this initiative.[19] Senator Roger Kahn was even more explicit in the distinction he drew between Michigan's experiment and the ACA. He told his colleagues "this is not Obamacare or the Affordable Care Act. [It is instead] a national model" that other states might adopt, following Michigan's lead.[20]

Critics inside and outside of state government did not readily accept this attempt to reframe an expansion of a government program that is intimately tied to the ACA. Instead, the Michigan chapter of Americans for Prosperity—a Koch brothers–funded group that opposed Medicaid expansion in several states—launched waves of robocalls to pressure Republican legislators over their votes.[21] At least one critical billboard appeared in the district of Republican Representative Mike Callton.[22] Other members encountered more face-to-face opposition, including Senator Howard Walker, who was accused at a political gathering by a conservative talk-radio host of being a "weak Republican," to which Walker responded, "Screw you."[23] Speaking directly to the issue, Annie Patnaude, spokesperson for the Michigan chapter of Americans for Prosperity, insisted in August 2013 that "we firmly believe a vote to support Medicaid expansion is a vote to support the president's healthcare law."[24]

Once the bill was signed into law in September 2013, the state agency requested a federal waiver to allow Michigan to implement the cost-sharing mechanisms called for by the legislation. The U.S. Department of Health and Human Services granted the waiver in December, and the Healthy Michigan Plan took effect in April 2014. The chief difference between Healthy Michigan and conventional Medicaid was the monthly premium of 2 percent of an enrollee's monthly income, a payment that could be halved or eliminated based on setting and meeting healthy behavior goals. This premium reduction was at the heart of what supporters referred to as a personal financial stake for recipients. Naturally, questions arose about the assumptions behind this cost sharing and incentive structure and about the evidence underlying these assumptions. Michigan's waiver request only briefly laid out the logic of how cost sharing might be useful, and the document did not elaborate exactly how those enrolled in the program would react to cost sharing, nor did the document cite any research supporting the claim that co-payments would engender consumer-like behavior. Instead, the request stated that one of the "hypotheses" of the research imbedded in this policy innovation would be to "evaluate what impact incentives for healthy behavior and the completion of an annual health risk assessment have on increasing healthy behaviors and improving health outcomes."[25] The individualized health account (MI Health Account), funded mainly by state contributions, was "intended to be a tool to encourage beneficiaries to become more active consumers of their health care, to save for future healthcare expenses and become more aware of the cost of the services they receive."[26] Further, the document explained that "the administration and operation of the MI Health Accounts will be designed to encourage beneficiaries to use high-value services, while discouraging low-value services such as non-urgent use of the emergency room."[27]

The gloss of individual financial accountability that was so instrumental for Michigan Republicans' support for this expansion (or "reform," as many of them insisted) turned out to rest on a foundation that was, arguably, little more than an ideologically driven hunch. When asked about the consumer behavior research that legislators were provided to help them understand how enrollees might respond, Republican Representative Mike Callton, chair of the Health Policy Committee, responded, "We got no information on that."[28] Granted, the bill was handled by Representative Shirkey's Competitiveness Committee rather than by Callton's Health Policy Committee (at the speaker's request), but as a committee chair and a chiropractor by profession, one would expect the leadership to have provided Callton with more evidence as part of the legislative process. Callton was not alone in this respect. Other important state officials echoed this. When asked about the expectation that the premium and co-payments would turn Medicaid recipients into savvier shoppers (in the language in the waiver request "designed to encourage beneficiaries to use high-value services"), Elizabeth Hertel, director for policy and innovation at the Department of Health and Human Services, explained that there was no real expectation that the structure of the program would do this; rather, the agency relied on relationships with physicians to steer patients in therapeutic directions. When asked to point to the empirical evidence on which her staff relied to design the cost-sharing structure, she said there was none and that these were simply legislative decisions.[29]

Time and evidence will tell if the imposition of cost sharing will lead Michiganders to use Medicaid in systematically different ways. Regardless of the federal funding for Medicaid into the future, many states will likely adopt some form of cost sharing in pursuit of what they see as individual accountability. In Lansing's case, the state's social service agency arranged for the University of Michigan's Institute for Healthcare Policy and Innovation to track developments, though it will likely take a few years of data to make any conclusive determinations. Among the various outcomes to be tracked are changes in uncompensated care, a reduction in the number of uninsured, the impact on healthy behaviors and outcomes, subjective beneficiary views of the program, the impact of contributions requirements, and the impact of health accounts on service usage.[30]

If Michigan's experience is typical of such cost-sharing arrangements, it may encounter what the state of Oregon found after imposing monthly premiums of up to $20 and co-payments of up to $5 on Medicaid in 2003. Following this, enrollment declined by half in one of Oregon's managed care Medicaid plans, and many patients reported skipping services. Kentucky, New Hampshire, and Wisconsin experienced similar declines in children's health services under cost sharing.[31] Reduced service use may save the state money in the short term, but two problems arise here. First, if high-value services or useful preventative services are deferred along with other types of treatments, this reduction will not in fact optimize participants' health treatments. Second, if the theory behind cost sharing is correct, consumers who are exposed to more of the costs will consume in more prudent and effective ways. Curtailing consumption across the board is different from refocusing consumption on high-value services, and this is precisely what the RAND health insurance experiment found in the 1980s. Throughout that study, participants did not systematically gravitate toward more-effective rather than less-effective treatments.[32] Given this, it seems unlikely that Medicaid recipients in Michigan will indeed become savvier shoppers. When asked about this refocusing on optimal services, social service agency director Hertel commented that she was "not sure what a person will do differently" under cost sharing but that the staff in her agency hoped recipients would "appreciate their services more" and that service choice would be enhanced through better doctor-patient relationships.[33] In light of the almost complete lack of evidence in the legislative process of the creation of the Healthy Michigan Plan, such hope seems to have been enough to justify the pragmatic move to expand Medicaid, despite deep ideological misgivings on the part of many Michigan Republicans.

The Healthy Indiana Plan

Indiana's experience tells a somewhat different story about how would-be opponents of a Medicaid expansion came to champion this move. As in Michigan, Republicans controlled the governorship and both chambers of the legislature at the time of the expansion. Also like Michigan, concerns about distressing public health statistics and a large uncompensated care bill borne by the state's medical providers helped overcome ideological objections to accepting this key component of the Affordable Care Act. However, unlike in Michigan, Indiana's Medicaid program previously had included a cost-sharing pilot project prior to the passage of the ACA, and modestly favorable results from this project provided an evidentiary basis on which to expand Medicaid in a way that carried the imprimatur of localism and individual accountability. Indiana officials were able to plausibly argue that their way of making Medicaid available to persons above the federal poverty level was homegrown and characterized by conservative principles, even if the impact of cost sharing was not terribly strong.

The Healthy Indiana Plan, in its first incarnation (HIP 1.0, as Hoosiers refer to it), was approved by the legislature in 2007 and implemented by Republican Governor Mitch Daniels's administration in 2008. HIP 1.0 involved personalized accounts made available to adults aged 19 to 64 and with income under 200 percent of the federal poverty level. The accounts were the source of payment for the first $1,100 of medical services annually, and participants were required to contribute between 2 and 5 percent of their income as a monthly premium. This Personal Wellness and Responsibility, or POWER, account was designed to mimic a private health savings account (HSA). However, unlike HSAs, most of the dollars flowing into these accounts come from the state's Medicaid budget; thus, for enrollees, the account vaguely resembled Monopoly money.[34] In addition to the trappings of individual accountability, the program emphasized regular use of preventative medicine. The first $500 of preventative services each year could be accessed without any deduction from one's POWER account. Indiana was the first state to employ personalized accounts for Medicaid beneficiaries. Although dressed up to look like an individually financed health insurance program, it is important to note that enrollees had to exhibit only minimally changed behavior in order to enjoy a significant financial consequence. If they complied with the preventative care incentive, a portion of their remaining account balance could be rolled over to the next year, effectively reducing their premiums.

HIP 1.0 was popular. By the end of 2012, over 105,000 individuals enrolled, and an impressive 94 percent regularly paid their premiums during that year.[35] Surveys indicated that 95 percent of participants reported being either somewhat or very satisfied with the program. As to the effectiveness of the financial incentives, the state monitored only a few indicators, but these showed positive trends. HIP enrollees visited emergency departments (EDs) less often than Hoosiers enrolled in traditional Medicaid in 2012 (31 percent of them, compared to 38 percent of traditional program participants). Further, in 2012, 5 percent of HIP enrollees reported seeking care at a walk-in clinic rather than the ED due to the required co-payment.[36] Among the many documents posted online by the state regarding HIP, none of them indicates improved health or enhanced patterns of shopping for more- versus less-effective services.

After four years of operation, Governor Daniels requested a federal waiver to extend HIP as Indiana's vehicle for the (initially mandated) Medicaid expansion.[37] This occurred prior to the 2012 Supreme Court decision that made expanded Medicaid optional for states. Shortly after this ruling, Daniels left office and was succeeded by Republican Mike Pence, elected in November 2012. Neither man supported using traditional Medicaid as a way to extend coverage to those living above the federal poverty level, nor did either support the creation of a state-run insurance exchange, citing high costs and concerns about burdensome federal regulations.[38]

Skeptical as he was of federal involvement, Governor Pence entered office in January 2013 eager to address uncompensated care costs and access the hundreds of millions of federal Medicaid dollars available under the ACA. He was able to leverage not only the documented results of HIP 1.0 but also the expertise of longtime State Senator Patricia Miller, chairperson of the Senate's Health and Provider Services Committee. Miller had written the legislative language for HIP 1.0 and took a leading role in authoring this second iteration of the program. Because the earlier version of the Healthy Indiana Plan targeted only those below the federal poverty level, the state needed a new waiver to apply the same market-based principles to the population above the poverty level. Pence was determined not to use traditional Medicaid as the vehicle for the expansion, insisting that "Medicaid isn't just broke, it's broken" and that the Indiana way of extending coverage was superior.[39]

The legislation creating HIP 2.0 passed the legislature with bipartisan support. Democrats backed it because it represented the expansion of care for low-income families, and most Republicans came on board because of the successful branding of the program as pro-market and Indiana specific. The state's social service agency followed up with a pair of public input sessions in May, which were said to elicit overwhelmingly positive feedback.[40] With this part of the process complete, Indiana requested a federal waiver on July 1, 2014. In his cover letter, the governor noted that HIP's "consumer-driven model incentivizes patients to take greater ownership over their health care decisions" and that this makes it a positive model and one worthy of building upon.[41] The governor insisted publicly that this was not simply an expansion of traditional Medicaid; rather, it was a program structured around significant individual accountability.

Perhaps because of the speedy (less than six months) approval of the waiver for HIP 1.0, Indiana officials became frustrated at what they saw as the slow pace of approval of HIP 2.0. Several letters went back and forth between Indianapolis and the Department of Health and Human Services; in October 2014, Governor Pence wrote the president asking for timely approval. He insisted that "our administration will not support efforts to remove or water down the Healthy Indiana Plan's core principles, essentially changing this proven program into an expansion of traditional Medicaid."[42] The following month the governor requested a meeting with HHS secretary Kathleen Sebelius in order to hammer out an agreement. He cited data indicating reduced emergency department use and heightened access to preventative services under HIP compared to traditional Medicaid.[43]

The HHS approved Indiana's waiver for HIP 2.0 in January 2015. The program launched the next month, making Indiana the tenth state with GOP leadership to adopt the Medicaid expansion under the ACA. HIP 2.0 became available to all adults aged 19 to 64 and with income under 138 percent of the federal poverty level so long as they make prescribed monthly payments.[44] These premiums for nonmedically frail individuals range from $1 per month for the poorest individuals up to $27 per month for persons with income at 138 percent of the federal poverty level. Federal law allows cost sharing up to 5 percent, and Indiana elected this as the upper threshold. Enrollees who fail to pay their premiums face co-payments, including $4 for an out-patient visit, $75 for an in-patient service, $4 for a prescription, and up to $25 for a nonemergency use of an emergency department.[45] The program also has an augmented component— HIP Plus—that covers dental and vision services. If enrollees fail to make their monthly POWER account contributions, they lose access to their dental and vision coverage and experience slightly higher co-payments. For those above the poverty level, missing payments would lead to a six-month lockout from the program. This was the first time the federal Centers for Medicare and Medicaid Services allowed a lockout on waiver-based Medicaid demonstration.[46] For conservatives, this provides another element of personal accountability. As of July 2015, more than 297,000 people had enrolled, and 72 percent were making the required contributions, according to the state.

The logic of charging co-payments, in the words of Brian Neale, the governor's health policy director, was "aspirational." He noted that the administration believed "that individuals, if offered the opportunity, will make the right choices."[47] The sheen of personal buy-in, arguably more stringent in Indiana's plan than in Michigan's, lent the program credibility among conservatives. Governor Pence, on the day he announced the waiver approval, evoked both humanity and antiwelfare sentiments. He remarked that HIP 2.0 is "about members of our family. It's about coworkers, friends. The truth is these hardworking Hoosiers don't want a handout. But they could use a hand up."[48] Elsewhere, harping on the individual accountability theme, Pence said this new program would give Hoosiers "the dignity to pay for their own health insurance."[49]

In explaining the politics of this expansion, senior Republican senators spoke of Medicaid enrollees having "skin in the game" and professed their belief that even the small amount of individual accountability involved in their program makes people more price sensitive and attentive to the services they obtain. Generally speaking, GOP legislators did not, however, exhibit a deep understanding of the research on consumer-driven health care. Senator Patricia Miller, the author of the legislative language that became HIP 2.0, professed a good deal of knowledge of consumer behavior in health care, though she said that most of her colleagues were generalists and knew quite a bit less. As the Senate's self-identified "guru" of health care policy, others trusted her policy judgments.[50] Confirming this assessment that most state legislators in Indiana are not particularly acquainted with health policy, Senate Floor Leader Brandt Hershman, a supporter of the new Medicaid, responded to questions about the role of evidence in the passage of the legislation by noting that he was not an expert on health policy and that he and others tended to "work from anecdotes" when it came to understanding consumer behavior. Both of these senior senators professed a strong belief in price sensitivity among Medicaid participants and that even co-payments of a few dollars would go a long way toward leading people to make better health care decisions.

Unlike states that were new to imposing cost sharing on Medicaid recipients, policy makers in Indiana had several years of evidence available. In line with other research that shows people to be only marginally sensitive to price in health care purchases, HIP found small reductions in nonemergency ED use and greater use of preventative care services.[51] Relying on five years of administrative data, Indiana could document that HIP enrollees used preventative services at comparable rates to persons on private insurance (at approximately a 60 percent rate) and that in 2012, 61 percent of enrollees who were required to make POWER account contributions received at least one recommended preventive service, compared to only 53 percent among those on traditional Medicaid. The use of generic drugs also edged slightly higher among HIP enrollees—about 80 percent of the time—compared to 65 percent among comparable populations under commercial insurance policies.[52]

Given these data, Indiana was in a stronger position to claim that its policy innovation worked, at least judging from its few measures of program performance. ED use declined, preventative care rose, and participants professed satisfaction with the program and tended to meet their cost-sharing obligations at a high rate. The larger claim, that individuals appreciated the Medicaid program more and that they became savvier consumers, proved much more difficult to substantiate and was one that Indiana officials had not documented as of 2016.

As tempered as Indiana's policy makers were, their work did not escape criticism. Among the detractors was John Davidson at the conservative Federalist Society, who wrote in early 2015 that Indiana's program bore the veneer of a market-driven system but that the state's decision to use taxpayer dollars to almost entirely supply the individualized accounts put them on the hook to expand welfare for thousands.[53] The Heritage Foundation also opposed the Indiana move, citing concerns over costs, continued federal funding for the expansion, and whether the Supreme Court might rule that first-dollar funding, which Indiana withdrew via this innovation, might be tied to receipt of any Medicaid dollars.[54] To such criticisms, Senator Hershman said there will always be ideologically charged up people "who aren't practical."[55]

Republican officials in Indiana plotted a pragmatic approach to using the state-federal partnership in Medicaid to cover 20 percent of their population (as of 2015), reducing their uninsured rate by 27 percent from 2013 to 2015 alone.[56] They overcame largely external criticism to craft a program that they could call their own and that was designed to include a nominal element of personal accountability. Conservative commentators in national venues, such as *Forbes Magazine* on the one-year anniversary of HIP 2.0, still belittled the minimal cost-sharing provisions as an instance of "little personal responsibility for enrollees, and higher costs for taxpayers."[57] Despite this, Hoosier state leaders found a way to live with the big-government program of Medicaid prior to Barack Obama's presidency and leveraged even more from the program under the Affordable Care Act, despite the insistence by some that they "hated" the ACA.[58] Mostly because of the program-specific evidence they brought to bear, expansion proponents had a fairly easy time of coming to live with a Medicaid expansion, despite the costs to the state (covered by a cigarette tax and new fees imposed on hospitals) and the political furor over the program among free-market conservatives in the media and think tanks at the national level. Hoosier Republicans found a way to live with Obamacare.

Other Republican States Found Their Own Ways to Expand Medicaid

The years 2014 and 2015 were pivotal for state decisions about the Medicaid expansion. While the vast majority of Democratically controlled states moved ahead with the enlarged program as soon as they were able (effective January 1, 2014), Republican state officials needed more time to mull their options and ability to customize their programs before they could soften their opposition to all things regarding the ACA. As GOP officials in several states pivoted away from their initial staunch opposition, this trend effectively gave a measure of political cover to leaders in other conservative states to find their own ways to broaden health coverage for low-income persons. By the end of 2016, fully 31 states and the District of Columbia had decided to expand their programs. Ten of these states had Republican governors. Even in deeply red Wyoming, GOP governor Matt Mead asked his legislature to support an expansion on the basis of covering an estimated 20,000 state residents and receiving more than $100 million annually from the federal government. State senators, many of whom had campaigned on promises to oppose an expansion, turned him down, but the governor continued to press.[59]

Looking beyond the particular states discussed here, there emerged a pattern to the expansion of Medicaid under the ACA. In order to understand why certain Republican states moved toward this expansion while others did not, it is useful to recall how strongly partisanship drove popular approval and disapproval of the ACA among the general public. As shown in Chapter 2, party identification proved to be a more powerful predictor of overall attitudes toward the law than other factors such as insurance status, age, or income. Similar findings of the importance of partisanship over other characteristics emerged from other recent studies as well.[60] The influence of partisanship among state electorates also helps explain which states acted on the Medicaid expansion and health insurance marketplaces and which did not.[61] Measuring state partisanship by the percentage of presidential votes cast in 2012 for Obama (the year immediately prior to when the initial expansion decisions had to be made), the figures in Table 4.1 show a clear correspondence between the Obama vote and how states responded on the Medicaid issue. Three-quarters of the states that gave Obama the least support in 2012 declined the expansion offer. States that offered Obama a moderate amount of support split somewhat more evenly between refusing the expansion and pursuing a cost-sharing, waiver-based program. Not quite one-fifth (19 percent) of these states pursued a traditional expansion. In sharp contrast, among the states that lent Obama the strongest electoral support in 2012, fully 83 percent adopted a traditional expansion and only 11 percent declined this offer altogether. Just as perspectives on the ACA were heavily driven at the individual level by partisanship, so were state actions.

Partisanship goes a long way in explaining state governments' decisions to extend Medicaid to those above the federal poverty level. In fact, the gubernatorial partisanship of states and the 2012 Obama vote percentage each explained more of the cross-state variation in whether or how states expanded their Medicaid programs than did a key objective measure of need: the percentage uninsured by state in 2013. When included in a multivariate analysis designed to explain the type of Medicaid expansion under way as of the end of 2015 (none, waiver-based, or traditional), the party of the governor and the Obama vote percentage taken together explained over half (55 percent) of the cross-state variation, with both of these variables

Table 4.1 **State Responses to the Medicaid Expansion Option, by the 2012 Presidential Vote**

	Low Obama Support (25–41%)	Moderate Obama Support (42–52%)	High Obama Support (53–71%)
No Medicaid expansion	75%	44%	11%
Waiver-based expansion	6	38	6
Traditional expansion	18	19	83
	N = 16	N = 16	N = 18

Figures in cells are column percentages showing the percentage of states within each level of support for Obama that responded to the expansion option in each manner.

Source: Author's calculations based on Medicaid expansion outcomes as of the end of 2015. State status at www.nashp.org/states-stand-medicaid-expansion-decisions/ (accessed December 31, 2015).

independently exerting significant explanatory power. The rate of state residents who were uninsured in 2013 did not contribute significantly to this explanation.[62] This is to say that states' uninsured rates did not systematically prompt their governments to extend Medicaid; rather, the explanation for such actions rests on partisanship. Any pragmatist hoping that states would base their decisions on objective human needs rather than partisanship should find this pattern disappointing.

Near-Term Prospects

The failure of the Democrats to win the presidency in the 2016 election threw the future of Medicaid into profound uncertainty. As of late 2016, it seemed unlikely that the Medicaid expansion offer made by the ACA would continue in the same form as before. Certainly, pride of ownership over cost-sharing plans designed by state officials—as described earlier—has been important. However, the continuation of the entitlement-based national funding for the program will have to compete with widespread calls from congressional Republicans to shift Medicaid funding to a fixed block grant. When President Reagan proposed this in the early 1980s, he failed to find a single congressional sponsor for the idea.[63] However, times have changed, calls for sweeping entitlement reform have grown, and Medicaid costs have escalated dramatically over the years. Moving to block grant funding would be a momentous change because it would constrain state governments to control program spending on their own or face potentially catastrophic budget implications. The spigot of federal dollars would no longer continue to match state contributions to program funding. Unlike the abolition of entitlement-based welfare funding in 1996, which was followed by a precipitous drop in program use by poor people (owing to a robust economy, the imposition of lifetime limits on program use, and other efforts to push people off of the program), no such decline in Medicaid use could be expected.

In the midst of this uncertainty, it is important to consider that the lessons learned under the Republican Medicaid expansions with cost sharing will likely have a lasting effect on program functioning going forward. Congressional Republicans will likely feel emboldened to consider cost sharing as a regular feature of the program. State officials may also embrace this more broadly. What was, prior to the passage of the ACA, a rare practice may become de rigueur. Despite the evidence presented in Chapter 3 that such cost sharing has only a marginal impact on individuals' behavior, the political appeal is likely to be powerful. Furthermore, linking Medicaid eligibility to behavioral requirements may also become common.

Under the ACA, Arizona took a step further to limit access for these newly eligible persons (those in households with income above the federal poverty level) and to seek permission to impose a work, school, or training requirement on able-bodied adults, as well as a five-year lifetime limit, with some exceptions.[64] Such a time limit for Medicaid was a first, echoing the five-year limit that faces adult recipients of cash welfare, or Temporary Assistance to Needy Families.

For better or worse, Medicaid has become the nation's largest health care assistance program, serving over 58 million as of the summer of 2015.[65] Given this, talk of seriously curtailing the program carries with it an element of political theater. To talk about significantly scaling back the program neglects how much many constituencies appreciate the program, even when colored with the pejorative of the ACA in places where that was unpopular. To illustrate how talk of hating the ACA while liking its Medicaid expansion became distorted and plain ignorant, consider the case of Kentucky. The residents of Kentucky widely embraced new ways of providing access to care. A survey of Kentuckians in 2013 with incomes below 133 percent of the federal poverty level found that approximately 80 percent of them supported the Medicaid expansion under the ACA.[66] A person tasked with helping Kentuckians shop for insurance shared a story with a journalist about how he typically avoided talking about the ACA when helping others use the commonwealth's exchange, called Kynect. In the spring of 2015, he noted that "I don't ever mention the ACA [when helping people.] . . . I had one guy say, 'I'm so glad I found you and didn't have to go through that Obamacare stuff.' "[67]

This disconnect between individual interest and political support for the government program that provided that support—the phenomenon of the submerged state—will likely continue to plague U.S. health care policy discourse so long as the policies, their origins, and their implications are intentionally jumbled by politicians who are more intent on denying their opponents a victory than they are in fixing the remaining problems of cost, quality, and access.

Looming over the near future of national health policy are, of course, numerous questions for health policy. How will national policy makers grapple with an ever more expensive Medicaid program as baby boomers enter nursing homes? Medicaid, as the nation's primary method of payment for such long-term care, can hardly be wished away or even significantly curtailed without dramatic implications for the nation's growing elderly population. Of course, the non-aged population faces significant questions about cost as well. Recent history indicates that America's political institutions are not positioned to confront aggressively the problems of costs, as our bicameral Congress shows itself to be exceedingly challenged to grapple with complicated issues in coherent ways.[68] The significant challenges to containing health care costs will almost certainly persist as part of our dysfunctional politics surrounding health care. These issues are taken up in Chapter 5.

CHAPTER FIVE

The Cost of Health Care

The preceding chapters have argued that the politics of the Affordable Care Act (ACA) proved to be an obstacle to a productive public discourse about the pressing issues surrounding the cost and quality of and access to medical services. Perhaps nowhere is this truer than regarding cost. Since at least 1960, spending on health care has risen faster each year than has the nation's gross domestic product. While these annual surplus expenditures have varied across time, they have outpaced overall economic growth for so long that overall health care spending currently consumes approximately one-sixth of the nation's economic production, compared to only one-twentieth in 1960. Americans spend considerably more on health care than any other nation both on a per capita basis and as a portion of GDP.[1] While steep price inflation in health care has, perhaps, come to be seen as normal to casual observers, the prospect of such expenditures rising to consume more than one-third of GDP within a generation ought to catalyze serious policy movement to address them, but as it turns out the dysfunctional public discourse surrounding health care has done little in recent years to move the nation toward a healthier health care politics.

This chapter presents an overview of recent patterns in American health care spending. The levels of health care costs are alarming, the trajectory is unsustainable, and Congress has demonstrated poor ability to respond productively. Peter Orzag, director of the Office of Management and Budget under President Obama, wrote in 2011 that "it is no exaggeration to say that the United States' standing in the world depends on its success in constraining this health-care cost explosion; unless it does, the country will eventually face a severe fiscal crisis or a crippling inability to invest in other areas."[2] While Orzag was part of the team that developed the ACA and had an incentive to raise an alarm, other observers not so situated concur. Scholars writing in the *National Tax Journal* in 2010 and working from data generated by the non-partisan Congressional Budget Office (CBO) explained that "rising costs for health care will cause federal spending to grow much faster than revenues, putting the federal budget on an unsustainable path."[3] This broadly shared view that recent trends are not tenable served as a primary catalyst for the passage of the ACA back in 2010. However, at least two problems persist. The ACA was not designed to do enough to aggressively confront rising health expenditures, though it helped; and repealing it without replacement would, in the CBO's estimation, contribute to heightened federal deficits.[4] An overview of Americans' health expenditures serves as a useful starting point for our discussion.

Overall Health Care Expenditures

The best data on overall health expenditures come from the National Health Expenditure Account tabulated by the U.S. Department of Health and Human Services. These annual figures are comprehensive and non-duplicative, and the agency has utilized a consistent methodology since 1960, allowing for meaningful longitudinal comparisons.[5] Based on this accounting, overall health care spending stood at 5 percent of GDP in 1960. By 2015, this figure had reached 17.4. Adjusting for inflation, the annual growth rate of health expenditures averaged 4.7 percent over this period. From the late 1970s to the year Barack Obama was elected president, health expenditure inflation outpaced GDP growth by an average of 2.2 percent annually.[6] Although spending has leveled out somewhat since the late 2000s, it has still continued to grow faster than the GDP and is expected to do so into the foreseeable future.

Looking below the surface of these aggregate figures, health spending growth has been uneven across time. In inflation-adjusted terms, from the early 1960s through the early 1980s, overall spending grew between 6.5 and 7.5 percent annually. The creation of Medicare and Medicaid in 1965 steepened expenditure growth rates but lowered the personal rate of spending, since these new programs allowed many Americans to reduce their out-of-pocket expenses. Overall spending slowed in the 1990s, averaging 4.7 percent annually between 1993 and 2002, in part due to the introduction of managed care arrangements, which limited consumers' choices, and low rates of general inflation. From 2003 to 2013, average annual spending rose at a rate of 3.2 percent. Various factors account for the recent slowdown, including fewer blockbuster drugs entering the market and the emergence of more generic drugs, a contraction in overall spending due to the recession post 2008, and some savings created by the implementation of the ACA, including reduced Medicare reimbursement rates. However, despite this diminished inflation rate, in 2014, Americans still managed to spend some $3 trillion on health care, an average of $9,523 per person.[7] The Centers for Medicare and Medicaid Services (CMS) projects future health care spending at an annual growth rate of 5.8 percent from 2014 to 2024, or about 1.1 percent more than GDP annually. If realized, this means that health spending will rise from its current 17.4 percent of GDP to 19.6 percent by 2024.[8]

Beyond burdening the overall economy, health expenditures also stress government budgets. Mainly due to the growth of Medicare and Medicaid, health care expenses in 2014 consumed 23 percent of the federal budget. Medicare accounted for 14 percent and Medicaid for another 9 percent.[9] In recent years, Medicare spending increased between 5 and 6 percent annually, reaching $618 billion in 2014. Medicaid, despite its humble origins in the 1960s, now serves more persons than does Medicare, though it spends a solid majority of its funds on an elderly minority of its clientele, specifically those participants who live in long-term care facilities. Its expenses having grown over the past two decades at an average annual rate of 6 percent, Medicaid spending jumped 10 percent during 2014, largely due to program expansions at the state level. Medicaid consumed $485 billion in 2014.[10] Because both Medicare and Medicaid are entitlements, governments' financial obligations for them remain open ended. This spending significantly implicates the nation's debt load. As of 2015, the U.S. national debt slightly exceeded America's GDP.[11] Multiple factors will influence this GDP-to-national-debt ratio in the future, but health expenditures will surely play a highly significant role.

Nongovernmental spending accounts for approximately half of Americans' health costs. These expenditures have also risen significantly over recent years. In 2014 alone, private health insurance spending grew 4.4 percent to $991 billion, and out-of-pocket spending rose 1.3 percent to $329 billion.[12] The cost of employer-sponsored health insurance policies, a major component of nongovernmental health spending, has risen steeply over the past couple of decades. Between 1999 and 2015, premiums rose 203 percent, outpacing both wage growth and general price inflation. In 2014, the average employer-sponsored policy for family coverage premium topped $17,500, with workers shouldering 19 percent of this expense. Premium costs are expected to moderate between 2017 and 2024, with a projected inflation rate of 5.4 percent annually due to the proliferation of high-deductible insurance plans.[13]

Rising prices have clearly impacted Americans' usage patterns and financial stress levels surrounding health services. For instance, when a 2015 survey asked about services foregone and prescriptions not filled due to high cost, one-fifth of respondents indicated they skipped a needed service over the previous year, and fully 40 percent said they had faced cost-related access problems to care.[14] The pressures of rising costs are not merely abstractions that can be hidden by government borrowing. For many Americans, they constitute matters of fundamental wellness.

Why Are Costs So High?

Several factors contribute to rising health care costs. Three of them stand out as primary culprits. First, advancing technology clearly has added a lot of value to modern diagnostic and treatment regimens, saving and extending lives. However, technology has also been a heavy driver of medical inflation. Second, pharmaceuticals play an important role. While many medications allow patients to reduce their overall use of other expensive treatments, prescription medications accounted for just under $300 billion in 2014, growing 12.2 percent in that year alone.[15] Third, patterns of overutilization paint a picture of routine waste in service delivery driven by technology, defensive medicine, perverse incentives built into payment systems, and other factors. What follows is a brief examination of these three factors underlying recent health care inflation.

Advancing Technology

Many studies have attempted to quantify the impact of new technologies on overall health expenditures. Modeling this question is difficult due to the challenges of measuring expenditures attributable to particular treatments and the specific roles of older and newer technologies. This said, several studies place this figure near 50 percent. Research examining spending in 18 developed nations from 1981 to 2009 concluded that new technologies accounted for approximately 43 percent of the growth in health care spending over this period.[16] Another study, focusing on the United States, concluded that between 25 and 50 percent of inflation-adjusted per capita spending from 1960 through the 2000s was attributable to new technologies.[17] Examining an earlier period, Peden and Freeland estimated that new technologies were responsible for approximately 70 percent of the increase in health spending between 1960 and the early 1990s.[18] Despite some differences in these estimates, scholars agree that technology is the prime driver of health care inflation.

Of course, not all technology is created equal. Some interventions are highly successful and unambiguously add value in terms of illnesses cured and lives extended: antibiotics for bacterial infections, beta-blockers for heart attacks, and anti-retroviral drugs for people with HIV/AIDS. A second class of treatments may hold great promise for a minority of patients but have not been broadly efficacious. Stents for stable angina, for example, fall into this category. A third group of treatments includes procedures that are not particularly efficacious or for which little scientific evidence exists to support their effectiveness, including vertebroplasty (involving cement injected to stabilize vertebrae[19]) and certain radiation treatments for prostate cancer.[20] The recent push for—and the ACA's funding of—comparative effectiveness research may help identify and promote the use of highly effective technologies while minimizing the use of less effective ones. While recent federal law includes grant programs to enable the National Institutes of Health, the federal Agency for Healthcare Research and Quality, and the Veterans Administration to gather evidence as to treatment effectiveness and better practices, concerns about how such information might be used to direct particular courses of treatment lead members of Congress to prohibit these findings from limiting payments under Medicare.[21] While some medical professionals were relieved to have been able to sidestep any mandates that would influence or coerce their care regimes, others see this firewall between good information and Medicare spending patterns as a lost opportunity.

Pharmaceuticals

Prescription drug costs represent another sector of health care spending that has seen high rates of inflation in recent years. From 1999 to 2003, prescription drug spending grew at an average annual rate of 13 percent. This slowed between 2003 and 2013 to an average of 5 percent per year but then accelerated after that, rising 12 percent in 2014 alone. Given many very large price increases for select drugs still under patent protection, particularly in the last few years, this rate may persist at a high level over the near term.[22]

Some pharmaceutical corporations experienced sales declines during the 2000s, as their drugs were either eclipsed with newer products or replaced by generics. A common tactic on the part of these companies has been to radically increase the prices of the patented drugs they still control and to claim that the revenue is needed to fund current and future research. Some of the more extreme examples help explain why this became a political hot-button issue. GlaxoSmithKline raised the wholesale price of

Albendazole, an anti-parasitic, from $5.92 for a typical daily dose in 2010 to $119.58 by 2013.[23] Sanofi manufactures the cancer drug Zaltrap and in 2012 began charging $11,000 per month for this medication. As of 2016, Celgene's cancer drug Revlimid costs $150,000 per year. In 2014, Gilead Sciences was called before Congress to explain its $1,000-a-day price tag on the hepatitis C medication Sovaldi, a drug that cost the Medicare program over $3 billion in 2014.[24] Novartis's leukemia drug Gleevec cost $3,000 per month (adjusted for inflation) in 2001. By the end of 2015, its price tag had grown to over $9,000.[25] Turing Pharmaceuticals in 2015 set what may be a record price increase, for the drug Daraprim, a 62-year-old medicine used to treat infections in persons with compromised immune systems, from $18 to $750 per pill, meaning that a course of treatment (typically about 100 pills) reached a cost of $75,000.[26] Why the sudden price increase on a 62-year-old drug whose research and development costs were long ago paid for? Profit, explained then-CEO Martin Shkreli in August 2015. While he was certainly working in a capitalist economy, Shkreli's public relations incompetence cost him his job. Within a few months of this tone-deaf public explanation, he left Turing.[27] As satisfying as Shkreli's downfall may be to his critics, the more general pattern across pharmaceutical companies is toward very high profits. Valeant Pharmaceuticals International generated $8.25 billion in revenue during 2014, up 43 percent from 2013.[28]

Directors of pharmaceutical corporations show an awareness of the political consequences of unbridled price increases. The threat of new government regulations tends to catch their attention. During the summer of 2015, Vertex Pharmaceuticals reduced the wholesale price of Orkambi, for cystic fibrosis, from $311,000 to $259,000, apparently in an effort to placate investors who feared backlash from Congress.[29] The CEO of Massachusetts-based Biogen, James Mullen (who stepped down in 2010), was asked at a conference about his company's steep price increases during the 2000s. He responded that "if there are price increases that can be taken and delivered to shareholders, we'll go get it, but I do think that we got to make sure we take a long enough view and you don't start to . . . get backlash."[30] More systematic evidence on this point comes from research into the effect of political scrutiny of drug price increases. For instance, drug makers slowed their price increases during the health policy reform discussions of 1993–1994, apparently concerned that if those reforms had been successful they could have imposed new regulation on drug prices.[31]

The backlash Mullen referenced continued during 2016 in Congress and the presidential campaign, as candidates promised action. In turn,

PhRMA responded by letting it be known that it would spend aggressively on lobbying and public relations after the 2016 elections to discourage what it saw as punitive regulation of their industry, arguing in part that other health care players would have to take some responsibility for rising prescription expenditures.[32] One other highly visible battle has been over the steeply rising retail cost of Mylan Pharmaceuticals' EpiPen, an injector to stop allergic reactions. The list price for a two-pack of this product rose from less than $100 in 2007, when Mylan acquired the patent, to over $600 by late 2016. For the Medicare program, this translated to skyrocketing spending, rising from $7 million in 2007 to nearly $88 million in 2014. (The spending increase was mainly due to the per-package price increase, though sales also increased.)[33] Congressional hearings were clearly designed to pressure Mylan into backing off its pricing strategy. However, exactly what form this next round of political combat will take remained an open question as of the end of 2016.

Overutilization

Because insurance programs typically allow medical providers wide latitude over how to address any given ailment, providers face choices about how intensively—or expensively—to pursue treatments. Despite years of conversation about how fee-for-service payment systems incentivize overutilization, they continue as the norm.[34] This problem is not new; in fact, the conversation about overutilization among health policy experts on this point is long running. While overutilization has been used as part of a political-economic narrative about the need to share costs with patients and to cut service delivery, it also persists as a significant problem that does not appear to have abated despite much recent discussion.[35] One recent and widely cited report of this problem indicates that one-third or more of U.S. health care expenditures are wasted due to over-diagnosis, overtreatment, the use of intensive end-of-life care, the use of higher-priced services than are necessary, inefficient care, and other factors.[36]

Patterns of overutilization in the United States are illustrated by the wide variation in spending across providers and regions of the country. Looking at Medicare spending per recipient, the regions of the country with the highest spending consume 30 percent more per person than the regions with the lowest spending.[37] Per-recipient Medicare spending in 2009 ranged from $9,278 in Massachusetts to $5,031 in Utah. Several states—Massachusetts, Alaska, Connecticut, Maine, and Delaware—experienced Medicare per capita spending that was 25 percent above the national average that year.[38]

This regional variation prompted calls for greater scrutiny of providers who may be systematically overutilizing treatments in ways that are, frankly, wasteful. These have taken the form of articles in popular media,[39] governmental reports,[40] and scholarly writings.[41]

Beyond overuse driven by local preferences, traditions, or the differences in available facilities, one particular problem encourages treatment that can be more intensive than is required. Physicians tend to work within a customary practice framework, meaning they do what other physicians in their neighborhoods or specialties customarily do. Sometimes, these treatments are driven by significant data on better practices, but often they instead reflect local norms. For instance, Dr. John Wennberg compared rates of various types of treatments and outcomes of those treatments in New Haven, Connecticut, and Boston, Massachusetts, during 1982. He found that patients in New Haven were twice as likely to undergo a coronary bypass operation as patients in Boston but that patients in Boston were much more likely to have their hips or knees replaced. New Haven residents were much more likely than Bostonians to undergo back operations and hysterectomies.[42] These differences suggest local preferences that likely correspond to the availability of specialists more than they have to do with evidence-driven practices.

The cross-regional and cross-provider expenditure differences seen in Medicare data clearly exceed what can be readily explained by the health conditions of Medicare recipients in different parts of the country or even neighborhood consumption patterns.[43] While the history of Medicare and Medicaid law clearly prohibits government policy makers from interfering in the doctor-patient relationship, the resulting wide variation in providers' access to these public dollars poses a chief challenge for both of these programs, especially given the expansion of Medicaid under the ACA and the growth of Medicare rolls caused by an aging population. Though counter to the long-standing tradition of these two programs, closer guidance on courses of treatment could produce significant savings.[44]

Congress's Limited Predisposition to Control Costs

Despite a long history of Americans admiring Congress as the preeminent expression of their republican democracy, this image has changed considerably over the past decade. While Congress long has struggled to achieve coherent collective action, heightened party polarization has acted as a key obstacle to effective legislation in numerous areas.[45] Since the end of the Cold War, Congress struggled to follow the Pentagon's advice on military base closures because those installations provide employment in congressional districts.[46] In only four years since 1970 has Congress passed a balanced budget.[47] It has struggled to enact campaign finance reform.[48] Similarly, it has revealed itself to be largely, but not entirely, incapable of controlling government spending on health programs. Interest-group pressure and fundamental conflicts over the government's role in service provision and financing typically frustrate policy making.

To illustrate just how complex these problems can be, this section examines two cases of health policy making from recent years. Controlling Medicare Part B expenditures for out-patient services proved exceedingly difficult, but in 2015 Congress reformed a policy that might prove productive and lasting, insomuch that this new approach was designed to incentivize quality over quantity. The second case shows, however, continuing inability to stop the hemorrhaging of billions of dollars annually as well as active political resistance to an obvious solution. In the end, Congress shows itself to be not *completely* incapable of addressing these major problems, but years of delay and tremendous expense tended to precede concerted action.

Medicare's Sustainable Growth Rate Formula

In the late 1990s, Congress recognized an unsustainable growth path for Medicare spending and created the Sustainable Growth Rate Formula (SGR) for Medicare Part B, covering out-patient services.[49] This system aimed to limit program expenditures, allowing them to rise annually no faster than the overall growth of the economy. A formula would reduce payments to providers (mainly physicians) in order to keep Medicare Part B payments in line. Oddly, at its center, the SGR relied on uncoerced collective action. Somehow, doctors were supposed to curtail their billing of the program or face a collective reduction in payments. This program's failure should not surprise anyone even vaguely familiar with collective action problems. While in 2002 Congress allowed the automated cut to take effect, from 2003 through 2015, Congress intervened each year to suspend the cuts prescribed by the formula.[50] This was a clear case of Congress kicking the can down the road, repeatedly.

Members of Congress were responding to pressure from organized medicine. Typically, the patch involved medical providers facing an automated cut of several percentage points but instead receiving a very modest increase as a result of Congress's intervention. For example, in 2004, the law called for a 6.6 percent cut, but Congress legislated a 1.7 percent increase in its place. In 2008, there should have been a 4.5 percent reduction in payments, but Congress approved a 0.5 percent increase.[51] Similar reversals occurred each year—17 times in all—as Congress implemented what colloquially came to be known as the "doc fix."

Of course, the decision each year to defer the legislated cut meant that over years these planned reductions piled up. By 2015, the automatic reduction was to be 21.2 percent.[52] The system had reached what could fairly be called a crisis, for implementing such a payment reduction all in one go would likely have led to many physicians either to accept many fewer Medicare beneficiaries or to pull out of the Medicare market altogether. Finally, sensing this disastrous possibility, in 2014 members of Congress began work on a replacement for the SGR but could not agree on how to budget the estimated $144 billion in additional government spending that such a fix would have required over its first decade. Attempting once again to repeal part of the ACA, a Republican proposal would have tied a funding formula for the doc fix to a delay of the individual mandate. This was not successful, and once again Congress legislated a short-term fix for out-patient Medicare payments.[53]

After years of hobbling along, in April 2015, Congress approved a new system that called for annual raises of 0.5 percent through 2018.[54] By that year, a system was to be in place tying payments to quality performance, practice improvement, and the meaningful use of information technology.[55] This arrangement involved some additional government spending: $214 billion over 10 years, according to the CBO. In order to offset these expenses, the law reduced Medicare payments to hospitals and post-acute providers, and it raised the Medicare premium for high-income beneficiaries (with annual income above $133,000). An estimated $70 billion of the new costs would be offset by these changes, with the CBO estimating this change to save the federal government money over the long run.[56]

Throughout this lengthy episode, despite the obvious need to control Medicare spending, Congress regularly demonstrated its unwillingness to stick with the solution it created in 1997 and instead resorted to a string of temporary patches that nursed along its relationship with medical providers and more than 40 million program enrollees.[57] While one might take some solace from the 2015 legislation, it remains to be seen if Congress will uphold this agreement any better than it did the last. The new law's quality measures may prove more difficult to adhere to than legislators anticipated, and the political pressure for annual increases of more than one-half of 1 percent will almost certainly be significant, given typical rates of overall cost escalation.

Medicare's Prescription Drug Benefit

When Congress enacted a nonhospital prescription drug program under the Medicare Modernization Act of 2003, it provided a large measure of security to Medicare recipients, though it proved hugely controversial at the time. Democrats had searched for a way to offer this coverage since Medicare became law in 1965. Republicans, finally in control of both chambers of Congress, found a way to enact, according to their own principles, what became Medicare Part D, which was created in 2003. Liberals harbored significant misgivings about the new law's coverage gap—specifically the so-called doughnut hole between $2,250 and $3,600 in annual prescription drug expenses in which the program initially offered participants no assistance—and in the end only 16 House and 11 Senate Democrats voted for the bill on final passage. The majority of the public—and a plurality of seniors, who wanted more comprehensive coverage—initially disapproved of the program. However, President Bush signed it into law in December 2003.[58] The program took effect in 2006.

While certainly a help to the elderly, Medicare's prescription drug benefit also provided a windfall for the pharmaceutical industry. The consensus in Congress at the time of enactment was that program costs should not exceed $400 billion over the first decade.[59] The administration's estimate conveniently came in at $395 billion. This was enough to help GOP members approve the package. Unhappily, within a couple of months of passage, the HHS released a revised cost estimate, this one at $534 billion, or just over one-third again as much as the original estimate. Some conservatives in Congress complained, claiming that the Bush administration intentionally withheld the higher estimate until after passage, but beyond scattered grievances Congress did nothing to curtail the program's cost.[60] As it turned out, the first decade of Part D cost approximately one-third less than expected, partly because of lower enrollment in Part D, but mostly due to a slowdown in drug purchasing.[61]

The fortuitous break, however, should not mask the fact that this additional benefit is very expensive and will likely continue to be a source of profiteering for pharmaceutical companies for years to come. In an ironic twist, lawmakers included a provision in the Part D statute explicitly prohibiting the Centers for Medicare and Medicaid Services from using its bulk purchasing power to negotiate directly with drug makers for lower prices.[62] This transparently anti-competitive provision, borne of a concern about government bureaucrats interfering in markets,[63] threw open a door to price increases that were nothing short of abusive. One observer at the time of the bill's passage, commenting on the nature of the new coverage with its reliance on private plans and for-profit drug companies fed by billions of public dollars, remarked, "that's not competition; that's corporate welfare."[64] Republican Senator John McCain at the time found this anti-competitive provision "outrageous."[65] More than a decade later, drug companies still have their way on this point, despite the September 2016 Kaiser Health Tracking Poll finding that fully 82 percent of respondents supported allowing government to negotiate prices.[66]

Beginning in 2013, several instances of radical price increases caught the attention of policy makers, health providers, and consumer advocates. The slowdown in drug purchasing caused by the recession of the late 2000s and other factors seemed to have led many pharmaceutical companies to seek profits by other means. In light of lagging sales, drug makers responded by steeply raising prices on many of their products. Because the Medicare program cannot refuse to pay for a drug that the Food and Drug Administration (FDA) has approved for consumer use, the industry has the government in a vulnerable position. While the Affordable Care Act required rebates to states and the federal government under Medicaid and to consumers under Medicare, pharmaceutical companies can game this system by raising prices on the drugs upfront and then offering a rebate on the back end, with details about earnings on any particular drug typically held in secret.[67] In January 2016, the Centers for Medicare and Medicaid Services finalized a rule designed to wring savings for consumers and states, but establishing best prices under this rule remained a fundamentally ambiguous exercise, leaving considerable discretion to drug makers.[68]

Washington's limited tools hobble government efforts to lower pharmaceutical prices. The story of Genentech and its pair of drugs—Avastin and Lucentis—shows just how severe price gouging can become. These two drugs are, molecularly, very similar, and according to six side-by-side trials, they work equally well to combat macular degeneration in the eye. Avastin costs about $50 per injection; Lucentis costs about $2,000. Although Genentech manufactures both drugs, it works to minimize Avastin's market share among ophthalmologists. When doctors prescribe Avastin for treating macular degeneration, they do so by using the drug off-label, which is permitted by the FDA. (Avastin was originally approved as a cancer drug.) Despite Genentech's best efforts, Avastin for macular degeneration is a popular treatment, as evidenced by Medicare data that show that it is used in 56 percent of such cases. Further, in a survey of the American Society of Retinal Specialists, 61 percent of respondents preferred Avastin. However, in order to discourage this, Genentech asked the FDA for permission to change Avastin's labeling to steer doctors away from its off-label use, but the FDA refused because there was no scientific evidence to support this change. Genentech's alternative effort has been to sell Avastin only in large quantities, which are suitable for cancer patients but much less so for ophthalmologists. In October 2007,

Genentech stopped selling Avastin to repackaging firms that sought to prepare it in smaller doses. The company clearly was determined to steer patients and providers toward the more expensive drug.[69]

Various voices have urged reform to allow the CMS to negotiate prices. In 2014, the former senior official at the CMS called for this.[70] In the spring of 2015, President Obama chimed in, and in November of that year the CMS held a day-long forum to gather ideas about how to control drug prices.[71] The Congressional Budget Office has suggested that Medicare use the lower Medicaid drug reimbursement schedules for persons who are dually eligible for Medicaid and Medicare, a move that, according to the CBO, could save between one-quarter and one-third of the cost.[72] Because the departments of Veterans Affairs and Defense are permitted to negotiate lower drug prices, another proposal has been to use this bargaining power for Medicare enrollees who are veterans.[73] California voters considered but rejected a ballot initiative in November 2016 that would have limited payments by state agencies to the prices paid by the U.S. Department of Veterans Affairs.[74] This seems likely to be an ongoing conversation.

Opponents to the idea of the CMS negotiating prices cite a reluctance to allow government to assume such a powerful role in markets. George W. Bush's secretary of health and human services, Michael Leavitt, insisted during his time in office that if given the power to negotiate prices he would not do so unless required by law. Many congressional Republicans, as well as some Democrats, still appear highly sensitive to the opposition of the pharmaceutical industry to such negotiating power. PhRMA, the industry's lead lobbying organization, has heavily focused its contributions on GOP members since 2010, when Republicans took control of the House, but it has also been practical when the times call for that. In 2008, a winning year for Democrats, PhRMA directed all of its more than $1.5 million in political giving to Democrats.[75] Given this field of forces and the program's continuing prohibition on direct negotiation, it is fair to conclude that Medicare's prescription drug program is and will remain at least as much a profit-making machine for pharmaceutical companies as it is a help to Medicare enrollees.[76]

The ACA's Cost Control Provisions

Various provisions of the Affordable Care Act were designed to address some of these spending problems by attempting to control both the cost and volume of services delivered.[77] How well these provisions might have worked had the ACA been allowed to work its influence over medical markets, uninterrupted by the 2016 elections, may never be known. The law's primary emphases were on expanding insurance coverage, but its architects also included various provisions to control costs. Although all of these provisions are subject to extensive rewriting by the 115th Congress and the Trump administration, a brief review of the ACA's cost-control measures helps to establish a point of comparison from which near-term health policy will almost certainly diverge.

In 2010, the Congressional Budget Office recognized in the ACA's provisions both new expenditures and budget offsets, due to spending reductions and new revenue, for a total budget deficit reduction of $140 billion over the first decade.[78] While the overall rate of health care spending fell after 2010, this trend had been under way for several years prior, due in significant part to the curtailed spending of the Great Recession. Reductions in Medicaid and Medicare reimbursements were to account for much of the expected savings under the ACA. These cuts were estimated to be $196 billion over 10 years to Medicare Parts A and B, $136 billion in reductions through Medicare Advantage (managed care) plans, and a trimming of payments to hospitals that treat low-income patients by $36 billion.[79]

The ACA's planned 2018 introduction of a 40 percent excise tax on expensive employer-sponsored health plans was a key strategy to place downward pressure on insurance prices. This excise tax—or Cadillac tax, as it came to be called—was initially designed to apply to employers whose plans cost on average more than $10,200 for individual coverage or $27,500 for a family. (The tax was designed to apply only to the cost in excess of these thresholds.) Initially envisioned as both an incentive to control the prices of employer-provided health policies and as a source of revenue to help fund other coverage expansions, the Cadillac tax quickly became deeply unpopular, as employers and their workers realized how expensive this could become. In response, in 2015 Congress intervened to delay by two years the implementation of the tax. This amendment also softened the impact of this charge by making it tax deductible for employers obliged to pay it. Further, the 2015 change added inflation escalators and heightened the thresholds for workers in high-risk occupations, such as construction and law enforcement.[80] Though various observers differ on whether the delay was warranted, it stands as a prime example of Congress's tendency to succumb to pressure, even if this means shorting the planned revenue stream to help fund service expansions.

Other steps to help reduce overall spending targeted service providers. Hospitals came to face stronger incentives to improve quality of outcomes. Under the ACA, the Centers for Medicare and Medicaid Services extended both carrots and sticks. The CMS reduced Medicare reimbursements for hospitals in the top 25 percent of the distribution of hospital-acquired infections. Similarly, hospitals with high readmission rates experienced reduced Medicare reimbursement.[81] On the positive side, the law created an opportunity for high-performing hospitals to share in the Medicare savings they create by maintaining their populations' health more efficiently. Such Accountable Care Organizations (ACOs) spread quickly, with 287 of them forming by the spring of 2013, and over 420 by April 2015.[82] While their performance was mixed, with a significant minority of them not meeting quality benchmarks by 2013, in many categories ACOs drove down risk rates, including falls and hospital-borne infections. On the matter of overall efficiency, by 2013, 24 percent of ACOs decreased savings sufficiently to earn premiums under the Shared Savings Program, and another 27 percent achieved lesser savings, though not enough to qualify for premiums.[83] As of late 2014, the CMS reported an overall savings of $417 million under this system, a modest amount but perhaps a promising start.[84]

One of the ACA's more controversial approaches to tightened control over Medicare reimbursement rates came in the form of the new Independent Payment Advisory Board (IPAB), a 15-member commission responsible for monitoring a revamped payment system for Parts A and B of Medicare as well as Medicare Advantage. Starting in 2014, the IPAB recommended reimbursement reductions that take effect unless Congress acts to modify Medicare payments in other ways that align its spending with overall growth of the economy.[85] Members of Congress voiced resistance because they saw this as usurping their power, and the American Medical Association called for the repeal of the IPAB due to its concerns about how these automated reductions can affect physicians.[86] Like other previous efforts to reduce overall spending by targeting a well-organized set of stakeholders, this one seems likely to run afoul of Congress members' weakness of will, a problem triggered by the political pressures that they will experience.

Repealing the ACA?

As of this writing in early 2017, Congress and the Trump administration are busy working to turn back parts of the Affordable Care Act, though these provisions will likely take some time to unwind. Further, due to the significant differences among congressional Republicans discussed in earlier chapters profound conflicts have arisen as to how to accomplish this and how far these changes can go. Congressional Republicans cannot, as their January 2011 bill envisioned, simply repeal the ACA and pretend that it never happened. The administrative and regulatory implications of that would be vast and complex for governments, employers, providers, insurers, and families.[87] More likely is that the most controversial parts of the law—the Cadillac tax, Medicare's Independent Payment Advisory Board, the individual mandate, the Medicaid expansion, the medical device tax—will be removed. New ideas have arisen from the consumer-driven strategies discussed in Chapter 3. At the very least, insured Americans should expect much higher deductibles and co-payments in the years to come, but they may also enjoy the tax benefits of expanded health savings accounts.

Whether these changes will produce the better health care at lower prices that Donald Trump promised during his campaign and as president is highly debatable and something Americans will only discern over time. The costs of repealing the ACA without a replacement have been studied by the Congressional Budget Office. This is a difficult set of calculations, and the CBO acknowledged this directly in its June 2015 report.[88] Reductions in government spending, of course, have direct impacts on budget deficits, but they also create economic feedback; hence, they create indirect effects. Not spending federal funds on prescription drugs will lead to a contraction in the pharmaceutical industry, which in turn will pay fewer corporate income taxes. Given the uncertainty of these indirect effects, the CBO offered a range of possible impacts on the federal budget. Considering only the direct effects, it estimated that repealing the ACA would increase the deficit by $353 billion over the years 2016 to 2025. Alternatively, including budgetary feedback consequences, repealing it would enlarge the deficit by $137 billion over the same period.

Naturally, government budget deficits are not the only way to gauge the ACA's impact on the nation's financial state. The law, whether in its 2010 form or under some revised version, will affect economic activity in various ways, including individuals' and employers' behavior in service utilization, sales, investments, and other financial activities. The CBO estimated that repealing the ACA would slightly increase economic activity, principally because more employers would be able to hire more workers and to pay higher wages if not obliged to provide health insurance. This impact was estimated to boost the GDP by an annual average of 0.7 percent up through the year 2025. This enhanced economic growth would lower federal budget deficits by some $216 billion between 2016 and 2025. However, this gain would not be enough to overcome the other deficit-enlarging effects of repealing the ACA.[89]

Repealing the ACA without a replacement plan would lead immediately to several very tangible consequences. Medicare expenditures would rise due to the removal of the incentive programs discussed earlier. The number of uninsured Americans would swell by approximately 22 million from 2017 to 2019, and by an estimated 24 million more from 2020 through 2025.[90] This would mark a powerful reversal of a downward trend in the number of uninsured individuals that began in 2014 with the implementation of the insurance requirement and Medicaid expansion. In 2013, just over 41 million Americans lacked insurance. By the end of 2014, that figure dropped to 32 million, and by the first quarter of 2016, it fell just under 28 million.[91]

By most reckonings, in early 2017, the ACA was on track to tame health care's cost curve somewhat, though not uniformly across categories of services. Pharmaceutical expenditures have risen steeply in the last few years and will almost certainly continue to do so, absent a regulatory intervention. However, simply repealing the law would feel like a tremendous political victory for its opponents, but this would take the nation back to the days of many millions more uninsured, along with the public health and cost-shifting consequences that created a broad consensus for reform in the late 2000s. The general public, however, has been deeply conflicted about such a move, in part because approximately 70 percent of adults in the United States obtained their insurance through employers during 2016, a figure that has remained largely stable over the past decade. Most Americans who had private insurance outside of the ACA did not feel much over the past few years in the way of direct effects of the law's coverage-expanding provisions.[92] Consequently, the plurality of respondents to surveys asking about whether the ACA will make them personally better off, worse off, or leave them unchanged indicated the latter. For instance, in the Gallup Poll in May 2016, 39 percent of respondents said that the law made no difference to their family's health care situation.[93] Interestingly, though, similar pluralities expressed a belief that the law had made the nation worse off.[94] While this last part likely reflects mostly conjecture, as most people lack the factual knowledge to answer such a complex question about costs and benefits, this certainly helps explain the general public's enduring skepticism toward the Affordable Care Act. Chapter 6 examines what the public learned about the law from 2010 to 2015 and how that knowledge, along with partisanship, helps to explain why so many Americans were reluctant to embrace it over this period of time.

CHAPTER SIX

A Frustrated Search for the Public's Voice

The literature on "the rational public" does not claim that public opinion is always right or wise, even when it is sensible. Rather, the public is only as wise as the available information enables it to be.
—Shapiro and Bloch-Elkon[1]

A considerable amount of evidence shows that the public is capable of acquiring and applying knowledge about politics, particularly if provided with information that is reasonably accurate and complete and accompanied by relevant conceptual frameworks within which to apply that information. But finding this knowledge, so important to the development of the public's voice, requires some help from experts. As a broad generalization, modern scholars of American politics have widely adopted the perspective that meaningful democracy requires not only information but an ongoing partnership between ordinary citizens and opinion leaders. In the absence of quality information or diverse sources of opinion, the stage is instead set for public ignorance, elite manipulation, or worse.[2]

The politics surrounding the Affordable Care Act (ACA) from the time of its passage to the end of the Obama administration provided a test of, or at least a challenge to, modern theories of democracy. The issues have been—and still remain—complex and terribly expensive, the public has a great deal to learn, and politicians have strong electoral incentives to deny their opponents anything that looks like a partisan victory, as the earlier chapters of this book have illustrated. While these factors do not necessarily portend outright failure for health care reform as an exercise in democracy, they provide the threads of a debate that, if not successfully resolved, could end either in policy failure—meaning an attempted but later aborted set of innovations—or in deepened resentment and hostility between partisans, or both. Central to the argument of this book is the claim that citizens can learn what they need to know to form reasonable opinions if provided a constructive environment but that the polarized political atmosphere in which this debate has taken place interfered with that learning. In order to document the trajectory of the public's knowledge about the ACA, this chapter examines longitudinal evidence on what the public learned about the law and how the contours of public opinion toward the ACA changed over its first several years.

Unfortunately, the news is not good. Instead of fostering a more informed public, the politics of the Affordable Care Act produced essentially static knowledge levels over a half-decade and a public sharply divided by party identification. Instead of making up their minds based on their insurance status or health condition, Americans largely defaulted to using party identification as their lens on the ACA. Because so many politicians at both the state and the national levels framed their discourse in partisan terms, ordinary citizens had little in the way of alternative perspectives on the very serious problems Americans face or on how these problems might be solved. Instead of a constructive and substantively issue-centered debate, party-line votes characterized the passage of the law and, after a reversal of congressional control, dozens of attempts to repeal it. As Chapter 4 documents, Medicaid expansion followed a course in the states that was far more responsive to partisan control than it was to the objective needs of state populations. Among the broader public, evaluations of the law patterned themselves along strongly partisan lines.[3] Much of the animus expressed in the opening years of the ACA has persisted.

Because of the starkly partisan nature of this debate, the general public has not come to grips with the shortcomings and inefficiencies of our health care systems and has instead defaulted to bumper-sticker discourse. For example, while experts widely recognize the perverse incentives of our predominantly fee-for-service payment systems, partisan discourse rarely engages citizens about pay-for-performance alternatives. That the majority public came to approve of many key provisions of the ACA while disapproving of the law as a whole suggests that the latter distaste was directed toward the law's proponents rather than toward its functionality. Fault lies on both sides, as Democrats largely failed to market their product, and Republicans used health care as a stalking horse for arguments over distrust in government and electoral advantage.

The Possibility of Public Competence

A very large body of academic literature paints a complicated mosaic of both the possibilities for and obstacles to what scholars variously refer to as deliberation, considered public judgment, or participatory democracy. Of course, these perspectives differ on both the processes and the expected outcomes of rich public discourse. Limited space does not allow for a detailed discussion of these schools of thought, though readers can locate a sampling of these writings by consulting the endnotes. We can, however, begin by considering three broad and somewhat overlapping schools of thought. First, the optimists see great potential for thoughtful public judgment that emerges from deliberation. The more people experience face-to-face conversation with neighbors and fellow citizens, the more likely they will come to understand themselves and others, resist the pull of language framing, and even align their own expressed interests with broader community interests.[4] Second, another group of scholars works from a mixed perspective, searching for meaningful democracy that thrives so long as citizens are provided with a good deal of substantially accurate information and a discursive environment that routinely involves competing perspectives. This allows individuals to sort through what are, for most people, competing considerations on issues. Heuristics, or cognitive shortcuts, may provide a solution.[5] Cues or signals from public officials and experts can be valuable.[6] People can learn quite a lot through effort and a supportive environment.[7] The epigraph at the top of this chapter nicely captures an important part of this perspective. Quality public judgments rely on good information. Third, there are the pessimists—or the realists, depending on the eye of the beholder—who adopt dimmer views of the general public and the possibilities of meaningful public knowledge.[8] For some, the problem is elite manipulation; for others, it is institutional contexts that exclude broad participation. Sometimes, the limitations simply come down to what these observers see as cognitive limitations that are widespread among ordinary citizens. As Giovanni Sartori wrote in the 1980s, "the average voter seldom acts, he reacts."[9] And as Joseph Schumpeter bluntly asserted in the 1940s,

> Information is plentiful and readily available. But this does not seem to make any difference. . . . ignorance will persist in the face of masses of information however complete and correct. It persists even in the face of the meritorious efforts that are being made to go beyond presenting information and to teach the use of it by means of lectures, classes, discussion groups. Results are not zero. But they are small. People cannot be carried up the ladder.[10]

Even if we choose to reject such pessimism regarding citizens' cognitive abilities, there persists a fundamental tension between deliberation and partisanship.[11] Briefly, deliberation requires individuals to both talk and listen, with openness to hearing the other side. At minimum, deliberation must foster an appreciation of those with whom one disagrees, but ideally it also involves openness to the occasionally changed mind. In contrast, partisanship, while certainly a useful guide in electoral contexts, typically leads individuals either to persuade or to vanquish the other side.[12] As it turns out, deliberation, which is supposed to occur when people voluntarily come together to discuss politics, stands little chance of arising between people of different political perspectives because of the voluntary sorting that usually occurs among citizens, particularly among those who are politically aware and active.[13] Because knowledge tends to congregate among those with strong ideological commitments, it is difficult to bring together people who are in need of knowledge, interested in acquiring it, and open to competing perspectives. It is one thing to accomplish this in a laboratory, but quite another to expect it will occur naturally.[14]

Health care policy making involves complex decisions, and evidence indicates that the general public is often not up to the job of skillfully handling the necessary trade-offs so often involved.[15] As Vincent Price and colleagues demonstrate, in order to understand the thorny issues here, citizens need multifaceted information, including knowledge, a sense of subjective importance, and active participation. Unfortunately, demographic, medical, and knowledge variables do not often align in useful ways. Factual knowledge tends to concentrate among persons of higher socio-economic status. More broadly, many surveys find that most of the public misunderstands key aspects of policy, including the Affordable Care Act. Actual medical need (such as experience with recent services) and medical-financial stress both vary inversely with health care knowledge, meaning that persons who objectively should be paying attention to health policy tend to do so less than others. Furthermore, males and less-educated persons disproportionately account for those with strong opinions on health care policy.[16] Sadly, ignorance does not seem to inhibit advocacy. Those who actually possess good knowledge tend to engage in selective exposure, reinforcing their beliefs and driving what has been called a "spiral of conviction."[17]

With these perspectives as foreground, a careful examination of some of the existing evidence on public knowledge will allow a better understanding of what the public knows, how partisanship helps to structure that knowledge, and what the prospects for a robust public discourse might be.

What the Public Learned about the ACA

What the public came to know about the Affordable Care Act is central to the argument of this book. If our politics is to be empowering for ordinary Americans, public discourse must foster citizen knowledge of the law. Because, as earlier chapters here have argued, the politics of the ACA was carried on largely in bumper-sticker terms, we might expect flat levels of public knowledge across time. As it turns out, a large body of evidence can be marshaled on this question. The Kaiser Family Foundation and other organizations polled Americans over the years about their factual knowledge of the ACA, starting the month after its passage. Examining these findings gives us a good idea of what the public knew over time, how this knowledge changed, and what the strong filter of party identification had to do with this.

In order to investigate public knowledge about the ACA, I gathered 194 questions that researchers posed to the public between April 2010 and early 2016, in 32 nationally representative surveys. Each of these surveys involved more than 1,000 respondents. This allows an analysis of approximately six years of data across a period when numerous challenges to the law attracted vast media attention, several election cycles provided opportunities for candidates to stake out positions, and through which the public should have had ample opportunity to learn quite a lot about this landmark legislation. These polling data come mainly from the Kaiser Family Foundation's monthly Health Tracking Poll (96 percent of the questions), though a few come from other organizations.[18] The collection consists of 66 different questions. Eleven of them were asked five or more times, accounting for 99 of the 194 items. Thirty-four of the questions were asked only once. The questions range from when the tax penalty for the individual mandate was to take effect, to whether the ACA called for the closure of Medicare's prescription drug coverage gap, to whether a respondent's state had expanded Medicaid, and many more. The large majority of the questions named a provision and asked respondents if, to the best of their knowledge, this was built into the law or not. On average across these 194 questions, 52.8 percent of respondents offered the right answer. This distribution of correct answers has 25th and 75th percentile scores of 43 and 63, respectively. Only two questions were answered correctly by more than 85 percent of respondents, and only two other questions were answered correctly by fewer than 20 percent. Hence, over these numerous and varied queries, the public displayed what can be considered a middling level of knowledge.

Most of the questions—178 of them—occurred in clusters within a given month's tracking poll. This clustering lends itself to aggregation, specifically averaging of the percentage of correct answers in a given month. Focusing on these 178 items finds a fairly steady level of knowledge. Because nearly all of the questions involved dichotomous response

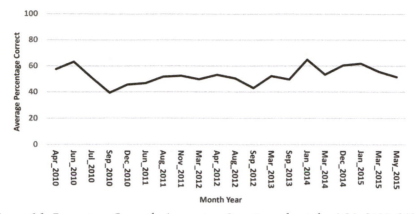

Figure 6.1 Percentage Correctly Answering Questions about the ACA, 2010–2015

Note: Based on 178 questions, with a minimum of 4 questions per time point.

options (i.e., yes or no), one might harbor suspicion, given that the result-ing average approximates a coin-toss result. However, the cross-item vari-ation, as explained below, suggests otherwise. Figure 6.1 shows the percentage of correct answers for each month in which at least four knowledge questions were asked.

Strikingly, the trend line in Figure 6.1 is fairly flat and ends lower than it begins. In the first survey in this series, conducted one month after the law's enactment, the Kaiser poll asked 18 knowledge questions, and an average of 57.5 percent of respondents answered correctly that month. By the end of this series, in May 2015, the average percentage correct stood at 51.4 (based on five questions that month).[19] By this reckoning, the pub-lic actually performed slightly worse in 2015 than it had five years prior.

Looking behind the overall performance, these knowledge questions can be sorted into three categories: questions that asked respondents about a provision that was actually in the law, such as the Medicaid expansion (there are 147 questions of this type); questions that asked respondents about a provision not in the law, such as government panels to direct end-of-life care (30 of these); and questions that were multiple choice, such as when the individual mandate would take effect (17). Over-all, respondents performed significantly better at affirming provisions that were in the law (55.7% of the time) than they did at recognizing pro-visions that were not (42.7% of the time). Respondents fared nominally better on the multiple-choice items (46.4 percent correct) than they did at rejecting false provisions.[20]

The difference in performance between the questions affirming actual provisions versus denying erroneous ones may be attributable in part to respondents' tendency to agree with the implicit proposal embedded in the question wording, or response acquiescence. However, partisan pride of ownership/opposition also plays a role. As discussed in earlier chapters, the politics of the ACA has been so pervasively framed as a case of partisan conflict that nonexpert citizens were encouraged to use party identification as a cover-all heuristic when evaluating the law's provisions. A similar dynamic occurred during the 1990s push for Clinton's reforms.[21]

Examining accuracy by party identification, 50.4 percent of their answers were correct among self-identified Republicans, compared to 57 percent among Democrats.[22] Independents (including leaners) scored a middle position, with 53.1 percent of their answers correct.[23] At least two possible explanations exist for this cross-party difference in the pattern of correct answers given. First, Democrats may have displayed some pride of ownership when asked about some of the ACA's provisions, especially the popular ones, such as allowing parents to carry their grown children on the parents' insurance policies up to age 26. Democratic respondents, in hearing about various benefits that appealed to them, might have been more prone to credit the law for including such provisions. In contrast, Republican respondents, likely to have been defensive and critical during the interview, may have been reluctant to attribute anything useful to Obamacare. We might call this a pride-of-ownership explanation, driven by response acquiescence among Democrats.

A second explanation posits that in their enthusiasm for health care reform, Democrats actually learned more than critics who were eager to dismiss the ACA. If the cross-party differences were entirely or substantially attributable to response acquiescence among Democrats, we should expect differences in the rates of correct responses by party identification across types of questions. Specifically, we would look for attenuation in the cross-party gap on the questions about false provisions relative to questions about the actual ones. This does not occur. The gap remains at 7 percentage points for both types of questions. Further, we would expect the cross-party gap to disappear on the multiple-choice questions (given that saying "yes" was not an option). This essentially occurs, as the gap in this category of questions drops to an insignificant 2.5 points. Hence, we can conclude that part of the cross-party gap in correct answers overall is attributable to Democratic respondents who were prone to affirm provisions more than Republicans, but this is a limited phenomenon, given that Democrats also displayed a greater ability to identify erroneous features of the law compared to Republicans. This suggests that Democrats indeed took the time to learn more about the ACA than did their

Republican counterparts. This pattern holds across the entire period. One recent example of this tendency comes from the September 2016 Kaiser Health Tracking Poll, which asked respondents if they were aware that the nation's uninsured rate had fallen to an all-time low. Overall, 26 percent recognized this. However, only 17 percent of Republicans did, compared to 38 percent of Democrats.[24]

Because only about one-half of all of the data points in this collection come from questions that were asked more than a few times, there is possibly some statistical noise in Figure 6.1, as potentially more challenging questions entered and exited the series. In order to measure and account for this, it is useful to focus on the 11 questions that Kaiser asked five or more times. These questions accounted for 99 of the 194 items. Comparing the scores on these frequently asked questions to the entire collection reveals that this subset produced very similar proportions of correct answers: 55 percent versus 52.8 percent over the entire collection and 50.7 percent on only those items that were not asked at least five times. The range of correct answer rates was broader on the overall collection (76 percentage points from the best to the worst performance on individual questions) compared to the subset of frequently asked questions (showing a range of 54 percentage points). Thus, while the overall central tendencies of the different subsets of the data were quite close, the range of error varied significantly.

Given this variation in accuracy across questions, we next can focus on the public's performance on these 11 repeated questions as a way of controlling for question difficulty. Despite the somewhat lesser variation in the rate of offering correct answers on this subset of questions, the overall trend of correct answers is almost identical to that shown in Figure 6.1. The rate of correct answers on the frequently asked questions begins the series at just over 60 percent in early 2010, it falls to the mid-40 percent range up through 2011, and it then fluctuates around the mid-50 percent range to the end of the series. Democrats and Republicans move substantially together on this subset of questions (as they also do on the larger set of questions), though in 2015 Republicans' knowledge declined slightly to 57 percent correct while that of Democrats rose to just over 70 percent correct.[25] While there is some instability introduced by the single-shot questions in the larger collection, this does not substantially limit what we can say about public knowledge of the ACA's provisions across time. On the whole, Democrats know more than Republicans, but even they do not perform at a level that inspires confidence.

Tracking the evolution of knowledge on the 11 repeated questions one at a time for as long as their presence in surveys allows reveals a surprising finding. Only three of them show a longitudinal increase in public knowledge. The percentage of correct responses (including all respondents, regardless of party identification) on the individual mandate rose from 71 to 77 percent; on the employer mandate, the percentage correct rose from 61 to 67 percent, and that on the absence of a government insurance plan showed an increase from 27 to 32 percent. Three of the topics showed no discernable change (the Medicaid expansion, end-of-life panels, and subsidies for undocumented immigrants). The other five items actually showed a significant decrease in knowledge over time, by an average of just over 11 percentage points.

Looking at these 11 frequently asked questions in one other way reveals a pattern that suggests both motivated learning and partisan credit claiming. In Table 6.1, the 11 often-polled provisions of the ACA are arranged in order of the size of the gap between Democrats' and Republicans' knowledge. From the top, Democrats were about 20 percentage points more likely than were Republicans to recognize that the law included tax credits for small businesses and that insurance subsidies were made unavailable to undocumented immigrants. Moving down, Democrats were somewhat more likely than Republicans to recognize that the ACA was designed to gradually close Medicare's coverage gap (the doughnut hole), was to offer subsidies for low-income persons in the online marketplaces, and offered a Medicaid expansion. Four of these five provisions (the issue of withholding subsidies from undocumented immigrants is less clear) are ones that, per recent history, Democrats could easily support. On these issues, Democrats appeared to enthusiastically claim ownership.

In the middle section of Table 6.1 are five items on which there was essentially no difference in knowledge across party identification, though apparently for mixed reasons. This group of provisions includes those that experienced high visibility, such as the question about Medicare (not) paying for end-of-life counseling sessions (Sarah Palin's apocryphal "death panels") and the ban on consideration of preexisting conditions by insurance companies, but also ones that received much less public and media discussion, such as raising the Medicare tax rate for upper-income individuals. The overall level of public knowledge does not correlate with the magnitude of the cross-party gap in knowledge. The absence of a cross-party gap for this middle category of items remains something of a puzzle. At the bottom of Table 6.1 is the individual mandate, the most offensive part of the law in critics' eyes. Republicans appeared quite enthusiastic to attach this controversial provision to the ACA, akin to a ball and chain, doing so at nearly 8 percentage points higher than Democrats.

Table 6.1 **Percentage Correct by Party Identification on 11 Frequently Polled Provisions**

	Democrat Percentage Correct	Republican Percentage Correct	Difference
Tax credits for small businesses (N = 5)	72	51.4	20.6*
No subsidies for undocumented immigrants (N = 5)	43.6	23.6	20*
Closing Medicare's doughnut hole (N = 12)	57.7	41.8	15.9*
Subsidies for low-income persons (N = 12)	69.4	58.1	11.3*
Medicaid expansion (N = 11)	63.9	54.7	9.2*
No end-of-life panels (N = 9)	45.6	41	4.6
Ban preexisting exclusion (N = 7)	59	56.3	2.7
No government insurance option (N = 4)	36.3	38	–1.7
Raise Medicare tax rate for wealthy (N = 8)	50.8	53.9	–3.1
Employer mandate (N = 5)	66.8	71.6	–4.8
Individual mandate (N = 10)	69.6	77.5	–7.9*

*Difference significant at better than 99 percent confidence level.

Taking one last look at knowledge, we can leverage the power of individual-level survey data from April 2010 and again from March 2014. At both these times, the Kaiser Health Tracking Poll included many knowledge questions (16 in the former, 11 in the latter), measuring personal characteristics such as age, income, education level, insurance status, and party identification. Using multivariate analysis, we can examine the impact of single characteristics on individual knowledge levels while controlling for the effects of other characteristics. Individual knowledge is measured here by calculating the percentage of knowledge questions correctly answered for each of more than 1,200 respondents. Perhaps not surprisingly, education and household income positively correlate with knowledge levels, though their influence is modest. In the 2010 survey, respondents' age did not correlate significantly with knowledge, though it rose to significance by 2014. The observation made earlier that Democrats knew somewhat more than Republicans continues to be true even after controlling for income, age, insurance status, and education level. Interestingly, insurance status does not correlate with knowledge in this multivariate analysis of either survey. To a modest extent, these factors explain higher knowledge of the ACA; the objectively important characteristic of insurance status takes a back seat to the factors of being a Democrat, education level, and age, in this order.[26]

Returning to the trend line in Figure 6.1, it is striking that despite the passage of time and volume of argument over the ACA, Americans did not learn more. This marks not only a failure of Democratic leaders to educate the public but also a disappointing lack of citizen engagement. Illustrating persistent ignorance are two items from Table 6.1, showing that large majorities of the public did not understand that the ACA did not create a government-run insurance program (the so-called public option favored by the Democratically controlled House of Representatives during the time of the drafting of the law but which was not included in the final version) as well as the confusion over the so-called death panels, which were associated with so much furor during the summer of 2009. While congressional Republicans and their allies are guilty of sowing erroneous information about the law, Democratic leaders and their allies largely failed to set the record straight.

As a result of this, Republicans in the general public appeared willing to have engaged in a measure of willful ignorance about numerous provisions in the law, failing to recognize or perhaps refusing to acknowledge them. On the other hand, Republicans were very willing to recognize the immensely unpopular individual mandate. Democrats knew more than did Republicans, though their overall knowledge levels were still modest and may have involved wishful thinking, ready to acknowledge pleasant-sounding provisions, whether or not those were actually part of the law authored by politicians in their own party.

While there are other aspects of public knowledge about the law that we cannot readily gauge, this large body of survey-based indicators strongly suggests that knowledge overall did not noticeably increase across the first five years of the law's implementation. To the great extent this failure is attributable to unhelpful elite and public discourse, policy advocates have their work cut out for them.

Public Opinion toward Health Care Reform

The public's skepticism toward the ACA appears to be a symptom of its modest knowledge of the law. This is a common phenomenon, and deliberative polls conducted by James Fishkin and others have strongly tended to find that as people learn more about the workings of government programs, they show greater appreciation for them.[27] While a majority of the public supported the idea of government providing universal access to basic services in the abstract throughout the 2000s, that sentiment waned from 2008 forward as the public discourse became more contested.[28] Critical elite rhetoric combined with declining confidence in Congress and uncertainty about the Obama administration's intentions for reform all contributed to majority public opposition to the ACA by the time of its passage.[29]

Public support for health reform was quite dynamic during the mid- to late 2000s. As recently as 2006 and 2007, polls showed that solid majorities of the public—69 percent in Gallup's November 2007 poll—looked to "the federal government to make sure all Americans have health insurance."[30] In 2008, 56 percent of Gallup respondents indicated trust in the Democratic Party to address the issue, compared to only 29 percent who placed their trust in the GOP.[31] A September 2008 Marist College poll found that 78 percent of respondents wanted the next president to deal with health care reform even if this required increased government debt, and 70 percent of respondents said that reforming health care was more important than cutting taxes.[32] When asked by Harris Interactive which issues Congress should work on, health care ranked near the top of respondents' list from the mid-2000s forward.[33] Harris's questions found that in 2004 only 10 percent of respondents named health care as the most pressing problem. By the spring of 2007, that figure rose to 15 percent, and by autumn 2007 it reached 25 percent.

However, beginning in 2008 various measures captured a significant decline in public support for reform. By the time of Obama's inauguration, Harris's measure of how pressing a problem this was fell to 16 percent, down from 25 percent in 2007. Gallup's question about federal responsibility for universal coverage declined from its November 2006 high of 69 percent to 64 percent in late 2007, 54 percent the month of Obama's election, and 47 percent through 2009 and 2010. Other versions of this question showed similar declines in support through this period.[34]

Beyond the overall decline in support, a partisan divide emerged during the late 2000s. By the beginning of the Obama administration, Democrats in the general population ranked health reform as their second priority, independents placed it fourth, and Republicans positioned it no better than seventh.[35] Among Republicans, there was a significant drop in support from 2008 to 2010, as 45 percent of them shifted from supporting to opposing health reform.[36] This echoes the sharp decline for the individual mandate among Republicans shown in Figure 1.2. Into this pronounced partisan divide stepped Democrats intent on passing sweeping policy reform, their energy on this issue having been pent up for nearly a century. For years, the public has professed greater confidence in Democrats than in Republicans to handle the issue of health care. The downside of such issue ownership, however, is that it often leads parties to pursue specific policy innovations that are not necessarily in line with public preferences. This generally has a way of further dividing partisans, as more extreme party leaders move policies closer to their ideal points and further from the other party's (and sometimes the general public's) preferred position.[37]

The passage of the ACA fits this pattern. While the public expressed approval for various parts of the ACA, uncertainty and outright opposition to its other parts continued to drag down overall approval. Democratic leaders might take solace in, for example, the February 2010 Kaiser poll that found that 76 percent of respondents favored the insurance reforms, 72 percent approved of the small business tax credits, and 71 percent liked the idea of closing Medicare's doughnut hole.[38] However, the individual

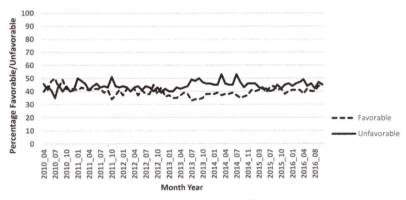

Figure 6.2　Favorable/Unfavorable Assessment of the ACA, 2010–2016

Question wording: "As you may know, a health reform bill was signed into law in 2010. Given what you know about the health reform law, do you have a generally favorable or generally unfavorable opinion of it?"

mandate and concerns that the law would drive up the price of health insurance undermined the ACA's overall popularity. The general public support for reform seen in the mid-2000s quickly gave way to negativity over its particulars. When surveys fielded during 2009 and 2010 asked about the bills being considered in Congress at the time, opponents almost always outnumbered supporters.[39]

Taking a longer view, the Kaiser series that tracked overall support and opposition beginning in 2010 shows a closely divided public. These figures appear in Figure 6.2, which shows trend lines for overall approval and disapproval of the law from 2010 to the autumn of 2016.[40] In order to understand these broad sentiments, it is useful to examine some of the reasons behind them. When respondents were asked in March 2015 by the Kaiser poll what they liked or disliked about the law, they congregated around a handful of issues. As might be expected, individuals holding generally approving outlooks listed very different concerns from those who generally disapproved. Table 6.2 shows the reasons offered by these respondents. Only those responses that garnered 5 percent or more of all mentions (multiple mentions accepted) are shown. Nearly half (47 percent) of those with overall favorable views of the law, almost all of whom identify as Democrats, pointed directly to expansions of access to care and financing. Many of Democrats' other comments related to the financial costs of health care: helping low-income people, making care more affordable, and likely many of the sentiments that were rolled into the other response options on the left side of the table. Opponents, whose responses appear on the right side of Table 6.2, saw very different prospects from the law. Approximately one-quarter of these respondents feared higher insurance and/or government costs, and at least one-quarter more envisioned overbearing government requirements.

Returning to the relatively stable trend lines in Figure 6.2, these can be interpreted in a couple of ways. First, the rising skepticism seen during 2008 and 2009 was later arrested. As the law took effect, portions of the public settled into their positions and changed very little over the following few years. Short-term fluctuations, such as the rise of opposition during 2013 over the failed launch of the healthcare.gov website, are couched within a longer pattern of substantial stability. This is potentially part of a narrative of a public with its mind made up. The small and shrinking percentages of those polled offering "don't know" responses on multiple versions of overall approval/disapproval questions offer some support to this perspective.[41] A second perspective sees this pattern as part of a public stuck on its way to learning about the law and profoundly unsure about how to move to what we might call considered judgment. In

Table 6.2 Reasons Given for Holding a Favorable or Unfavorable View of
the ACA

Reasons to Approve of the ACA (41% of total)		Reasons to Disapprove of the ACA (43% of total)	
Reason	Percentage Approved	Reason	Percentage Disapproved
Expands access to health insurance	28	Health insurance and health care will become more expensive	16
Expands access to health care services	19	Oppose mandatory insurance purchases	15
Will help one's self or family	11	Government-related issues	10
Will make health care more affordable/ control costs	10	The law will cost too much	8
Country/people will be better off generally	7	Inequitable/individuals should pay for their own insurance	8
Will help low-income families/ the poor	5	Limits choices and benefits/ hurts people's existing health care arrangements/ quality of care	7
Brings America in line with other advanced countries	4	Generally dislike of the law/ unnecessary	7
		Unfair to people who cannot afford insurance	6
		Opposed to the law's legislative process	5
		The law does not do what it was promised to do	5

Source: Kaiser Health Tracking Poll, March 2015

Question wording: "Could you tell me in your own words what is the main reason you have a favorable/unfavorable opinion of the health reform law?" multiple responses accepted (N = 1,503 national adults).

support of this view, we can observe that approval or disapproval of the ACA tracks very tightly with partisanship. As discussed earlier, using party as an election heuristic makes a certain amount of sense where the binary choice is about electing candidates to office, but it makes less sense in more complex choice or evaluation contexts where people need to sort out various elements of a bundle of policy reforms.[42] Arguably, given the many events that have unfolded over the life of the ACA, public opinion should have gestated more over this period, as, ideally, citizens learn about how the law works and what its legitimate shortcomings are.

Herein lies the rub. Given the poor state of public knowledge documented in the aforementioned text, we see that only slightly better than half of the public could correctly answer factual questions, and this pattern substantially held across more than five years of polling. Learning was scant, and it did not generally improve. Again, this points back to a dysfunctional politics surrounding health care reform. The passage and implementation of the ACA called for the public to learn more, but our political discourse did not foster such learning.

One specific example of the lack of learning had to do with the benefits that the ACA produced. A widely shared perception persisted that these reforms did not make much difference in people's lives. When asked "so far, has the new law helped you and your family, not had an effect, or has it hurt you and your family?" 60 percent of May 2014 respondents to a Kaiser poll indicated that it had had no effect. This percentage remained between 55 percent and 63 percent or higher in seven other polls up through April 2015. This figure later fell into the mid to high 50 percent range but still persisted as a major obstacle to the public's embrace of the ACA, particularly since fewer than 20 percent of respondents said that the law had actually helped them across this entire period. One-fifth to one-quarter of respondents said the law had hurt them.[43]

Looking at these responses by party, Republicans claimed harm at higher rates than Democrats during 2014 and 2015. For instance, in May 2014, fully 37 percent of Republican respondents indicated harm, compared to only 8 percent of Democrats. As time passed, Republicans tended even more strongly to point to harm. By March 2015 these figures stood at 40 percent of Republican respondents and 8 percent of Democrats. Of course, it is difficult to imagine how one's partisanship aligns with actual help or harm from the law. Clearly, selective perception played an important role here.

Changing the focus, when polls asked whether the ACA had made things better or worse off for the nation, the trend is pessimistic. In March 2010, 45 percent of respondents believed the law had made the nation "better off." By November 2010, this figure fell to 38 percent and then to the mid-30s through 2011, where it settled through the end of 2013.[44] By January 2014, this figure stood at 28 percent.[45] While most nonexperts would be hard pressed to evaluate the impact of the law on the nation, especially given the poor knowledge levels presented earlier, the growing subjective pessimism made the successful GOP attacks on the law during the 2016 campaign season understandable.

This discussion has made much of the role of partisanship in explaining approval of the Affordable Care Act. As the earlier chapters document, this focus is justified. The explanation, however, for approval or disapproval of the ACA at the individual level is not entirely symbolic. Other correlates play important roles, such as age and income.[46] Older and wealthier Americans were less approving. Senior citizens remained understandably skeptical of changes that could have adversely affected their Medicare benefits, and if curtailed reimbursements to medical providers were to reduce the number of providers willing to service Medicare patients, older Americans' skepticism is warranted. To the extent the ACA's design called for some redistribution of income in order to enhance health care coverage for the less wealthy, it is understandable that upper-income Americans opposed it. Naturally, both of these demographic characteristics contribute to party identification, meaning that party identification is itself not entirely symbolic. However, the strong linkage of party identification, even statistically controlling for the influence of age and income, with approval of the law and the partisan patterns of knowledge explained earlier certainly raise persistent questions about the bias in individuals' assessment of the ACA and the extent to which public approval relied so little the actual performance of the law. The path toward considered public judgment on the ACA seems to have been predominantly paved with notions of skepticism toward government and partisan considerations rather than how well this landmark legislation achieved it intended goals. Sadly, the development of significant policy knowledge seems a distant prospect, which dims our view of a meaningful public discourse surrounding health care reform.

Party Loyalty or Policy Knowledge: What Does the Public Need?

Quite a lot of research over the past couple of generations has made the case that, for most citizens, knowledge about politics tends toward the modest end of the scale. As Philip Converse stated, "the two simplest truths . . . about the distribution of political information in modern electorates are that the mean is low and the variance is high."[47] Given this, public opinion analysts place a great deal of importance on the role of elites, whether those are policy experts or competitive politicians. John Zaller's *The Nature and Origins of Mass Opinion* (1992), one of the most influential books ever written on the subject, bases its model of opinion formation on how and under what circumstances ordinary citizens respond to cues from elites. Because cue givers tend to be partisan, most of the messaging that citizens receive seeks to push them in partisan directions. My contention is that partisanship, in the absence of policy

knowledge, is an inadequate heuristic by which to evaluate the complicated nature of health care policy. Americans are not faced with simply a
series of binary choices. Reform will succeed or fail not based on whether
we elect to spend *more* or *less* money but rather *how* those funds are
spent.[48] Expanding access to health insurance does not map neatly onto a
big-government versus small-government dimension. As Chapter 4 demonstrated, there is a significant partisan disjuncture between policy
reform at the federal versus the state level. Thus, framing the debate over
the ACA in little more than partisan terms—"job-killing Obamacare,"
"socialized medicine," "a Washington takeover of health policy," "death
panels"—leaves citizens bereft of the cues they need to engage in meaningful conversations.

As much as this argument is central to the claims of this book, it does
not settle the matter of how we know when a citizen wrongly endorsed
one side or the other of the debate over the ACA. Should citizens judge
the law by its merits or instead according to ideological or partisan considerations? There are sound responses on both sides of this question. On
the former, rational citizens ought to care about the benefits they as individuals or members of their families received from the law. On the latter,
the idea of belief centrality implies that if one is liberal (or conservative) at
one's core, one should be liberal (or conservative) on a wide variety of
issues and that this is a reasonable way to order one's belief set.[49] However, sorting out decision rules, or in this instance the question of erred
policy support, is methodologically problematic. Asking whether a vote or
a policy endorsement is correct or not, as Converse put it years ago, is to
pose an "impossibly formulated" question.[50] Giovani Sartori pushed the
conundrum one step further; he "wonder[ed] if it should be formulated at
all,"[51] for in his view, democracy is best defined as an electoral exercise
between parties, not a striving for public mastery or sovereignty over particular policy mechanisms. Sartori was not alone in this stance, as other
recent scholars of democratic theory and practice have documented significant shortcomings in the public's ability to sort through policy facts,
typically resulting in a default to partisan cues.[52] From this perspective, to
freight a theory of democracy with the public obligation to discern *how* to
achieve a smarter health policy is simply a bridge too far.

As fundamentally ambiguous as the question of right versus wrong
votes or endorsements is, there is value in struggling with this puzzle.
Presumably, no one would argue for less public knowledge of health policy. Whether such knowledge assists individuals in expanding their
understanding of how payment and delivery systems work or helps them
to refine their overall ideological positions, more information is better.

While there is certainly a point of diminishing returns with information quests for the non-specialist (after all, parents still need to find the time to take kids to soccer games, people need to go to their jobs, etc.), a good working knowledge will unarguably help people to better understand the stakes, some possible solutions, and how these affect individuals such as themselves. Hence, the central issue here is whether the general public can learn what it needs to know about health policy, specifically moving beyond knowledge of partisan alignments on the ACA. Despite the essentially static trend in public knowledge documented here, a good deal of evidence shows that, under the right circumstances, people can learn a considerable amount about politics. For instance, Prior and Lupia show that when financially incentivized, study subjects perform much better at drawing correct inferences about the veracity of others' statements than when not so incentivized.[53] When surveys press for an answer, instead of readily accepting "don't know" responses, survey respondents perform significantly better on political knowledge questions.[54] Zaller and others show that when presented with diverse elite perspectives, knowledgeable individuals make appropriate use of competing cues to separate into meaningful ideological camps.[55] In an experiment involving both partisan cues and policy information, Bullock shows that information can influence individuals' policy attitudes as much as or even more than elite cues.[56] Clearly, the right opportunities can foster good quality learning.

Unfortunately, the evidence shows that the very thin public discourse surrounding the ACA did not provide these opportunities during its first five-plus years. Instead, from 2010 to 2015, the public, in the main, simply maintained its mediocre knowledge about the various provisions of the law, it continued to assess it in highly partisan terms, and collective opinion seemed to fall into a closely divided rut instead of evolving in response to what is now years of experience with these policy reforms. This situation is at odds with the generally optimistic tenor of the rational public literature referenced at the top of this chapter, though here one has to decide how readily information can make its way to members of the general public. In this particular instance, changes in public opinion on health care track closely with changes in elite rhetoric.[57] To the great extent that rhetoric traffics mainly in themes of electoral advantage instead of policy knowledge, Americans face a significant obstacle to a straightforward assessment of the facts. The public could do better if it enjoyed a richer information environment.

If the general public is to find its voice and achieve something like what the educator and philosopher John Dewey long ago referred to as the Great Community, good quality information and time for public reflection will be necessary.[58] If the hope is that the public can learn effectively, the findings in this chapter stand as a disappointment. However, this disappointment ought to be specifically directed at the poor framework for public discussion, not at citizens themselves. If politicians and policy experts were to amplify their discussion of the practicalities of one versus another approach to health reform, the public could grasp not only the broad issues but also many of the nuances.[59] The point of deliberation is about problem solving, not about victory or defeat. But of course, in a highly polarized environment, many office holders see partisan victory as essential, given the great ideological distance of the other side. Going forward, it stands as a great tragedy that this inhibits public learning and discourse on one of the great issues of our time. The final chapter grapples with near-term prospects for the public as a partner with policy makers and for constructive policy evolution.

CHAPTER SEVEN

Repealing the Affordable Care Act: Now What?

The first seven years of the Affordable Care Act (ACA) mainly represented a time of lost opportunity for Americans to constructively discuss and learn about useful policy directions as the nation confronted complex and evolving health service delivery and financing challenges. This unhelpful public discourse was significant in several ways. Distorted descriptions of the law warped the public's understanding of the problems, possible solutions, and how those solutions do or do not fit with values held by a majority of Americans regarding health care issues. These widely shared values include universal access to basic services and a willingness to spend more tax dollars to achieve this, but also a reluctance to have government become the insurer for all.[1] Some of the discourse fostered superficial understandings of how treating patients like shoppers will, purportedly, solve most of our problems. This issue will likely gain even more traction that it already has as consumer-driven health plans spread over the coming years. The states-rights rhetoric surrounding important parts of the law encouraged state officials to prioritize political gamesmanship over coverage expansions, at the cost of tens of millions of Americans not receiving the services they need. The politics of this reform episode did not improve public knowledge of the ACA. Consequently, the mass public was unable to play the important role it deserved to play regarding one of the more pressing policy issues of the era.

Some of the blame for these problems lies at the door of the law's architects. In 2009 and 2010, they failed to legislate in ways that would generate widespread public support. They misrepresented a few key aspects of the law. They foot-dragged on elements of the preparation for the launch of the healthcare.gov website in 2013, and they were somewhat ineffective in rhetorically defending the reforms. On the other hand, a significant portion of the political conflict over the law and the public's failure to embrace it arose from opponents' maligning rhetoric and actions, bent on undermining the law through mischaracterization of its provisions and how those provisions were intended to address significant problems in America's health care systems. Opponents spent a tremendous amount of energy challenging the law between 2010 and 2016—in legislatures, in courts, and rhetorically—while failing to advance a serious alternative during this time. Health care reform passed Congress largely due to a widely shared consensus in the late 2000s that to do nothing, previously many players' second preference, was no longer viable.[2] However, most of the critics of the ACA ignored this earlier consensus and instead acted as though repealing the ACA, seemingly to imagine that it never passed, would somehow be a responsible move. Calls—indeed, bills passed by the House of Representatives and positions taken by Republican candidates for president and Congress—to do exactly this would have been laughable if this were a less serious matter. But this is a very serious matter. The trajectory of U.S. health spending is unsustainable. Public health outcomes place the United States below most developed nations on many metrics. Far too many Americans die each year due to medical errors. Americans are not making the kind of progress they should toward building a first-class health care system.

This chapter summarizes the major obstacles to public engagement as documented in earlier chapters before turning to consider some near- and medium-term policy challenges. Given the public health shortcomings and the rates of financial consumption in the health care sector, neither kicking the can further down the road nor distorting the issues at play will do.

To begin, the design of the Affordable Care Act was arguably flawed in its heavy focus on systemic reforms and light on individual benefits. (Of course, reasonable people can disagree on the wisdom of systemic versus individual rewards and the political attractiveness of each.) The ACA's efforts at systemic change limited its ability to generate positive policy feedback.[3] Given Americans' penchant for asking what their politicians have done for them *lately*, a tendency fostered by short election cycles, many of the benefits of the law were designed in such ways that made it somewhat difficult for average citizens to see and appreciate.[4] Encouraging hospitals to treat Medicare beneficiaries more efficiently is important, but few elderly people are likely to become excited about these programmatic savings. Compelling insurance companies to spend at least 80 percent of their revenues on payments to providers is important but does not generally impassion customers. It seems improbable that Americans will take to the streets any time soon to celebrate the marginal public health improvements resulting from a tax on tanning salons or the revenue generated by a tax on medical device makers. These are certainly defensible systemic reforms, but they did not readily fire the public's imagination.

On the individual level, the ACA was designed to provide tangible benefits, but these never engendered the kind of grassroots support for the law that its architects anticipated. The $250 rebate sent to Medicare Part D enrollees in 2010 was a token. The Medicaid expansion was not directly relevant for the approximately 60 percent of Americans who obtain their health insurance through employment. Similarly, the online marketplaces cater to a limited clientele and increasingly lead enrollees into narrow provider networks at high prices. Polling of individuals who purchased insurance through an exchange showed very mixed assessments, with 48 percent in the spring of 2016 saying their plan provided either "excellent" or "good" value and 51 percent giving it lower ratings. This represented a downward shift from 2014, when nearly 60 percent considered their plan's value either "excellent" or "good."[5] None of this is to say that striving for systemic reform is unimportant; however, giving people more of what they want surely would have helped, and it might have spared the Democrats their loss of Congressional control in 2010 as electoral punishment over the law.

What indeed feels personal, albeit in a symbolic way for the majority of Americans, is the resentment fostered by the marriage of convenience between government and the private insurance industry, a move that blocked, almost certainly for years to come, a more equitable and less profit-driven approach to health care coverage. With or without the ACA's individual mandate, the private insurance industry is poised to maintain its centrality in American health care. The law's strategy of locking in this large for-profit entity as a key player will continue to have profound implications for who can afford coverage and what Americans on the whole will spend on health care for the foreseeable future. Further, reliance on private insurers hobbled state-level exchanges through 2016, and heading into 2017, many of them—if they survive at all—will face a severe contraction of offerings and competition. This heavy dependence on subsidized private coverage for households above the poverty level—instead of elevating the Medicaid eligibility threshold—ensures that the clientele for Medicaid will continue to be poor. This is a recipe for weak political mobilization around the Medicaid program, which will consequently remain underfunded and subject to cross-state variation of the kind explained in Chapter 5.

As these chapters show, opponents of the ACA played powerful roles in undermining public support for the law. As detailed in Chapters 1 and 2, conservatives moved from supporting mandated coverage with government subsidies to becoming intractable opponents of this strategy. By the time the ACA became law, congressional Republicans and others, determined to thwart a Democratic legislative victory, developed a substantial litany of complaints, some straightforward and others distorted, that proved easier for the general public to understand than did the Democrats' inadequate and largely systemically oriented defense.[6] The oppositional strategy immediately took on an overwhelmingly slash-and-burn tenor, far from one that offered constructive suggestions for improvement. The language of "Washington takeovers," "death panels," and legislation being "rammed down our throats" distorted the issues at stake and deprived the public the opportunity to learn what it needs to know.

In the midst of this terminological pandemonium, the public's learning about the law remained largely static, as illustrated in Chapter 6. Of course, the tragedy is that citizens cannot meaningfully debate what they do not meaningfully know. The complexity of the issues makes this a truly challenging—but not impossible—policy area in which to foster adequate public knowledge and a healthier public discourse. However, the opposition described in Chapter 2 had very little to do with enhancing understanding and much to do with defending ideological and partisan turf. People need narratives to make sense of politics, and if talk of insurance take-up rates, risk corridors, and medical loss ratios proves unattractive for many citizens, they will instead gravitate to more familiar decision rules. Party identification turns out to be a handy and powerful heuristic, even if it proves woefully inadequate for nuanced learning on a complex issue such as health care reform.

For decades, scholars have documented the sometimes-narrow confines of public knowledge about politics.[7] Even highly sympathetic observers recognize the serious limits of cognition, or put differently, interest and attention.[8] People are busy with jobs, children, aging parents, and everything else that fills their days. Taking the time to master the complexities of public policy, unless those complexities are immediately relevant to one's current situation, is simply not compelling. When pressed to state a preference, either by an election or a pollster, people unsurprisingly reach for information shortcuts. As Chapter 6 shows, party identification was that shortcut on health care reform. For at least a century, political scientists have viewed parties and interest groups as fundamental building blocks of American politics.[9] However, given the role reversals that parties have engaged in over the years on some of these issues—most prominently, the individual mandate—party identification hardly provides an ideal synecdoche.

As the 115th Congress and President Trump set about to rewrite national health policy according to their own vision, the public will potentially once again have the opportunity to play a guiding role. However, the recent track record is not promising. Some degree of popular policy knowledge will be necessary if reform ideas are to move from discussions among narrow stakeholder groups into the legislative process without abandoning public preferences and key values. Until this broader knowledge becomes diffused, critics can and will misrepresent the designs of various proposals with impunity and without popular consequence. Of course, they can also malign the history of the ACA. Hence, a requirement to obtain health insurance coverage (analogous to auto insurance) partnered with government subsidies to make those purchases affordable becomes a "Washington takeover" instead of an effort to eliminate inefficient free-riding. Efforts to wring savings from Medicare by trimming its reimbursement rates are not portrayed as savings but rather as an attempt to dismantle the program. Government regulation of the insurance industry to discourage minimalist policies that leave significant gaps become meddlesome steps away from "patient-centered medicine" instead of being seen as consumer protections. These are eye-of-the-beholder problems, but they could be ameliorated by clearer discourse about intentions and results.

A prime example of short-handing and exaggeration is the rhetoric surrounding consumer-driven health care (CDHC). As explained in Chapter 4, CDHC advocates tend to portray market transparency as a panacea, capable of focusing more personal spending on highly effective services that people value and generating competition among medical providers, thereby lowering prices for everyone.[10] However, evidence here and elsewhere strongly indicates that the gains to be obtained through aggressive cost sharing are marginal.[11] Talk of individual accountability, personal choice, competition, and skin in the game plays well in environments where nonspecialists can be convinced to draw an analogy between shopping for cars and shopping for emergency department services, as if there is very little difference between the two. However, thoughtful economists long have recognized how quickly the market comparison breaks down in the face of evidence, even if contemporary market-oriented thinkers, smitten with the notions of competition and consumerism, refuse to acknowledge this.[12] For these neo-conservatives, the power to shop is the ultimate freedom.[13] The idea of medical shoppers, however, founders on problems of information asymmetry, perverse incentives, emotion, and even the most rudimentary understanding of access to basic health care services as a human right. This misplaced metaphor gave rise to a consumerist argument that now acts as a talking point used to abate any sort of policy victory by advocates of universal health care that is both accessible and affordable. Such urging for more individual responsibility has fueled GOP calls for market-oriented health care reform, and, as explained in Chapter 4, they also helped state officials find the political cover they needed to implement waiver-based expansions of Medicaid in political environments that otherwise punish collaborators with Obamacare. More of this is likely to come under a Republican rewriting of the Medicaid contract with the states.[14]

Despite the controversies surrounding the legacy of the Affordable Care Act and the portions of it that survive the Republican ascendency to power following the 2016 elections, the law took significant strides toward closing the uninsured gap, which stood at 17 percent of the population in 2010 but was reduced to 9.1 percent by the summer of 2016.[15] It also pushed medical providers, especially hospitals, to implement more efficient and higher quality medicine under the Medicare program and by extension to all of their patients. Regardless of how quickly or extensively the ACA is repealed and replaced, this set of experiences will certainly inform health policy reform for years to come.

As this book went to press, President Trump was assembling his administration and struggling to shift from a campaign mode to governing. His statements on health care reform still tended to be of a rather general nature, calling for better insurance at lower prices, but seemingly not wedded to any particular replacement plan. Congressional Republicans were at odds with each other over how generous subsidies or tax credits should be to help Americans purchase health insurance.[16] The American Medical Association's House of Delegates issued a statement in mid-November of 2016 insisting that, while the organization was willing to work with the new administration on reforms, a line in the sand for doctors was that such reforms must not result in those who have insurance losing it.[17] In round terms, this referred to the 20 million people who gained coverage under the ACA between 2010 and 2016. The American Medical Association's insistence was a tall order indeed.

Future reforms will likely come in pieces, just as the ACA itself took only a limited number of steps in what will be a longer process of addressing enormous and still-unresolved challenges of health care costs, quality, and access. Despite the uncertainties these steps will involve, some brief discussion about developments to come may be useful. Two areas in particular deserve attention.

Individual Responsibility for Medical Expenses

Despite the substantial evidence summarized in Chapter 3 that consumer-driven health care plans do not strongly tend to induce consumer-like selective behavior, cost sharing has spread and will likely continue as employers search for ways to limit their premium costs. Republican thinking on health care reform is certainly poised to advance this movement. Deductibles, co-payments, and coinsurance grew significantly after the late 1990s and will continue to rise as a direct consequence of the pressure to control premiums. While no comprehensive archive of deductibles exists, analyses of tax returns and employers' insurance plans paint a striking portrait. According to Internal Revenue Service data, among workers at small firms (3 to 199 employees) with a deductible, the average deductible was approximately $1,800 in 2014. For larger firms, the comparable figure stood just under $1,000.[18] These amounts pose serious burdens to households with modest incomes. In 2013, fewer than one-half of households with incomes between 100 and 250 percent of the federal poverty level had on hand liquid resources sufficient to cover their deductibles. Hence, for these families the potential liability is enough to force them to sell off vital assets such as cars and homes.[19] An analysis by the Kaiser Family Foundation in 2016 found that since 2001 deductibles rose, on average, six times faster than wages.[20]

Another study examined a large volume of annual commercial claims data.[21] Personal spending to satisfy deductibles rose by 256 percent from 2004 to 2014, or from $99 on average to $353. Average spending on coinsurance rose 170 percent, from $117 to $242. Coinsurance expenses for workers in the top 15 percent of the population more than doubled over this period. Despite the out-of-pocket expense limits built into the ACA ($6,850 for an individual and $13,700 for a family for 2016), these direct costs weigh heavily for many.

Critics of the ACA managed to find fault even with these market-driven developments. Somewhat ironically, supporters of consumer-driven care blamed the ACA for the growing phenomenon of unexpected bills sent to patients for services delivered by out-of-network providers. For instance, a March 2016 column on the conservative website redstate.com blamed these surprise bills on the revolving door between the insurance industry and the Obama administration (a phenomenon that is common across government and has existed for decades).[22] A more tempered but still critical treatment appeared in the *Wall Street Journal*, with its June 2015 story implying that the growth of surprise billing was attributable to insurance companies trying to keep costs low for the sake of making them attractive in the online marketplaces.[23] Even if a patient's hospital and surgeon are in-network, perhaps the anesthesiologist is not. While the ACA's language limited out-of-pocket expenses under insurance policies, these limits did not apply to bills issued by out-of-network providers.[24] How is a patient to know the name of every provider who will be associated with a medical visit? This is exactly the type of question CDHC skeptics pose when critiquing the high knowledge demands on ordinary people when navigating complex billing systems. In turning the blame for surprise billing back to the ACA, market-oriented critics were engaging in a highly selective perception of the issues involved.

Narrowed provider networks, likely with us for the foreseeable future, arise from efforts by insurers to limit premium increases. As plans offer reduced payment levels to doctors and others, fewer providers consent to join such plans. The result is a rising number of insured patients who receive what are often alarmingly high bills that they thought would be covered by insurance.[25] In sum, the argument that consumers are best positioned to negotiate their own coverage, services, and payments turns out to be substantially a fiction in the face of what is referred to as balance billing.[26] State legislators, recognizing this problem, stepped in to regulate such billing. In 2015, New York began requiring insurers and providers that disagree on out-of-network payments to go through a dispute-resolution process.[27] California banned balance billing for emergency services for individuals covered by health maintenance organizations.[28] In October 2015, a bill was introduced in Congress to limit balance billing.[29] In December 2015, the Center for Medicare and Medicaid Services proposed a rule that aimed to compel insurance plans sold through online marketplaces to count out-of-network charges toward the out-of-pocket maximum allowed under the ACA, though this was thought to exert upward pressure on premium prices, as those insurance companies would have to absorb the excess amount of these surprise bills. This rule was finalized in March 2016, but could be reversed by the Trump administration.[30] This is a modest intervention compared to the problem of double-digit inflation on health insurance premiums from 2016 to 2017. For all the talk of a Washington takeover of health care, it turns out the government has very limited tools to control private insurance prices.

As Americans move into a new era of health care delivery and financing, they will need to learn a great deal about payment systems, insurance networks, and more. This is a tall order, but evidence indicates that nonspecialists can indeed learn, particularly if they have at hand the appropriate information shortcuts or the right incentives.[31] The problem thus far is that the discourse has offered warped perspectives of the ACA, complicating Americans' efforts to understand the stakes.

Moving Away from Fee-for-Service

Beyond pressures applied on the consumer-demand side of the billing equation, other efforts on the provider-supply side also seem poised to advance and to enhance service efficiency. To the extent the ACA was designed to nudge providers toward greater cost control, one key mechanism that has gained a footing is a shift away from fee-for-service billing under Medicare. Such efforts have been part of Medicare since the late 1980s regarding in-patient services. The Department of Health and Human Services under the Obama administration redoubled efforts to spread this model. The ACA invited hospital groups to become accountable care organizations that receive payment for bundles of services rather than on a fee-for-service basis. Bundled payments encourage providers to deliver the most efficient treatment regimens instead of the most lucrative ones. The expected savings are then shared with the Accountable Care Organizations. Obama's Health and Human Services Secretary Sylvia Burwell indicated in 2015 a preference to see Medicare payments increasingly tied to quality outcomes and these bundled payments. She articulated a goal of 85 percent of all Medicare payments based on quality outcome measures by the end of her time in office. Burwell expressed that this should involve financial rewards for delivering high-quality care, for encouraging improved coordination of service delivery across providers, for further expanded use of electronic medical records (a practice adopted by nearly 80 percent of U.S. physicians by 2013) and involve the creation of the Patient-Centered Outcomes Research Institute to share comparative effectiveness research.[32] Of course, it remains to be seen if these efforts will continue under the Trump administration.

Prospects for an Engaged Public

As much as this book critiques poor public discourse and learning, not all of these technical issues lend themselves to significant engagement by ordinary citizens. Bundling payments, figuring out how to digitize medical records, and disseminating comparative effectiveness research are, arguably, on par with discussions about the mechanics of space exploration. Some matters are best left to experts. However, many of the larger, value-laden issues discussed here can and should be subjected to a better quality and thoroughgoing public discourse than has occurred up through the Obama administration. The essentially vapid debate on health care during the 2016 presidential campaigns provided further evidence of the problem. Hillary Clinton rarely ventured beyond her very general calls to preserve the positive elements of the ACA and to fix the parts that have not worked well. For his part, Donald Trump hued closely to the superficial and well-worn GOP calls to repeal and replace, substantially devoid of details about what such a replacement might involve.

Looking forward, several steps could foster a more meaningful public discourse, engaged citizens, better public learning, and in the end a better fit between the public's broadly held values on health care policy and what Americans actually end up with. First, some brief background will be useful. As discussed in Chapter 6, various schools of thought differ on the desirability and practicality of close linkages between mass public preferences and policy making. Because democracy comes in many forms, the literature on these issues—even limiting this to scholarship generated in the past generation or so—is vast. Space here hardly allows for a fair summation. However, one useful approach to this body of thought is to envision a spectrum ranging from highly participatory processes on one end to more elite-driven politics on the other. Proponents of the former process, including such thinkers as Bruce Ackerman, James Fishkin, Frank Newport, and Daniel Yankelovich, imagine a significantly engaged citizenry, capable of deliberating, learning, and modifying stances to account for new knowledge but also able to accommodate themselves to a more temperate vision of the public good and to express themselves in ways that pollsters can share with policy makers.[33] Much of this thinking is predicated on public learning about policy and the presence of discursive institutions and practices that foster meaningful feedback, not simply partisan bickering at election time and horserace descriptions in the media.

On the other end of this spectrum lie those who describe democracy, in one way or another, as little more than competition between elites for the people's vote. In the 1940s, Joseph Schumpeter expressed this perspective bluntly, writing that "the electoral mass is incapable of action other than a stampede."[34] In a similar way, E. E. Schattschneider opined that the electorate is "a sovereign whose vocabulary is limited to two words, 'Yes' and 'No.'"[35] More recently, Christopher Achen and Larry Bartels offered an account of a myopic and ill-informed public and of political parties that do largely what parties want.[36] In another recent thoughtful analysis, Patrick Egan documents how parties, once elected, tend to overshoot their electoral mandates, legislating on the issues that the public sees them as owning but not necessarily in the ways the public prefers.[37]

In its broad outlines, this spectrum represents an argument between those who believe in what we might call *policy democracy* versus *electoral democracy*.[38] A central question is, do we look to our politics to deliver particular policies that the public endorses or rather to elect parties that share certain broadly defined orientations with the majority electorate? The former view would seem to require a different kind of politics than the ACA was either born into or generated. Occurring at a time of strong party polarization, the ACA revealed just how divided Americans were (and are) on questions of government activism generally. It also helped foster deep divisions across party lines by holding out the prospect of a resounding partisan victory for Democrats had it gone uncontested. In analyzing public support for Congress immediately before and after the passage of the ACA in March 2010, David Jones found that health policy reform opponents moved slightly downward in their assessments of the ACA and reform supporters moved up by 15 percentage points.[39] The shifts of public opinion here seem to be an instance of legislative enactment solidifying the partisan base. From this perspective, electoral democracy won out over policy democracy. A large body of evidence indicates that opposition to the ACA was at least as much about partisan advantage as it had to do with the merits of the law, and this makes a truly troublesome environment in which to work.

But this is not an impossible environment for health policy makers. I hold out hope that Americans can indeed discuss policy in meaningful ways. For instance, the first several years of experience with the ACA illustrated the viability of various key ideas embedded in the law. Insurance regulation to protect consumers and government subsidies to make coverage more affordable are two prime examples of widespread (though not complete) agreement. Even the notions advanced by Republicans tended to involve these policies to various degrees.[40] The goal of expanding insurance coverage also enjoyed significant success, with the uninsured rate falling from 18 percent in 2013 to approximately 9 percent by 2016.[41] As a direct consequence, hospitals experienced a large reduction in uncompensated care costs, down $6 billion during 2014, for instance, mainly due to the Medicaid expansion.[42] Broadened consumer protections—banning policy rescissions when people get sick and requiring insurers to sell policies to individuals who suffer from preexisting conditions—also seem to have gained purchase in the public mind since the passage of the Affordable Care Act. While any broad consensus over the many provisions of the ACA is clearly absent, narrower swaths of common ground can likely be found and should be pursued.

To pursue such common ground, it would be helpful if American politicians and journalists could pay more attention to these points of broad agreement, refining how these successful policies work, and, importantly, developing public support for the same. Instead of a distressingly standard strategy of merely voicing support for or opposition to proposals by one party or the other as whole packages, politicians and journalists could and should distinguish between those provisions they can support versus those they cannot. Such a discourse would spare Americans the wasted time and energy spent arguing over aspects of health reform that enjoy broad support, such as protecting people from insurance company abuses and moving toward universal insurance coverage. This would also allow advocates to focus their energy on those policy challenges that still divide liberals and conservatives. Ultimately, this would help citizens to understand exactly what the ACA was designed to accomplish, what it was not intended to do, what problems still confront Americans, and how the country should proceed. These chapters clearly indicate that the public needs this kind of better information.

Considerable evidence supports the idea that workable policies can flow from well-developed consensus, even if these discussions begin amidst deep controversy. One example of such constructive discourse occurred in Oregon during the 1980s and 1990s as that state sought to expand its Medicaid program to cover select individuals with income above the federal poverty level and to manage costs through a soft rationing system.[43] Oregon's approach involved wide-ranging public discussions, certainly including some controversy but also broad public and interest group consensus around core principles and acceptance once the program went into place. In this case, Oregon used extensive public discussions of the values involved in its proposed rationing arrangement as a way to generate the necessary public buy-in. Thousands of citizens participated in deliberations at numerous sessions, and many interest groups voiced their concerns. Naturally, not all won, including the tobacco industry, which opposed a tax increase on cigarettes, but many stakeholders came away from the protracted process knowing they had been heard.

The idea of deliberative forums, advanced particularly by James Fishkin at Stanford University, offers cross-sections of citizens opportunities to come together to talk, listen, learn, and develop what tend to be more moderate, community-oriented positions on complex issues.[44] Beyond direct participation, such deliberative forums can be shared on television and online, amplifying the audience and potentially the number of citizens who can learn, improve their political sophistication, hear other sides of issues, and, in many instances, increase their trust in government in the process. While there is some research that suggests that delibera-tive polls do not change attitudes as much as advocates such as Fishkin and his colleagues claim, there is enough evidence to strongly indicate that this is a worthwhile exercise.[45] Other such examples of intentionally fostered public discourse surrounding complex and controversial topics are the National Issues Forums run by the Kettering Foundation, the 1998 Americans Discuss Social Security gatherings organized by Ameri-caSpeaks, the study circles initiative supported by the Topsfield Founda-tion, and the educational work of Public Agenda.[46] Naturally, not all of these forums lead directly to consensual legislative agreements on their issues, and that was not always the goal, but a good deal of evidence from these initiatives shows that when citizens talk among themselves in struc-tured settings, the discourse strongly tends to be healthier than what we have seen manifested over the Affordable Care Act. People will disagree, even in the most well-engineered discursive environments, but they will also learn more of what they need to know, and they will likely come to appreciate the other side.

Journalism also has a vital role to play in fostering better public under-standing of complex issues. The civic journalism movement that gained prominence in the 1990s proposed that reporters consider, among other moves, intentionally writing from points of view to lead readers to see issues through different frames designed to broaden the range of consid-erations citizens bring to bear on political issues.[47] Such reporting might be expressed as a point/counterpoint juxtaposition of positions and voices. It can also assume the form of journalism with a point of view, nudging readers to think hard about objections, counterclaims, and per-plexing evidence. The latter strategy raised eyebrows in some newswrit-ing circles, as it was perceived to represent a break with a just-the-facts reporting tradition in professional journalism. However, the possibilities for a more purposeful public discourse—as opposed to spending an inor-dinate amount of time discussing little more than the horse-race nature of campaigns and legislative efforts—are significant and have shown evi-dence of success.

Naturally, ordinary citizens themselves also have a role to play in fos-tering more informative and consensus-seeking discourse. If you as a reader have made it this far, by now you must know that many of the short-handed criticisms of recent health care reform politics—both by progressive advocates and their detractors—have tended to neglect numerous important issues. When Democratic politicians talk about uni-versal coverage, you might ask them what level of coverage would be fea-sible, how much this would cost and who will pay for it, what personal responsibility the newly insured would bear, and what kinds of savings might be generated through regular access to preventative care. When Republican politicians talk about personal accountability for spending, you might ask them what kinds of citizens have the required disposable income to meet those cost-sharing provisions, what happens to people who do not, what kinds of specific evidence support their claims about consumer behavior, and to what extent access to basic health care services should be thought of as a citizenship right. There will be a lot of learning required here, but an insistence on facts over superficial rhetoric and sloganeering will push advocates to be more explicit about their plans and what the existing evidence tells us about likely outcomes.

This book calls for a more explicit acknowledgment of and greater public engagement on the problems with America's health care systems. Some of the key problems include, but are not limited to, a discourse led by politicians that has been long on heat and short on light (as discussed in Chapter 2), escalating costs (summarized in Chapter 5), and a general public that did not improve its knowledge of the ACA between 2010 and 2015 (documented in Chapter 6). Neither burying heads in the sand and denying the crisis, nor arguing that market-based mechanisms will solve all of our problems, nor undertaking an undifferentiated defense of what the ACA was designed to accomplish will do. We will need a more open political discourse than the one that characterized the failed Clinton plan of the 1990s.[48] Further, Americans will need both their parties to remain at the negotiating table as they grapple with costs and quality of services, problems that the design of the ACA did not sufficiently address.[49] The health care inflation rate still exceeds GDP growth, and medical errors were, as of 2015, the third leading cause of death in the United States, associated with over 250,000 fatalities annually.[50] American politicians have work to do, and the public will need to be an active partner in these conversations. To date, the most involved citizens have tended to be those with strong opinions, a pattern that works against open deliberation, but experience also tells us that with effective leadership, ordinary citizens can play vital roles in healthier health care politics.[51]

The issues discussed here are difficult, expensive, value laden, and often literally involve matters of life and death. The spectrum of democratic theories referenced in preceding text—ranging from policy democracy to electoral democracy—might tempt some politicians to steer American political institutions and processes in a direction that takes the general public for granted in broad terms, wagering instead that, if alternatives are framed compellingly by party leaders, citizens will buy into the resulting legislated responses.[52] However, variations on this hyper-partisanship, as detailed in these chapters, have not moved the American public any closer to knowing more about national health policy or coming to appreciate the majority of steps the federal government took under the Patient Protection and Affordable Care Act to improve matters. The nation's ability to advance and embrace the kinds of solutions it will need in order to address our many unresolved problems will require a more engaged public, and that will require political leadership that catalyzes a more open, constructive public discourse.

Notes

Preface

1. Key 1961, 1966; Page and Shapiro 1992; Zaller 1992; Lupia and McCubbins 1998.
2. Munro 1996, p. xx.

Chapter 1 Designing the Affordable Care Act: Fateful Decisions

1. Bill signing comments at www.whitehouse.gov (accessed January 13, 2015).
2. Oberlander and Weaver 2015.
3. Gruber 2011.
4. "Uncompensated Care for Uninsured in 2013: A Detailed Examination," Teresa Coughlin, John Holahan, Kyle Caswell, and Megan McGrath, Kaiser Family Foundation, May 2014, at www.kff.org (accessed February 16, 2015); "Uncompensated Hospital Care Cost Fact Sheet," from the American Hospital Association, at www.aha.org (accessed February 16, 2015). See also Gruber 2008, p. 577.
5. McDonough 2011, p. 24.
6. McDonough 2011, Chapter 3; see also Jacobs and Skocpol 2010 for a thoughtful discussion of the creation of the ACA.
7. For example, WellPoint's profit margin in 2008 was 4.07 percent; in 2007, it was 5.47 percent; and in 2006, it was 5.42 percent. See Uwe Reindhart, "How Much Money Do Insurance Companies Make? A Primer," at www.economix.blogs.nytimes.com/2009/09/25 (accessed February 20, 2015).
8. Potter 2010.
9. McDonough 2011, pp. 35–37; Pear 2009, p. A16.
10. See www.kaiserhealthnews.org/news/selling-insurance-across-state-lines/ (accessed May 18, 2016).
11. Shaw 2010.

12. See www.medicaid.gov/chip/eligibility-standards/chip-eligibility-standards.html (accessed May 18, 2016).

13. See www.nasbo.org/sites/default/files/State%20Expenditure%20Report%20%28Fiscal%202013–2015%29S.pdf (accessed May 18, 2016).

14. McDonough 2011.

15. See www.kff.org/medicaid/state-indicator/federal-matching-rate-and-multiplier/ for state and federal shares of Medicaid funding (accessed February 10, 2017).

16. McDonough 2011.

17. See www.kff.org/interactive/uninsured-gap/ (accessed March 12, 2015).

18. Kaiser Family Foundation, "Key Facts about the Uninsured Population" at www.kff.org.

19. Americans spent $1.1 trillion in 2015 on private insurance. Centers for Medicare and Medicaid Services, "National Health Expenditure 2014 Highlights," at www.cms.gov/research-statistics-data-and-systems/statistics-trends-and-reports/nationalhealthexpenddata/downloads/highlights.pdf (accessed February 10, 2017).

20. Obama speech to the Illinois AFL/CIO, June 30, 2003, at www.youtube.com/watch?v=LhEX3rHssJI (accessed October 25, 2016). See also Cohn 2010, p. 16.

21. Starr 2013, pp. 182–83; Kirsch 2011, p. 83.

22. Starr 2011, p. 11.

23. Ibid., p. 11.

24. Ibid., p. 12.

25. Brill 2015, p. 51.

26. Board statement by America's Health Insurance Plans, "Now Is the Time for Health Care Reform: A Proposal to Achieve Universal Coverage, Affordability, Quality Improvement and Market Reform," December 5, 2008, at www.ahip.org (accessed February 10, 2017); McDonough 2011, p. 55; Brill 2015, pp. 51–52.

27. Cohn, "The Operator," 2009, pp. 21–23; Brill 2015, pp. 91–92.

28. Daschle 2010, p. 83; Cohn, "The Operator," 2009.

29. Pear, "Insurers Offer to Soften a Key Rate-Setting Policy," 2009, p. B1.

30. Suzy Khimm, "AHIP Insists It's Still a Friend of Health Reform. Really!" *The New Republic*, October 22, 2009 (at www.newrepublic.com; accessed February 20, 2015).

31. Sarah Ferris and Megan Wilson, "Aetna's Defection Comes with Risk," Thehill.com, January 7, 2016.

32. McDonough 2011, pp. 78–79.

33. Ibid.

34. Murray and Kane 2009, p. A-1.

35. Ipsos-Public Affairs/McClatchy Poll, "Which of the remaining parties involved in health care reform do you trust the least to make sure that all Americans have access to quality healthcare? . . . Doctors and other health practitioners, President Barack Obama, Republicans in Congress, Democrats in Congress,

health insurance companies, pharmaceutical companies," August 2009
(N = 1,057 national adults). Available at the iPOLL Databank, Roper Center,
Cornell University.

36. Marmor 2000.

37. McDonough 2011; Brill 2015.

38. In February 2012, the Fairleigh Dickinson University Public Mind Poll
asked, "A key question the (Supreme) Court will answer is whether the U.S. Congress can legally require every adult to have health insurance—and if they don't
have health insurance, to pay a tax penalty. What's your view? Can Congress
require everyone to have health insurance or pay a tax penalty?" Sixty-five percent said "no," 29 percent said "yes" (N = 1,185 national adults).

39. In May 2010, the IMS Health National Survey asked, "Apart from decisions made by your doctor, whom do you trust to guide overall health care policy about how health care is delivered to you? On a scale of 1–10, with 1
indicating no trust at all and 10 indicating a maximum level of trust." Fifty-five
percent of respondents rated health insurance companies at 4 or below, and only
24 percent rated them at 6 or above. Twenty percent picked the middle position.
Two percent said "don't know" (N = 1,000 national adult 2008 voters).

40. In October 2013, the Democracy Corps/Women's Voices Poll asked, "Now
I'm going to read you a list of concerns some people have about the new [2010]
health care law—the Affordable Care Act or Obamacare. After I read each one,
please tell me whether you are very concerned about this, somewhat concerned,
a little concerned, or not at all concerned . . . I just won't be able to afford the
insurance I will be required to have." Thirty-one percent were "very concerned,"
and another 15 percent were "somewhat concerned." Two percent said they did
not know (N = 950 national voters).

41. Butler 1989, p. 3. See also Butler and Haislmaier 1989 for a book-length
exposition of this perspective.

42. Pauly et al., 1991. See also Pauly 1994.

43. Ezra Klein, "An Interview with Mark Pauly, Father of the Individual Mandate," at www.washingtonpost.com (accessed May 18, 2016).

44. "Summary of a 1993 Republican Health Reform Plan," Kaiser Health
News, February 23, 2010, at www.kaiserhealthnews.org (accessed July 2, 2012).

45. Ezra Klein, "In Interview with Mark Pauly, Father of the Individual Mandate," at www.washingtonpost.com, February 1, 2011 (accessed May 18, 2016).

46. Congressional Quarterly Weekly Report, September 18, 1993, p. 2456.
Congressional Quarterly Press, Washington, D.C.

47. Johnson and Broder 1996, pp. 363, 371–74.

48. Jacobs et al. 1998, p. 30.

49. Friedman 1991.

50. Alex Seitz-Wald, "Why Hillary Clinton Was Not a Fan of the Individual
Mandate," *National Journal*, March 3, 2014, at nationaljournal.com (accessed
February 3, 2015). See also David Nather, "Hillary Clinton Dissed Individual
Mandate, Docs Show," www.politico.com (accessed February 3, 2015).

51. Clinton address to National Governors Association, August 16, 1993, at www.americanpresidencyproject.org (accessed March 5, 2015); Pauly 1994, p. 29.

52. Skocpol 1996.

53. Blendon et al. 2008.

54. Appleby 2005, p. 3B.

55. Monahan 2005, p. A1.

56. Gruber 2011; Brill 2015, Chapter 2. See also Peter Dizikes, "How Jonathan Gruber Became 'Mr. Mandate'" (MIT News Office press release), at newsoffice.mit.edu (accessed December 15, 2014). See Gruber 2008 and Lambrew and Gruber 2006/2007 for an elaboration of the logic of the individual mandate.

57. Rampell 2012, p. B-1.

58. Brill 2015, p. 30.

59. McDonough 2011, p. 39.

60. Blendon et al. 2006, pp. 642–43.

61. Appleby 2005, p. 3B.

62. Arvidson 2005.

63. Cohn, "Mass Appeal," 2009, pp. 10–11. See also Brill 2015, pp. 29–45 and McDonough 2011, pp. 37–43.

64. Gruber 2011.

65. Brill 2015, p. 35.

66. Pugh 2006, p. 4A.

67. Higgins 2006, p. A1.

68. Broder 2006, p. B7; Gavant 2006, p. 17.

69. Higgins 2006, p. A1.

70. Edmund Haislmaier, "The Significance of Massachusetts Health Reform," report by the Heritage Foundation, April 11, 2006. Washington, D.C.

71. Ibid.

72. Heritage Backgrounder #1953, Owcharenko and Moffit, "The Massachusetts Health Plan: Lessons for the States," July 18, 2006. Washington, D.C.

73. Kurtzman 2007.

74. Solomon 2007.

75. See Frakt 2011 for an argument and evidence that hospital cost shifting is not such a significant problem.

76. Friendersdorf 2012.

77. Romney commented during an October 2011 discussion at the Western Republican Leadership Conference. See Iowa Republican Debate Blog, *The New York Times*, December 10, 2011 (available via Lexis-Nexis). See also Avik Roy, "How the Heritage Foundation, a Conservative Think Tank, Promoted the Individual Mandate," at www.forbes.com (accessed May 8, 2012).

78. Lee 2008, p. A10.

79. Brill 2015, p. 36, quoting Stern.

80. Brill 2015, at p. 61, notes that this conversation occurred on June 7, 2008.

81. Daschle 2010, p. 102.

82. Klein 2012. See also McDonough 2011, p. 60.

83. Moffit 2008.

84. Ibid., p. 229.

85. Jacobs et al. 1998; Jacobs and Shapiro 2000; Shapiro and Jacobs 2010.

86. Johnson, "Republican Rivals," 2007.

87. Johnson, "A Year Later," 2007.

88. Many national survey organizations asked about the mandate, generally each using its own language. A graph showing response patterns by party appears in Figure 1.2. Opinion data come from the Roper Center's iPOLL Databank and from the survey organizations. Further details are available from the author.

89. McDonough 2011, p. 81.

90. Ibid., pp. 63–64.

91. Quoted in document at the website of Physicians for a National Health Program at www.pnhp.org/news/2009/may/frank_luntzs_the_l.php (accessed February 10, 2017).

92. For the FreedomWorks quote, see Eggen and Rucker 2009, p. A1; for discussion of the phrase, see Markham 2005.

93. Starr 2013, p. 215.

94. Author's interview with Robert MacGuffie, March 14, 2015 (telephone). See Hacker 2010 for discussion of personal attacks.

95. Kirsch 2011, p. 212.

96. Starr 2013, p. 114; Eggen and Rucker 2009.

97. Farley 2009.

98. Randy Barnett, Nathaniel Stewart, and Todd Gaziano, "Why the Personal Mandate to Buy Health Insurance Is Unprecedented and Unconstitutional," legal memorandum #49, Heritage Foundation, December 9, 2009, at www.heritage .org (accessed March 4, 2015).

99. *National Federation of Independent Businesses v. Sebelius*, 567 U.S. ___ (2012).

100. Ponnuru 2012.

101. Rowan Callick, "The Singapore Model," at www.aei.org/publication/ the-singapore-model (accessed October 25, 2016).

102. Lee 2008, p. A10; Kirsch 2011, p. 88.

103. Shalit 1994.

104. James Taranto, writing in *The Wall Street Journal* (February 8, 2012), accused Butler of attempting to "rewrite history" (no page numbers in online story "Heritage Rewrites History").

105. Butler 2012.

106. Butler 1989, quotes at p. 6.

107. Epstein 2014.

108. A January 2010 Pew Research Center asked 1,504 adults whom they trust more to decide what kinds of medical procedures insurance should cover. Sixty-five percent of Republicans sided with insurance companies and only

10 percent with the government. In stark contrast, only 32 percent of Democrats sided with insurance companies and fully 47 percent with the government (January 6–10, 2010, conducted by Princeton Survey Research Associates).

109. See interactive chart on confidence in government at www.people-press .org/2014/11/13/public-trust-in-government/ (accessed October 26, 2016).

110. Based on Lexis-Nexis searches of AP stories mentioning the terms "require" or "mandate," "health insurance," and "individual."

111. Kaiser Family Foundation poll, February 2011. Majority support was expressed for each of these specifically named provisions among the 39 percent of respondents who separately stated that they would support the repeal of the law. Data available at www.kff.org (accessed March 20, 2015).

112. Lynch and Gollust 2010.

113. Interactive chart showing tracking poll results at www.kff.org/interactive/ health-tracking-poll-exploring-the-publics-views-on-the-affordable-care-act-aca/.

114. "Please tell me whether that proposal is acceptable or unacceptable. . . . Require everyone to have health insurance coverage. Those people with low and moderate incomes would receive government assistance. Those people who can afford it would have to buy their own health insurance or pay a penalty or fine if they do not." July 24–27, 2009, NBC News/*Wall Street Journal* (N = 505 national adults).

115. NBC News/*Wall Street Journal*, June 6–15, 2009 (N = 1,008 national adults).

116. Lynch and Gollust 2010; Gelman et al. 2010; Brady and Kessler 2010; Oakman et al. 2010.

117. Brodie et al. 2010; Blendon et al. 2010.

118. See Commonwealth Fund report card on outcomes by nation at www .commonwealthfund.org/publications/fund-reports/2014/jun/mirror-mirror (accessed October 26, 2016).

Chapter 2 Fighting Obamacare

1. Béland et al. 2016; Trapp 2010, p. 5.

2. Helderman 2010b, p. A1.

3. Kaiser tracking poll data at kff.org/interactive/kaiser-health-tracking-poll-the-publics-views-on-the-aca/#?response=Favorable—Unfavorable& aRange=twoYear (accessed February 11, 2017).

4. Page and Shapiro 1992.

5. Brodie et al. 2010.

6. Oberlander 2003 and Marmor 2000 for a discussion of public views toward Medicare and Béland 2005 for a discussion of Social Security.

7. For the list of repeal votes, see www.washingtonpost.com/blogs/the-fix/ wp/2014/03/21/the-house-has-voted-54-times-in-four-years-on-obamacare-heres-the-full-list/ (accessed October 25, 2016).

8. Klein 2015, p. 5.

9. HR 2 passed on January 19, 2011; text is at www.gpo.gov/fdsys/pkg/
BILLS-112hr2eh/pdf/BILLS-112hr2eh.pdf (accessed October 25, 2016).

10. Congressional Budget Office 2013, 2015.

11. Federal spending chart at www.usfederalbudget.us/budget_pie_gs.php
(accessed October 25, 2016). For state spending figures, see www.nasbo.org/
sites/default/files/Summary_State%20Expenditure%20Report.pdf (accessed July
7, 2015).

12. See Michel Cannon, November 13, 2008, at www.cato.org/blog/blocking-
obamas-health-plan-key-gops-survival (accessed October 25, 2016).

13. Pethokoukis 2008.

14. See www.freedomworks.org/content/coalition-letter-congress-must-honor-
sequester-savings-and-defund-obamacare-it-too-late (accessed October 25,
2016).

15. See Congressional Quarterly's *America Votes* (various years) for national
vote data.

16. For state legislative seats, see www.pewresearch.org/fact-tank/2015/03/02/
ahead-of-redistricting-democrats-seek-to-reverse-statehouse-declines/ (accessed
July 8, 2015). For governors, see www.multistate.com/state-resources/governors-
legislatures (accessed October 25, 2016).

17. Bacon, Jr., 2010b.

18. Bacon, Jr., 2016a.

19. Bacon, Jr., 2010b.

20. Béland et al. 2016, p. 57.

21. For an exception to this pattern, see Roy 2014, though even this proposal
did not provide congressional Republicans a plan around which they could
coalesce.

22. Heritage Foundation, Backgrounder report #2847, October 31, 2013,
Washington, D.C.

23. Video at www.obamacare.heritage.org/the-conservative-alternative-to-
obamacare/ (accessed June 24, 2015).

24. Sherman and Allen 2012.

25. *Congressional Quarterly Almanac*, 2012, page 8-3. Congressional Quarterly
Press, Washington, D.C.

26. Weisman 2013, p. A1; Mike Zapler, "Boehner Unloads on GOP's 'False
Prophets,'" at www.politico.com/story/2015/09/john-boehner-gop-false-prophets-
214120 (accessed October 18, 2016).

27. Stolberg and McIntire 2013, p. 1.

28. Ibid.

29. *Congressional Quarterly Almanac*, 2012, page 8-3. Congressional Quarterly
Press, Washington, D.C.

30. Cornyn 2013.

31. Volsky 2013.

32. Ibid.

33. Kane 2013, p. A1.

34. Costa 2014, p. A1.

35. O'Keefe 2013, p. A3.

36. Tumulty and Hamburger 2013, p. A1.

37. Montgomery and Helderman 2013, p. A1.

38. "Do you think the shutdown was a good thing for the country or a bad thing for the country?" CNN, October 18, 2013 (N = 841 national adults). A nearly identical question was asked by ABC News and *The Washington Post* in early January 1996 (N = 852 national adults). The gap between the percentage of Democrats and Republicans believing the shutdown to be "a bad thing" grew from 27 to 36 points. The cross-party gap on the "good thing" response grew by 9 percentage points.

39. Dreyfuss 2001.

40. Polling by the Kaiser Family Foundation showed 42 percent disapproval in August 2013. This level rose to 50 percent by January 2014 and did not settle back to 42 percent until June 2015. Tracking poll data available at www.kff.org (accessed October 18, 2016).

41. Brill 2015, pp. 335, 343–44.

42. For a detailed account of this episode, see Brill 2015. For the House Republicans' assessment, see U.S. House of Representatives, Committee on Oversight and Government Reform 2014.

43. *Federal Register*, "Health Insurance Premium Tax Credit," August 17, 2011. U.S. Government, Washington, D.C.

44. Brill 2015, p. 241.

45. Ibid., p. 259.

46. Ibid., p. 292.

47. Ibid., p. 294.

48. Ibid., p. 295.

49. Ibid., p. 276.

50. Based on Lexis-Nexis news archive searches for the terms "health" and "website."

51. ABC/*Washington Post*, "Do you think this is an isolated incident or do you think it's a sign of broader problems in implementing the healthcare law?" October 17–20, 2015 (N = 1,002 national adults).

52. Health Tracking Poll data at www.kff.org.

53. DHHS, "Health Insurance Marketplace: Summary Enrollment Report," May 1, 2014. DHHS, "2015 Plan Selections by Zip Code in the Health Insurance Marketplace," April 8, 2015.

54. www.usatoday.com/story/news/politics/2013/11/11/fact-check-keeping-your-health-plan/3500187/ (accessed October 25, 2016).

55. Brill 2015, p. 206.

56. www.healthcare.gov/health-care-law-protections/grandfathered-plans/ (accessed October 25, 2016).

57. Brill 2015, pp. 366–67.

58. Lisa Clemans-Cope and Nathaniel Anderson, "Health Insurance Policy Cancellations Were Uncommon in 2014," Urban Institute, March 12, 2015, at

www.hrms.urban.org/quicktakes/Health-Insurance-Policy-Cancellations-Were-Uncommon-in-2014.html#fn5 (accessed September 28, 2015).

59. Story at www.nbcnews.com/news/other/exclusive-obama-personally-apologizes-americans-losing-health-coverage-f8C11555216 (accessed September 18, 2015). See also Eilperin 2013, p. A1.

60. Brill 2015, pp. 380, 397.

61. Helderman 2010a, p. B1.

62. Hunley 2010.

63. Barnett 2010, p. B2.

64. Richey 2010. See *State of Florida v. U.S. Department of Health and Human Services* in U.S. District Court for the Northern District of Florida, January 31, 2011, for Vinson's ruling.

65. "McCain Camp Distorts Obama's Tax Policies," *The Washington Post*, June 11, 2008.

66. Rosen 2012, p. 11; Brill 2015, p. 206; Emanuel 2014, pp. 190–93.

67. *Congressional Quarterly* Almanac, 2012, page 9-3. Congressional Quarterly Press, Washington, D.C.

68. *NFIB v. Sebelius* 2012, p. 2.

69. Ibid., p. 6.

70. NFIB document at www.nfib.com/foundations/legal-center/healthcare-lawsuit/ (accessed July 27, 2016).

71. *NFIB v. Sebelius* 2012, p. 5.

72. Emanuel 2014, p. 198.

73. For example, "Regardless of your feeling about the law itself, do you approve or disapprove of the U.S. Supreme Court ruling on the health care law last week?" 42% approve, 44% disapprove. ABC News/*The Washington Post*, July 5–8, 2012 (N = 1,003 national adults).

74. Confidence in government ratings at www.gallup.com.

75. Jen Gunter, "The Medical Facts about Birth Control and Hobby Lobby—From an OB/GYN," www.newrepublic.com/article/118547/facts-about-birth-control-and-hobby-lobby-ob-gyn, July 6, 2014 (accessed October 18, 2016).

76. These included two types of intra-uterine devises and two types of morning-after pills that, they said, act to prevent fertilized eggs from attaching to the uterine wall.

77. "5 Things to Know about Hobby Lobby's Owners," *The Seattle Times*, July 1, 2014.

78. The methods are Plan B (morning after pill), Ella (a similar drug), Cooper Intra-Uterine Device, and IUD with progestin.

79. Quoted in *National Review Online*, at www.nationalreview.com, June 30, 2014.

80. Brill 2015, p. 194.

81. Online summary at www.kff.org/health-reform/issue-brief/are-premium-subsidies-available-in-states-with-a-federally-run-marketplace-a-guide-to-the-supreme-court-argument-in-king-v-burwell/ (accessed October 18, 2016).

82. See Cross 2009 for a general discussion.

83. *King v. Burwell* 2015, section IIA, p. 9.

84. *King v. Burwell* 2015. See also www.kff.org/health-reform/issue-brief/are-premium-subsidies-available-in-states-with-a-federally-run-marketplace-a-guide-to-the-supreme-court-argument-in-king-v-burwell/ (accessed October 18, 2016).

85. At this early stage, the case was *King v. Sebelius*, as Kathleen Sebelius was still secretary of HHS.

86. *King v. Burwell* 2015, section IB, p. 4

87. Ibid., section II A, p. 14.

88. Ibid., Scalia's dissent, first paragraph.

89. Scalia 1997.

90. *King v. Burwell* 2015, Scalia's dissent, section V, p. 21.

91. *King v. Burwell* 2015, section IIB, p. 17.

92. www.kff.org/health-reform/issue-brief/are-premium-subsidies-available-in-states-with-a-federally-run-marketplace-a-guide-to-the-supreme-court-argument-in-king-v-burwell/ (accessed October 25, 2016).

93. "As you may know, the Supreme Court ruled that government assistance for lower-income Americans buying health insurance through both state-operated and federally-operated health insurance exchanges is legal. Do you support or oppose this ruling?" CNN/ORC International Poll, 6/21–28/15 (N = 1,017 national adults).

94. "'Judicial Tyranny' to 'A Great Day,' Candidates React to Health Care Ruling," NPR.org, June 25, 2015 (accessed July 27, 2016).

95. For discussion, see www.healthaffairs.org/blog/2014/12/05/section-1332-waivers-and-the-future-of-state-health-reform/ (accessed October 25, 2016).

96. Sinozich (forthcoming).

97. "Do you approve or disapprove of the way Obama is handling implementation of the new law?" ABC/*Washington Post*, 1/20–23/14 (N = 1,003 national adults).

98. "To the best of your knowledge, would you say the health reform law does nor does not establish . . .?" Kaiser Family Foundation, 12/2–9/14 (N = 1,505 national adults)

99. Kaiser Family Foundation poll, 12/2–9/14 (N = 1,505 national adults).

100. Ponnuru 2013, pp. 32–35, quote at p. 34.

101. Ferris 2015.

102. Klein 2015, p. 99.

Chapter 3   Will Markets Save Us?

1. Tanden 2014; Stuart Butler, "Why the GOP Needs an Alternative to the Obamacare Repeal Strategy," www.brookings.edu (accessed 8/1/16).

2. The Internal Revenue Code allows employers to exempt earnings spent on health insurance from their tax obligation, and allows employees to receive health insurance without this being counted as taxable income. Self-employed individuals do not enjoy this tax advantage.

3. See www.washingtonpost.com/blogs/the-fix/wp/2014/03/21/the-house-has-voted-54-times-in-four-years-on-obamacare-heres-the-full-list/ (accessed October 25, 2016).

4. This chapter owes a significant intellectual debt to Jost 2007.

5. See Schneider and Hall 2009 for elaboration of this point.

6. Herzlinger 1997, p. 258, 2004, pp. 102–21.

7. Epstein 1997.

8. Feldstein 1973.

9. Herzlinger 1997, pp. 64–69; Goodman and Musgrave 1992, p. 94; Cogan et al. 2011, p. 16; Cannon and Tanner 2005, p. 46.

10. Herrick and Goodman 2007, p. 2.

11. Schneider and Hall 2009; Gawande 2005.

12. Herzlinger 1997, p. 15; see also column by Peter Orzag at www.bloombergview.com/articles/2012–01–25/to-shop-smart-patients-need-to-know-price-of-care-peter-orszag (accessed October 25, 2016).

13. Cannon and Tanner 2005, p. 5.

14. Herzlinger 1997, p. 31; Cannon and Tanner 2005, pp. 6–7.

15. Brill 2014; Schneider and Hall 2009.

16. Herrick and Goodman 2007.

17. Arrow 1963; Schneider and Hall 2009.

18. General Social Survey, National Opinion Research Center, February 2000 (N = 1,408 national adults).

19. Jost 2007, p. 34; Goodman and Musgrave 1992, pp. 75–80.

20. Goodman and Musgrave 1992, p. 76; Jost 2007, p. 34.

21. Blendon et al. 2006.

22. Kim et al. 2014.

23. Strine et al. 2008; Friedman et al. 2013.

24. See www.statista.com/chart/3668/the-worlds-biggest-chocolate-consumers/ for chocolate consumption (accessed February 5, 2017).

25. Jost 2007, p. 35.

26. Cannon and Tanner 2005, p. 64; Jost 2007, p. 39.

27. Claxton et al. 2016.

28. IRS brochure on HSAs at www.irs.gov/pub/irs-pdf/p969.pdf (accessed October 25, 2016).

29. Ibid.

30. For overviews and critiques, see Stone 1993; Jost 2007; Schneider and Hall 2009.

31. Newhouse and the Insurance Experiment Group 1993, especially Chapter 11.

32. But see Nyman 2007 for a critique and Newhouse et al. 2008 for a rejoinder.

33. Newhouse 1993, pp. 339–40.

34. Ibid., p. 344.

35. Ibid., p. 341.

36. American Academy of Actuaries Consumer-Driven Health Plans Work Group 2009.

37. Dixon et al. 2008.

38. Fronstin and Roebuck 2014.

39. Parente et al. 2010, pp. 7–8.

40. Lo Sasso et al. 2010; Fronstin 2010, p. 22.

41. Fronstin 2010, p. 23.

42. Waters et al. 2011, p. 168.

43. See Rowe et al. 2008 for evidence that consumers distinguish, but see Parente et al. 2010 for contrary findings.

44. Fronstin and Roebuck 2014.

45. Michael Morissey, "Price Sensitivity in Health Care: Implications for Health Care Policy," National Federation of Independent Businesses, July 2005, at www.nfib.com/Portals/0/PriceSensitivity.pdf (accessed October 25, 2016).

46. Parente et al. 2004.

47. Dixon et al. 2008, p. 1129.

48. Morrisey 2005.

49. Ringel et al. 2005.

50. Newhouse 1992; Manning et al. 1987.

51. Centers for Disease Control and Prevention, at www.cdc.gov/nchs/fastats/emergency-department.htm (accessed August 1, 2016).

52. Ibid. for total costs; for average cost see Centers for Disease Control and Prevention, at www.cdc.gov/nchs/data/hus/hus12.pdf, Figure 29 (accessed October 25, 2016).

53. Newhouse and the Insurance Experiment Group 1993, Chapter 11.

54. Selby et al. 1996.

55. Wharam et al. 2007.

56. Sabik and Gandhi 2015; Tang et al. 2010.

57. Sabik and Gandhi 2015, Table II.

58. Mortensen 2010.

59. Tamblyn et al. 2001.

60. Soumerai et al. 1989.

61. Parente et al. 2008, p. 1552.

62. Dixon et al. 2008, Exhibit 5.

63. Fronstin 2010, p. 21.

64. Centers for Disease Control and Prevention data, at www.cdc.gov/obesity/data/adult.html (accessed October 25, 2016).

65. CBS/*New York Times* Survey, "Do you happen to know what your own blood pressure is, or is that something you usually don't keep track of?" February 2007 (N = 1,281 national adults). Available through the Roper Center's iPOLL Databank, Cornell University.

66. EBRI Health Confidence Survey (various months 2008–2012), at www.ebri.org/surveys/hcs/ (accessed February 13, 2017).

67. Another problem is optimism bias, or the exaggerated sense of health, competence, and other qualities that many people harbor. See Kahneman 2011.

68. James 2013 for an overview.

69. Hibbard et al. 2013; Veroff et al. 2013.

70. Nease et al. 2013; Kahneman 2011; Thaler and Sunstein 2008.

71. "How often does your doctor discuss with you his or her reasons for recommending a particular treatment?" Three percent did not know. Kaiser Family Foundation poll conducted in collaboration with the Harvard School of Public Health and National Public Radio, March 12–22, 2009 (N = 1,238 national adults).

72. Alexander et al. 2004; Schneider and Hall 2009.

73. Fronstin 2010, p. 20.

74. See Dixon et al. 2008, especially pp. 1124–25.

75. Gawande 2005, p. 44.

76. Brill 2014.

77. 2015 Medicaid Fee Schedule for Illinois, at www.illinois.gov/hfs/SiteColle ctionDocuments/032309mch.pdf (accessed October 25, 2016).

78. Personal communication, December 15, 2015.

79. Robinson 1999.

80. Sommers et al. 2013; Alexander et al. 2004.

81. Kaiser Family Foundation survey, January 3–23, 2008, conducted in collaboration with the Harvard School of Public Health and *USA Today* (N = 1,695 national adults). Available through the Roper Center's iPOLL Databank, Cornell University.

82. "Tell me whether you [this] always, often, sometimes, or never . . . shop around for the best price [on prescriptions]." Roper Public Affairs and Media Group survey, October 2004 (N = 1,001 over 50). Available through the Roper Center's iPOLL Databank, Cornell University.

83. "Which do you think would do a better job of keeping healthcare costs down? . . . Individuals, employers, government regulation . . ." CBS/*New York Times* Survey, January 2006 (N = 1,229 national adults). Available through the Roper Center's iPOLL Databank, Cornell University.

84. Stein 1983, p. 1.

85. Gawande 2009, p. 44.

86. *Differentials in the Concentration in the Level of Health Expenditures across Population Subgroups in the U.S., 2010,* at www.meps.ahrq.gov/mepsweb/data_ files/publications/st421/stat421.shtml (accessed October 25, 2016).

87. Fronstin and Elmlinger, "Health Savings Accounts and Health Reimbursement Arrangements: Assets, Account Balances, and Rollovers, 2006–2014," EBRI Issue Brief 409, January 2015.

88. Institute of Medicine 2001, p. 6; see also James 2013, p. 1.

89. See www.alec.org/publications/the-state-legislators-guide-to-repealing-obamacare/ (accessed October 25, 2016).

90. Orrin Hatch press release, March 4, 2015, at www.finance.senate.gov/ newsroom/chairman/release/?id=55250066–1241–4962–92d3–84ae1d3369b9 (accessed October 25, 2016).

91. See Klein 2015 for one version of this debate.

92. HR 3762; Sarah Ferris, "House Passes Partial Obamacare Repeal," *The Hill*, October 23, 2015.

93. Alexander Bolton, "Senate Approves Bill Repealing Much of Obamacare," *The Hill*, December 3, 2015.

94. Ramesh Ponnuru, "GOP Split: What to Hate about Obamacare," American Enterprise Institute, May 28, 2015.

95. Ibid.

96. See www.heritage.org/research/reports/2008/04/health-care-reform-design-principles-for-a-patient-centered-consumer-based-market (accessed October 25, 2016.

97. www.weeklystandard.com/articles/getting-there_804816.html?page=2 (accessed October 25, 2016).

98. Stuart Butler, "Two Cheers for the GOP's Burr, Hatch and Upton Alternative to Obamacare," Brookings Institution, at www.brookings.edu/blog/health 360/2015/02/09/two-cheers-for-the-gops-burr-hatch-and-upton-alternative-to-obamacare/ (accessed February 14, 2017).

99. Capretta and Levin 2014.

100. For one other conservative alternative built on this principle, see Roy 2014.

Chapter 4 Learning to Live with the Enemy

1. Ryan 2016. Heritage Foundation backgrounder, "A Fresh Start for Health Care Reform," October 30, 2014, at www.heritage.org/health-care-reform/report/fresh-start-health-care-reform (accessed February 14, 2017).

2. See Flagg 2016 for a discussion of the importance of both electoral pressures and insistence of the organized medical lobby.

3. Mettler 2011.

4. Ibid., p. 5.

5. Gantert 2013.

6. Hertel-Fernandez et al. 2016.

7. See Walker's website advocacy for a bill that would formally expand Alaska's Medicaid program, at www.gov.alaska.gov/Walker/priorities/accessible-healthcare/about-the-bill.html (accessed October 25, 2016).

8. Author's interview with Elizabeth Hertel, Michigan Department of Health and Human Services, July 20, 2015. See also Gray and Erb 2013.

9. "Michigan Panel Rejects" 2013.

10. Ayanian et al. 2014.

11. Martin 2013.

12. Davey 2013.

13. Oosting 2013; see also Davey 2013.

14. Quote from May 16, 2013, testimony of the Michigan Health and Hospital Association, at www.mha.org/advocacy/documents/mha_reform_testimony_lda.pdf (accessed August 2, 2016). See also Devitt 2013.

15. Gray and Erb 2013.

16. Ibid.

17. Author's interview with Rep. Andy Schor, July 7, 2015 (Lansing). See also Jack Lessenberry, "Michigan GOP Has Reasons to Be Optimistic in 2014," *The Blade* (Toledo, OH), September 27, 2013.

18. Interview at www.youtube.com/watch?v=q9qhhgk3T3U (accessed October 25, 2016).

19. Author interview with Rep. Andy Schor, July 17, 2015 (Lansing).

20. Davey 2013, p. A14.

21. Author's interview with Rep. Andy Schor, July 17, 2015 (Lansing).

22. Author's interview with Nick Wake, legislative assistant to Rep. Mike Callton, July 17, 2015 (Lansing).

23. McGillivary 2013.

24. Davey 2013, p. A14.

25. Michigan's waiver amendment request to HHS, November 8, 2013, p. 3, at www.medicaid.gov/Medicaid-CHIP-Program-Information/By-Topics/Waivers/1115/downloads/mi/Healthy-Michigan/mi-healthy-michigan-waiver-amend-req-11082013.pdf (accessed February 14, 2017).

26. Ibid., p. 8.

27. Ibid., p. 8.

28. Author's interview with Rep. Mike Callton, June 24, 2015 (telephone).

29. Author's interview with Elizabeth Hertel, July 20, 2015 (telephone).

30. "Medicaid Expansion in Michigan," Kaiser Family Foundation factsheet, January 8, 2016, at www.kff.org/medicaid/fact-sheet/medicaid-expansion-in-michigan/ (accessed February 14, 2017).

31. Levey 2015.

32. Newhouse and the Insurance Experiment Group 1993, chapter 11.

33. Author's interview with Elizabeth Hertel, July 20, 2015 (telephone).

34. For a summary of the program rules and history, see Healthy Indiana Plan 1115 Waiver Extension Application, submitted April 12, 2013, by the Indiana Family and Social Services Administration. For archive of documents relating to HIP, see www.in.gov/fssa/hip/2336.htm (accessed October 26, 2016).

35. According to 2012 annual report, at www.in.gov/fssa/hip/files/2012_HIP_Annual_Report.pdf (accessed October 25, 2016).

36. Ibid.

37. Daniels's letter, at www.in.gov/governorhistory/mitchdaniels/files/12–28–11_HHS_letter.pdf (accessed August 3, 2016).

38. Pence's letter to Daniels, at www.in.gov/fssa/hip/files/November_15_Pence_Letter.pdf (accessed October 25, 2016).

39. Pence's letter to state legislators, at www.in.gov/healthcarereform/files/GOV_HIP_201401301514.pdf (accessed October 25, 2016).

40. Summary of public input, at www.in.gov/fssa/hip/files/HIP_2_0_Waiver_(Public_Comment_Summary).pdf (accessed October 25, 2016).

41. Pence's letter, at www.in.gov/fssa/hip/files/HIP_2.0_Transmittal_Letter_to_Secretary_Burwell.pdf (accessed October 25, 2016).

42. Letter, at www.in.gov/fssa/hip/files/Governor_Pence_Letter_to_President_ Obama.pdf (accessed October 25, 2016).

43. Pence's letter, at www.in.gov/fssa/hip/files/Letter_from_Governor_Pence_ to_Secretary_Sebelius.pdf (accessed February 14, 2017).

44. POWER is an acronym for Personal Wellness and Responsibility.

45. See frequently asked questions document at www.in.gov (accessed August 3, 2016).

46. Karsish 2015.

47. Levey 2015.

48. Slavin 2015, state news section.

49. For quote, Dickson 2015.

50. Author's interview with Sen. Patricia Miller (Indianapolis), July 16, 2015.

51. See discussion in Chapter 3.

52. Points from www.in.gov/fssa/hip/files/Healthy_Indiana_Plan_Successes_ Dec2013.pdf (accessed August 3, 2016).

53. John Davidson, "Indiana Gov. Mike Pence's 'Alternative' Medicaid Expansion Is the Worse One Yet," at www.thefederalist.com (accessed August 3, 2016).

54. Nina Owcharenko, "Pence's Indiana Medicaid Decision a Disappointment," at www.heritage.org (accessed October 25, 2016).

55. Author's interview with Sen. Brandt Hershman (Indianapolis), July 16, 2015.

56. See www.healthinsurance.org/indiana-medicaid/ (accessed October 25, 2016).

57. Josh Archambault, "One Year Update of Indiana's Medicaid Expansion," at www.forbes.com (accessed December 17, 2015).

58. Author's interview with Sen. Patricia Miller (Indianapolis), July 16, 2015.

59. Brown 2015; Ruffin Prevost, "Wyoming Senate Rejects Obamacare Medicaid Expansion," Reuters, February 6, 2015, at www.reuters.com/article/us-usa-wyoming-medicaid-idUSKBN0LB04I20150207 (accessed February 14, 2017).

60. Christenson and Glick 2015.

61. Béland et al. 2016, Chapter 4; Jacobs and Callaghan 2013; Rigby and Haselswerdt 2013.

62. Because the dependent variable is ordinal, ordinal regression was used. Dependent variable: Medicaid expansion, 0 = none, 1 = waiver-based, 2 = traditional. Independent variables: 2012 Obama vote, party of governor in 2013 (Republican = 0, Democratic = 1), state's uninsured rate in 2013, taken from the Census Bureau's Current Population Survey (tabulated by Kaiser Family Foundation; see "Key Facts about the Uninsured Population," October 5, 2015). Cox & Snell R^2 = 0.55. This finding remains the same using updated data on gubernatorial control for 2015.

63. Coughlin et al. 1994.

64. Kaiser Family Foundation 2015.

65. Enrollment figures at www.medicaid.gov (accessed August 3, 2016).

66. Epstein et al. 2014.

67. Unger and Kenning 2015.
68. Mann and Ornstein 2006, 2012.

Chapter 5 The Cost of Health Care

1. Catlin and Cowan 2015; "National Health Expenditures Fact Sheet, 2015," Centers for Medicare and Medicaid Services, U.S. Department of Health and Human Services, at www.cms.gov/research-statistics-data-and-systems/statistics-trends-and-reports/nationalhealthexpenddata/nhe-fact-sheet.html (accessed February 20, 2017).
2. Orzag 2011, p. 42.
3. Manchester and Schwabish 2010, p. 285.
4. Congressional Budget Office 2015.
5. Catlin and Cowan 2015.
6. Ibid.
7. Ibid.; Centers for Medicare and Medicaid Services, "National Health Expenditures Fact Sheet, 2014" and "Brief Summaries of Medicare and Medicaid," at www.cms.gov (accessed August 3, 2016).
8. "National Health Expenditures Fact Sheet, 2015," Centers for Medicare and Medicaid Services, U.S. Department of Health and Human Services, at www.cms.gov/research-statistics-data-and-systems/statistics-trends-and-reports/nationalhealthexpenddata/nhe-fact-sheet.html (accessed February 20, 2017).
9. Chernew 2010; www.kff.org/medicare/fact-sheet/medicare-spending-and-financing-fact-sheet/ (accessed August 3, 2016).
10. "National Health Expenditures Fact Sheet, 2015," Centers for Medicare and Medicaid Services, U.S. Department of Health and Human Services, at www.cms.gov/research-statistics-data-and-systems/statistics-trends-and-reports/nationalhealthexpenddata/nhe-fact-sheet.html (accessed February 20, 2017).
11. St. Louis Federal Reserve Bank data, at www.research.stlouisfed.org/fred2/series/GFDEGDQ188S (accessed August 3, 2016).
12. "National Health Expenditures Fact Sheet, 2014," Centers for Medicare and Medicaid Services, U.S. Department of Health and Human Services, at www.cms.gov/research-statistics-data-and-systems/statistics-trends-and-reports/nationalhealthexpenddata/nhe-fact-sheet.html (accessed February 20, 2017).
13. Kaiser Family Foundation, "Visualizing Health Policy: Recent Trends in Employer-Sponsored Health Insurance Premiums" at www.kff.org/slideshow/recent-trends-in-employer-sponsored-health-insurance-premiums/ (accessed February 20, 2017). Centers for Medicare and Medicaid Services, U.S. Department of Health and Human Services, "National Health Expenditure Projections 2014–2024," available at www.cms.gov/Research-Statistics-Data-and-Systems/Statistics-Trends-and-Reports/NationalHealthExpendData/Downloads/proj2016.pdf (accessed February 20, 2017).

14. Commonwealth Fund, "How High Is America's Health Care Cost Burden?" November 2015, at www.commonwealthfund.org/publications/issue-briefs/2015/nov/how-high-health-care-burden (accessed February 20, 2017).

15. U.S. Department of Health and Human Services, "National Health Expenditure 2014 Highlights," at www.cms.gov/research-statistics-data-and-systems/statistics-trends-and-reports/nationalhealthexpenddata/downloads/highlights.pdf (accessed February 20, 2017).

16. Willemé and Dumont 2015, studying data from OECD countries.

17. Smith et al. 2009.

18. Chernew 2010; Peden and Freeland 1995.

19. For a discussion, see www.hopkinsmedicine.org/healthlibrary/test_procedures/orthopaedic/vertebroplasty_135,37/ (accessed August 3, 2016).

20. Cutler 2006; Chandra and Skinner 2012.

21. The 2009 American Recovery and Reinvestment Act earmarked $1.1 billion for comparative effectiveness research; see Health Policy Brief, October 5, 2010, at www.healthaffairs.org/healthpolicybriefs/brief.php?brief_id=27 (accessed October 26, 2016).

22. Congressional Budget Office 2014a; Centers for Medicare and Medicaid Services, U.S. Department of Health and Human Services, "National Health Expenditure Projections 2014–2024," at www.cms.gov/Research-Statistics-Data-and-Systems/Statistics-Trends-and-Reports/NationalHealthExpendData/Downloads/proj2016.pdf (accessed February 20, 2017); and "National Health Expenditures 2015 Highlights," at www.cms.gov/research-statistics-data-and-systems/statistics-trends-and-reports/nationalhealthexpenddata/downloads/highlights.pdf (accessed February 20, 2017).

23. Alpern et al. 2014.

24. CMS data at www.cms.gov/Newsroom/MediaReleaseDatabase/Factsheets/2015-Fact-sheets-items/2015–12–21.html (accessed February 23, 2016).

25. Bach 2015.

26. Cha 2015; Pollack 2015.

27. Angell 2015.

28. Morgenson 2015.

29. Silverman 2015.

30. Walker 2015.

31. Ellison and Wolfram 2006.

32. Karlin-Smith 2016.

33. Owens 2016.

34. Stremikis et al. 2008.

35. Levine and Mulligan 2015; Kale et al. 2013; Gawande 2009.

36. Health Affairs 2012.

37. Orzag 2011, working with data from the Medicare Payment Advisory Commission.

38. Centers for Medicare and Medicaid Services, U.S. Department of Health and Human Services, "National Health Expenditures Fact Sheet 2014," at www

.cms.gov/research-statistics-data-and-systems/statistics-trends-and-reports/
nationalhealthexpenddata/nhe-fact-sheet.html (accessed February 20, 2017).

39. Gawande 2009.

40. Government Accountability Office 2013.

41. Skinner et al. 2006.

42. Califano 1988, p. 44.

43. Zhang et al. 2012; Levine and Mulligan 2015.

44. Government Accountability Office 2013.

45. Mann and Ornstein 2006, 2012.

46. Davis 2013.

47. Historical Budget tables from the Office of Management and Budget, at
www.obamawhitehouse.archives.gov/omb/budget/Historicals (accessed February 20, 2017).

48. Samples 2006.

49. 1997 Balanced Budget Act (PL-105–33).

50. Laugesen 2009; Steinbrook 2015.

51. Laugesen 2009.

52. Reschovsky et al. 2015.

53. *Congressional Quarterly* 2014, pp. 8-3, 8-4.

54. Reschovsky et al. 2015; Sullivan and Ferris 2015.

55. Doherty 2015.

56. Sullivan and Ferris 2015.

57. Medicare enrollment reached this level in 2002.

58. Oliver et al. 2004.

59. Ibid.

60. Connolly 2004, p. A4. "Medicare Part D Spending Trends," Kaiser Family
Foundation Issue Brief, May 2012, at www.kff.org/health-costs/issue-brief/
medicare-part-d-spending-trends-understanding-key/ (accessed February 20, 2017).

61. Donohue 2014; Congressional Budget Office 2014a.

62. Shih et al. 2016.

63. Oliver et al. 2004.

64. Ibid., p. 319.

65. Ibid., p. 320.

66. Kaiser Health Tracking Poll, September 2016. "Please tell me whether you
would favor or oppose the following actions to keep prescription drug costs
down. . . . Allowing the federal government to negotiate with drug companies to
get a lower price on medications for people on Medicare" (N = 604 national
adults). Details at www.kff.org/health-costs/report/kaiser-health-tracking-poll-
september-2016/ (accessed February 20, 2017).

67. Herper 2012.

68. Centers for Medicare and Medicaid Services rule, at www.medicaid.gov/
medicaid-chip-program-information/by-topics/benefits/prescription-drugs/
downloads/drug-fact-sheet.pdf (accessed August 2016).

69. Whoriskey and Keating 2013.

70. Ornstein 2014.

71. Pear 2015a,b.

72. Frank and Newhouse 2008; Frakt et al. 2008; Congressional Budget Office 2013.

73. Lopert and Moon 2007; Frakt et al. 2008.

74. Ana Ibarra, "Voters Say Yes to Marijuana Legalization, Tobacco Tax; Reject Drug Price Initiative," at www.Californiahealthline.org (accessed November 14, 2016).

75. Political contribution data at www.crs.org (accessed February 20, 2017).

76. Lopert and Moon 2007.

77. Emanuel 2014, pp. 219–21.

78. Gruber 2011; Blumberg et al. 2014.

79. Orzag 2011.

80. Ibid.

81. Ibid.; Emanuel 2014, p. 229.

82. Emanuel 2014, p. 227; CMS information at www.cms.gov/Medicare/Medicare-Fee-for-Service-Payment/sharedsavingsprogram/Downloads/PioneersMSSPCombinedFastFacts.pdf (accessed February 22, 2016).

83. Abrams et al. 2015.

84. Reschovsky et al. 2015.

85. Emanuel 2014.

86. Orzag 2011; Oberlander and Weaver 2015; AMA explanation at www.ama-assn.org/ama/pub/advocacy/topics/independent-payment-advisory-board.page? (accessed August 3, 2016).

87. HR 2, 112th Congress, 1st session. See Chapter 2 for discussion.

88. Congressional Budget Office 2015.

89. Ibid.

90. Ibid.

91. Kaiser Family Foundation, "The Uninsured: A Primer," November 2015, at www.files.kff.org/attachment/primer-the-uninsured-a-primer-key-facts-about-health-insurance-and-the-uninsured-in-the-era-of-health-reform (accessed February 23, 2016). Centers for Disease Control and Infection data for 2015, at www.cdc.gov/nchs/data/nhis/earlyrelease/insur201508.pdf (accessed October 25, 2016). Press release from HHS, September 7, 2016, at www.hhs.gov/about/news/2016/09/07/statement-by-secretary-burwell-on-the-uninsured-rate.html (accessed November 15, 2016).

92. CDC data at www.cdc.gov/nchs/data/nhis/earlyrelease/insur201508.pdf (accessed October 26, 16).

93. Gallup Poll, "In the long run, how do you think the healthcare law will affect your family's healthcare situation? . . . Make better, not make much difference, make worse" (N = 1,549 national adults). Poll details available through the Roper Center's iPOLL Databank at Cornell University.

94. Corman and Levin 2016.

Chapter 6   A Frustrated Search for the Public's Voice

1. Shapiro and Bloch-Elkon 2008, p. 117.
2. Zaller 1992; Levendusky 2009; Schneider and Jacoby 2005.
3. Kriner and Reeves 2014.
4. Yankelovich 1991; Fishkin 1995; Druckman 2004.
5. Gigerenzer et al. 1999.
6. Dahl 1956; Popkin 1991; Page and Shapiro 1992; Zaller 1992; Lupia and McCubbins 1998.
7. Key 1961, 1966; Prior and Lupia 2008.
8. Lippmann 1922; Schumpeter 1942; Schattschneider 1960.
9. Sartori 1987, p. 123.
10. Schumpeter 1942, pp. 261–62.
11. Mutz 2006; Muirhead 2010.
12. Aldrich 2011.
13. Mutz 2006; Levendusky 2009.
14. Fishkin 1995.
15. Blendon et al. 2006.
16. Price et al. 2006; Brodie et al., 2010.
17. Friedman 2006; Holbrook et al. 2005.
18. Further information available from author.
19. Other knowledge questions were fielded into early 2016, but none of these later months saw at least four questions; therefore, they are left out of this part of the analysis.
20. A t-test for difference of means confirms a significant difference in comparing true and false provisions, but not when comparing false provisions to the multiple-choice items.
21. Kriner and Reeves 2014.
22. Based on t-test of difference of means, this gap is significant at better than a 99 percent confidence level; party identification based on Kaiser's question, excluding independents.
23. Independents included leaners.
24. Kaiser Health Tracking Poll, September 2016. "To the best of your knowledge, is the rate of Americans who do not have health insurance at an all-time high, at an all-time low, or about the same as it has been?" (N = 1,204 national adults). Details at www.kff.org/health-costs/report/kaiser-health-tracking-poll-september-2016/ (accessed February 20, 2017).
25. The percentage of correct answers from Democrats versus Republicans correlates at 0.7 across all items and at 0.65 among the frequently asked questions (Pearson r significant at better than 99 percent confidence level).
26. Based on the standardized coefficients produced by ordinary least squares regression. Independent variables include age, insurance status, household income during the prior year, education level, and dummy variables for Democrats and independents. The adjusted R^2 for 2014 was 0.133, and for 2010 it was

0.039 (F-test significant for both). The 2010 survey included 1,202 respondents, and the 2014 included 1,494. Data are available from the Roper Center's iPOLL Databank.

27. Ackerman and Fishkin 2004.

28. Corman and Levin 2016, Tables 1 and 3.

29. Brodie et al. 2010; Jacobs and Mettler 2011; Corman and Levin 2016, Tables 15, 19, 20.

30. Corman and Levin 2016, Table 1.

31. Henderson and Hillygus 2011.

32. Ibid.

33. Harris Interactive series asked, "What do you think are the two most important issues for the government to address?"

34. Corman and Levin 2016, Table 1.

35. Brodie et al. 2010.

36. Henderson and Hillygus 2011.

37. Egan 2013, especially pp. 82–83. See also Achen and Bartels 2016.

38. Brodie et al. 2010.

39. Corman and Levin 2016, Table 15.

40. Kaiser's Health Tracking Poll at www.kff.org (accessed February 20, 2017).

41. See, for instance, Corman and Levin 2016, Table 23.

42. Aldrich 2011.

43. Kaiser Family Foundation, "So far, would you say the health care law has directly helped you and your family, directly hurt you and your family, or has it not had a direct impact?" Polls span May 2014 to December 2015. Details at http://kff.org/health-reform/poll-finding/kaiser-health-tracking-poll-may-2014/ (accessed February 20, 2017).

44. Corman and Levin 2016, Table 28. "Do you think the nation will be better off or worse off under the health reform law, or don't you think it will make much difference?"

45. Kaiser Health Tracking Poll, January 2014 (N = 1,506 national adults). Details at /kff.org/health-reform/poll-finding/kaiser-health-tracking-poll-january-2014/ (accessed February 20, 2017).

46. Lynch and Gollust 2010; Brady and Kessler 2010; Gelman et al. 2010.

47. Converse 1990, p. 372.

48. House 2015.

49. Converse 1964.

50. Converse 1975, p. 125.

51. Sartori 1987, p. 110.

52. Achen and Bartels 2016.

53. Prior and Lupia 2008; Lupia and McCubbins 1998.

54. Mondak and Davis 2001.

55. Zaller 1992.

56. Bullock 2011.

57. Kriner and Reeves 2014; see also Abramowitz and Saunders 1998; Shapiro and Bloch-Elkon 2008; Blendon et al. 2010.

58. Dewey 1927.

59. Ackerman and Fishkin 2004.

Chapter 7 Repealing the Affordable Care Act: Now What?

1. Shapiro and Arrow 2009; Blendon et al. 2011.

2. McDonough 2011, Chapter 3.

3. See Oberlander and Weaver 2015 for a thoughtful discussion on this point.

4. See Achen and Bartels 2016 for a discussion of public myopia.

5. Based on polling by Kaiser Family Foundation, May 2016, at www.kff.org/health-reform/press-release/survey-finds-most-marketplace-enrollees-like-their-coverage-though-satisfaction-with-premiums-and-deductibles-has-declined-since-2014/ (accessed October 25, 2016).

6. For one example, see Republican Representative Eric Cantor's talking points, at www.nytimes.com/interactive/2013/11/21/us/politics/21republican-talking-points.html (accessed October 26, 2016).

7. Lippmann 1922; Converse 1964; Delli Carpini and Keeter 1996.

8. Ackerman and Fishkin 2004.

9. Bentley 1909; Berelson et al. 1954; Campbell et al. 1960.

10. For a strident statement, see Turner et al. 2011. For a more balanced treatment, see www.rand.org/pubs/research_briefs/RB9672/index1.html (accessed August 6, 2016).

11. Jost 2007; Schneider and Hall 2009.

12. Arrow 1963.

13. See Mirowski and Plehwe 2009.

14. Pear 2016.

15. See HHS testimony before Congress, 7/12/16, at www.hhs.gov/asl/testify/2016/07/t20160713a.html (accessed October 26, 2016).

16. Pear and Kaplan, 2017; Martin 2017.

17. Mary Ellen McIntire, "AMA Says New Health Policy Must Maintain Coverage for All Currently Covered," at www.morningconsult.com (accessed November 16, 2016).

18. Gary Claxton, Matthew Rae, and Nirmita Panchal, "Consumer Assets and Patient Cost Sharing," KFF, February 2015 Issue Brief, at kff.org (accessed August 6, 2016). This work uses the Federal Reserve Board's Survey of Consumer Finance data.

19. Ibid.

20. Altman 2016b.

21. Gary Claxton, Larry Levitt, and Michelle Long, "Payments for Cost Sharing Increasing Rapidly over Time," at www.healthsystemtracker.org (accessed October 20, 2016).

22. See www.redstate.com/california_yankee/2016/03/18/rise-obamacares-surprise-medical-bills/ (accessed October 20, 2016).

23. See *Wall Street Journal* article, at www.wsj.com/articles/surprise-bills-for-many-under-health-law-1434042543 (accessed October 25, 2016).

24. See www.healthaffairs.org/blog/2015/11/03/a-tale-of-two-deliveries-or-an-out-of-network-problem/ (accessed October 25, 2016).

25. See *Time* magazine story at www.time.com/4246845/health-care-insurance-suprise-medical-bill/ (accessed October 25, 2016).

26. Stone 1993; Schneider and Hall 2009.

27. Herman 2015.

28. Kaiser Family Foundation report, at www.kff.org/private-insurance/issue-brief/surprise-medical-bills/ (accessed October 25, 2016).

29. See www.consumerist.com/2015/10/21/lawmakers-introduce-legislation-to-curtail-surprise-medical-bills/ (accessed October 25, 2016).

30. See rule at www.federalregister.gov/documents/2016/03/08/2016–04439/patient-protection-and-affordable-care-act-hhs-notice-of-benefit-and-payment-parameters-for-2017 (accessed October 25, 2016).

31. Popkin 1991; Lupia and McCubbins 1998; Gigerenzer et al. 1999; Prior and Lupia 2008.

32. Burwell 2015. See Gerber et al. 2014 for discussion of the controversy.

33. Yankelovich 1991; Fishkin 1995; Ackerman and Fishkin 2004; Newport 2004.

34. Schumpeter 1942, p. 283.

35. Schattschneider 1942, p. 52.

36. Achen and Bartels 2016.

37. Egan 2013.

38. See Sartori 1987 for discussion.

39. Jones 2013.

40. For instance, the Hatch, Burr, Upton proposal retains these emphases. Other GOP proposals place much more emphasis instead on incentivizing consumer-like behavior. For an assessment of these alternatives, see Altman 2016a.

41. Based on large-sample polling by Gallup, at www.gallup.com/poll/190484/uninsured-rate-lowest-eight-year-trend.aspx (accessed August 6, 2016).

42. See Peter Cunningham, Robin Rudowitz, Katherine Young, Rachel Garfield, and Julia Foutz, "Understanding Medicaid Hospital Payments and the Impact of Recent Policy Changes," June 2016, at www.kff.org (accessed June 9, 2016).

43. Jacobs, Marmor, and Oberlander 1999; Sirianni and Friedland 2001, Chapter 4.

44. Fishkin 1995; Luskin et al. 2002; Sturgis et al. 2005.

45. Gastil and Dillard 1999; Goidel et al. 2008.

46. Fung 2003.

47. Rosen 1999; Roden and Steinberg 2003.

48. Hacker 1997; Sirianni and Friedland 2001, p. 166.

49. Washington Post Staff 2010; Starr 2013.

50. According to the Centers for Disease Control and Prevention; see summary in the *British Medical Journal*, at www.bmj.com/content/353/bmj.i2139 (accessed October 25, 2016).

51. Fishkin 1995; Fung 2003; Ackerman and Fishkin 2004; but see also Mutz 2006.

52. Jacobs and Shapiro 2000.

Suggested Further Readings

On the Passage and Impacts of the Affordable Care Act

Daniel Béland, Philip Rocco, and Alex Wadden. *The Obamacare Wars: Federalism, State Politics, and the Affordable Care Act.* University Press of Kansas, Lawrence, 2016.

Steven Brill. *America's Bitter Pill: Money, Politics, Backroom Deals, and the Fight to Fix Our Broken Healthcare System.* Random House, New York, 2015.

Lawrence Jacobs and Theda Skocpol. *Health Care Reform and American Politics: What Everyone Needs to Know.* Oxford University Press, New York, 2010.

John McDonough. *Inside National Health Reform.* University of California Press, Berkeley, 2011.

The Staff of *The Washington Post. Landmark: The Inside Story of America's New Health-Care Law and What It Means for Us All.* Public Affairs, New York, 2010.

Paul Starr. *Remedy and Reaction: The Peculiar American Struggle over Health Care Reform.* Yale University Press, New Haven, CT, 2013.

Critiques of the Affordable Care Act

James House. *Beyond Obamacare: Life, Death, and Social Policy.* Russell Sage Foundation, New York, 2015.

Grace-Marie Turner, James Capretta, Thomas Miller, and Robert Moffit. *Why Obamacare Is Wrong for America.* HarperCollins, New York, 2011.

On Consumer-Driven Health Care

Regina Herzlinger (editor). *Consumer-Driven Health Care: Implications for Providers, Payers, and Policymakers.* Jossey-Bass, San Francisco, 2004.

Timothy Jost. *Health Care at Risk: A Critique of the Consumer-Driven Movement.* Duke University Press, Durham, NC, 2007.

Historical Works on U.S. Health Care Policy and Politics

Philip Funigiello. *Chronic Politics: Health Care Security from FDR to George W. Bush.* University of Kansas Press, Lawrence, 2005.

Theodore Marmor. *The Politics of Medicare*, 2nd edition. Aldine de Gruyter, New York, 2000.

Jill Quadagno. *One Nation, Uninsured: Why the U.S. Has No National Health Insurance.* Oxford University Press, New York, 2005.

Greg Shaw. *The Healthcare Debate.* ABC/CLIO, Santa Barbara, CA, 2010.

Bibliography

Abramowitz, Alan, and Kyle Saunders. 1998. "Ideological Realignment in the U.S. Electorate." *Journal of Politics* 60 (3): 642–44.

Abrams, Melinda, Rachel Nuzum, Stuart Guterman, Mark Zezza, Jamie Ryan, and Jordan Kiszla. 2015, May 7. "The Affordable Care Act's Payment and Delivery System Reforms: A Progress Report at Five Years," The Commonwealth Fund, New York, NY.

Achen, Christopher, and Larry Bartels. 2016. *Democracy for Realists: Why Elections Do Not Produce Responsive Government.* Princeton: Princeton University Press.

Ackerman, Bruce, and James Fishkin. 2004. *Deliberation Day.* New Haven, CT: Yale University Press.

Aldrich, John. 2011. *Why Parties? A Second Look.* Chicago: University of Chicago Press.

Alexander, G. Caleb, Lawrence Casalino, Chien-Wen Tseng, Diane McFadden, and David Metzler. 2004. "Barriers to Patient-Physician Communication about Out-of-Pocket Costs." *Journal of General Internal Medicine* 19: 856–60.

Alpern, Jonathan, William Stauffer, and Aaron Kesselheim. 2014. "High-Cost Generic Drugs—Implications for Patients and Policy Makers." *New England Journal of Medicine* 371: 1859–62.

Altman, Drew. 2016a. "The Fundamentally Different Goals of the Affordable Care Act and Republican 'Replacement' Plans." *Wall Street Journal*, June 7.

Altman, Drew. 2016b. "The Missing Debate over Rising Health-Care Deductibles." *The Wall Street Journal*, September 18.

American Academy of Actuaries Consumer-Driven Health Plans Work Group. 2009. "Emerging Data on Consumer-Driven Health Plans" (May). American Academy of Actuaries, Washington, D.C.

Angell, Marcia. 2015. "Why Do Drug Companies Charge So Much? Because They Can." *The Washington Post*, September 25.

Appleby, Julie. 2005. "Mass. Gov. Romney's Health Care Plan Says Everyone Pays." *USA Today*, July 5, p. 3B.

Arrow, Kenneth. 1963. "Uncertainty and the Welfare Economics of Medical Care." *American Economic Review* 53: 941–73.

Arvidson, Erik. 2005. "Speaker Vows to Pass Health Reform," *The Berkshire Eagle* (Pittsfield, MA), October 8.

Ayanian, John, Sarah Clark, and Renuka Tipirneni. 2014. "Launching the Healthy Michigan Plan—The First 100 Days." *New England Journal of Medicine* 371: 1573–75.

Bach, Peter. 2015. "How the U.S. Could Cure Drug Price Insanity." *Forbes*, September 17 (accessed February 20, 2016).

Bacon, Perry, Jr. 2010a. "GOP Lawmakers, Candidates Promise to 'Repeal It.'" *The Washington Post*, March 18, p. A-4. The pledge can be found at www.therepealpledge.com/ (accessed October 25, 2016).

Bacon, Perry, Jr. 2010b. "Health-Care Bill Not Yet a Law, but Republicans Organize to Oppose It." *The Washington Post*, March 17.

Barnett, Randy. 2010. "Can the Constitution Stop Health-Care Reform?" *The Washington Post*, March 21, p. B2.

Barrilleaux, Charles, and Carlisle Rainey. 2014. "The Politics of Need: Examining Governors' Decisions to Oppose the 'Obamacare' Medicaid Expansion." *State Politics and Policy Quarterly* 14 (2): 437–60.

Béland, Daniel. 2005. *Social Security: History and Politics from the New Deal to the Privatization Debate*. Lawrence: University of Kansas Press.

Béland, Daniel, Philip Rocco, and Alex Wadden. 2016. *The Obamacare Wars: Federalism, State Politics, and the Affordable Care Act*. Lawrence: University Press of Kansas.

Bentley, Arthur. 1909. *The Process of Government: A Study of Social Pressures*. Chicago: University of Chicago Press.

Berelson, Bernard, Paul Lazarsfeld, and William McPhee. 1954. *Voting: A Study of Opinion Formation in a Presidential Campaign*. Chicago: University of Chicago Press.

Blendon, Robert, John Benson, Gillian SteelFisher, and John Connolly. 2010. "Americans' Conflicting Views about the Public Health System, and How to Shore Up Support." *Health Affairs* 29 (11): 2033–40.

Blendon, Robert, Mollyann Brodie, John Benson, and Drew Altman. 2011. *American Public Opinion and Health Care*. Washington, D.C.: CQ Press.

Blendon, Robert, Mollyann Brodie, John Benson, Drew Altman, and Tami Buhr. 2006. "Americans' View of Health Care Costs, Access, and Quality." *The Milbank Quarterly* 84 (4): 623–57.

Blendon, Robert, Tami Buhr, Tara Sussman, and John Benson. 2008. "Massachusetts Health Reform: A Public Perspective from Debate through Implementation." *Health Affairs* 27 (6): 556–65.

Blumberg, Linda, Timothy Waidmann, Fredric Blavin, and Jeremy Roth. 2014. "Trends in Health Care Financial Burdens, 2001 to 2009." *The Milbank Quarterly* 92 (1): 88–113.

Brady, David, and Daniel Kessler. 2010. "Who Supports Health Reform?" *PS: Political Science and Politics* 43 (1): 1–6.

Brill, Steven. 2014. "Bitter Pill: How Outrageous Pricing and Egregious Profits Are Destroying Our Health Care." *Time*, March 14.

Brill, Steven. 2015. *America's Bitter Pill: Money, Politics, Backroom Deals, and the Fight to Fix Our Broken Healthcare System*. New York: Random House.

Broder, David. 2006. "For Romney, A Healthy Boost; Insurance Plan an Asset for '08." *The Washington Post*, April 30, p. B7.

Brodie, Mollyann, Drew Altman, Claudia Deane, Sasha Buscho, and Elizabeth Hamel. 2010. "Liking the Pieces, Not the Package: Contradictions in Public Opinion during Health Reform." *Health Affairs* 29 (6): 1125–30.

Brown, Trevor. 2015. "Projections Show Medicaid Expansion Would Cover 20K in Wyoming." *Wyoming Tribune Eagle*, December 14.

Bullock, John. 2011. "Elite Influence on Public Opinion in and Informed Electorate." *American Political Science Review* 105 (3): 496–515.

Burwell, Sylvia. 2015. "Setting Value-Based Payment Goals—HHS Efforts to Improve U.S. Health Care." *New England Journal of Medicine* 372 (10): 897–99.

Butler, Stuart. 1989. *Assuring Affordable Health Care for All Americans*. Heritage Foundation, Washington, D.C., p. 3.

Butler, Stuart. 2012. "Don't Blame Heritage for ObamaCare Mandate." *USA Today*, February 6.

Butler, Stuart, and Edmund Haislmaier. 1989. *A National Health System for America*. Washington, D.C.: Heritage Foundation.

Califano, Joseph. 1988. "The Health-Care Chaos." *The New York Times*, March 20, p. 44.

Campbell, Angus, Philip Converse, Warren Miller, and Donald Stokes. 1960. *The American Voter*. New York: John Wiley and Sons.

Cannon, Michael, and Michael Tanner. 2005. *Healthy Competition: What's Holding Back Health Care and How to Free It*. Washington, D.C.: Cato Institute.

Capretta, James, and Yuval Levin. 2014. "Getting There: How to Transition from Obamacare to Real Health Care Reform." *Weekly Standard* 20 (2): 26–29.

Catlin, Aaron, and Cathy Cowan. 2015, November. "History of Health Spending in the United States, 1960–2013." Document available at the Centers for Medicare and Medicaid Services, Baltimore, MD.

Cha, Ariana Eungung. 2015. "Drug and Biotech Industry Trade Groups Give Martin Shkreli the Boot." *The Washington Post*, September 24.

Chandra, Amitabh, and Jonathan Skinner. 2012. "Technology Growth and Expenditure Growth in Health Care." *Journal of Economic Literature* 50 (3): 645–80.

Chernew, Michael. 2010. "Health Care Spending Growth: Can We Avoid Fiscal Armageddon?" *Inquiry* 47 (4): 285–95.

Christenson, Dino, and David Glick. 2015. "Issue-Specific Opinion Change: The Supreme Court and Health Care Reform." *Public Opinion Quarterly* 79 (4): 881–905.

Claxton, Gary, Larry Levitt, and Michelle Long. 2016. "Payments for Cost Shar-ing Increasing Rapidly." April 2, at www.healthsystemtracker.org/insight/ payments-for-cost-sharing-increasing-rapidly-over-time/ (accessed Octo-ber 25, 2016).

Cogan, John, R. Glenn Hubbard, and Daniel Kessler. 2011. *Healthy, Wealthy, and Wise: Five Steps to a Better Health Care System*, 2nd edition. Washington, D.C.: American Enterprise Institute Press.

Cohn, Jonathan. 2009a. "Mass Appeal." *The New Republic* 240 (4872): 10–11.

Cohn, Jonathan. 2009b. "The Operator." *The New Republic* 240 (4862): 21–23.

Cohn, Jonathan. 2010. "How They Did It." *The New Republic* 241 (4884): 16.

Congressional Budget Office. 2013. *Health-Related Options for Reducing the Deficit: 2014–2023.* December. Washington, D.C.: Congressional Budget Office.

Congressional Budget Office. 2014a. *Competition and the Cost of Medicare's Pre-scription Drug Program.* July. Washington, D.C.: Congressional Budget Office.

Congressional Budget Office. 2014b. *Payments of Penalties for Being Uninsured under the Affordable Care Act: 2014 Update.* June. Washington, D.C.: Con-gressional Budget Office.

Congressional Budget Office. 2015. *Budgetary and Economic Effects of Repealing the Affordable Care Act.* June. Washington, D.C.: Congressional Budget Office.

Congressional Quarterly [Various years]. *America Votes.* Congressional Quarterly Press, Washington, D.C.

Congressional Quarterly [Various years]. *Congressional Quarterly Almanac.* Con-gressional Quarterly Press, Washington, D.C.

Connolly, Cici. 2004. "OMB Says Medicare Drug Law Could Cost Still More." *The Washington Post*, September 19, p. A4.

Converse, Philip. 1964. "The Nature of Belief Systems in Mass Publics," in David Apter (editor) *Ideology and Discontent*, pp. 206–61. Glencoe, IL: Free Press.

Converse, Philip. 1975. "Public Opinion and Voting Behavior," in Fred Green-stein and Nelson Polsby (editors) *Handbook of Political Science, Volume 4*, pp. 75–169. Reading, MA: Addison-Wesley.

Converse, Philip. 1990. "Popular Representation and the Distribution of Infor-mation," in John Ferejon and James Kuklinski (editors) *Information and Democratic Processes*, pp. 369–88. Urbana: University of Illinois Press.

Corman, Juliane, and David Levin. 2016. "Support for Government Provision of Health Care and the Patient Protection and Affordable Care Act." *Public Opinion Quarterly* 80 (1): 114–79.

Cornyn, John. 2013. "Obama Must Engage Congress." *The Houston Chronicle*, January 4.

Costa, Robert. 2014. "Cantor Attempts to Rebrand the House GOP, and Himself." *The Washington Post*, March 25, p. A1.

Coughlin, Teresa, Leighton Ku, and John Holahan. 1994. *Medicaid since 1980: Costs, Coverage, and the Shifting Alliance between the Federal Government and the States.* Washington, D.C.: The Urban Institute Press.

Cross, Frank. 2009. *The Theory and Practice of Statutory Interpretation*. Stanford: Stanford University Law Books.

Cutler, David. 2006. "Making Sense of Medical Technology." *Health Affairs* 25 (2): 48–50.

Dahl, Robert. 1956. *A Preface to Democratic Theory*. Chicago: University of Chicago Press.

Daschle, Tom. 2010. *Getting It Done: How Obama and Congress Finally Broke the Stalemate to Make Way for Health Care Reform*. New York: St. Martin's Press.

Davey, Monica. 2013. "Michigan Passes Bill to Expand Medicaid." *The New York Times*, August 28, p. A14.

Davis, Christopher. 2013. *"Fast Track" Legislative Procedures Governing Congressional Consideration of a Defense Base Closure and Realignment (BRAC) Commission Report*. Washington, D.C.: Congressional Research Service.

Delli Carpini, Michael, and Scott Keeter. 1996. *What Americans Know about Politics and Why It Matters*. New Haven, CT: Yale University Press.

Devitt, Caitlin. 2013. "Michigan Senate Hands Snyder Victory with Medicaid Expansion." *The Bond Buyer*, August 29.

Dewey, John. 1927. *The Public and Its Problems*. New York: Henry Holt.

Dickson, Virgil. 2015. "Indiana's Medicaid Expansion Waivers Raises Lockout Concerns." *Modern Healthcare*, January 31 (available at www.modern healthcare.com/article/20150131/MAGAZINE/301319961 accessed February 22, 2017).

Dixon, Anna, Jessica Greene, and Judith Hibbard. 2008. "Do Consumer-Directed Health Plans Drive Change in Enrollees' Health Care Behavior?" *Health Affairs* 27 (4): 1120–31.

Doherty, Robert. 2015. "Goodbye, Sustainable Growth Rate—Hello, Merit-Based Incentive Payment System." *Annals of Internal Medicine* 163 (2): 138–39.

Donohue, Julie. 2014. "The Impact and Evolution of Medicare Part D." *New England Journal of Medicine* 371 (8): 693–95.

Dreyfuss, Bob. 2001. "Grover Norquist: Field Marshall of the Bush Plan." *The Nation*, April 26.

Druckman, James. 2004. "Political Preference Formation: Competition, Deliberation, and the (Ir)relevance of Framing Effects." *American Political Science Review* 98 (4): 671–86.

Egan, Patrick. 2013. *Partisan Priorities: How Issue Ownership Drives and Distorts American Politics*. New York: Cambridge University Press.

Eggen, Dan, and Philip Rucker. 2009. "Loose Network of Activists Drives Reform Opposition." *The Washington Post*, August 16, p. A1.

Eilperin, Juliet. 2013. "Obama Apologizes over Promise on Health-Care Law." *The Washington Post*, November 8, p. A1.

Ellison, Sara Fisher, and Catherine Wolfram. 2006. "Coordinating on Lower Prices: Pharmaceutical Pricing under Political Pressure." *The RAND Journal of Economics* 37 (2): 324–40.

Emanuel, Ezekiel. 2014. *Reinventing American Health Care.* Philadelphia: Perseus Books Group.

Epstein, Arnold, Benjamin Sommers, Yelena Kuznetsov, and Robert Blendon. 2014. "Low-Income Residents in Three States View Medicaid as Equal to or Better Than Private Coverage, Support Expansion." *Health Affairs* 33 (11): 2041–47.

Epstein, Reid. 2014. "Conservative Thinker Stuart Butler Leaves Heritage for Brookings." *Wall Street Journal*, July 25, at www.wsj.com (accessed February 20, 2015).

Epstein, Richard. 1997. *Mortal Peril: Our Inalienable Right to Health Care?* Reading, MA: Addison-Wesley.

Farley, Robert. 2009. "Palin Claims Obama Misled When He Said End-of-Life Counseling Is Voluntary." *St. Petersburg Times* (FL), August 13.

Feldstein, Martin. 1973. "The Welfare Loss of Excess Health Insurance." *Journal of Political Economy* 81 (March/April): 251–80.

Ferris, Sarah. 2015. "GOP Divided on ObamaCare Replacement." *The Hill*, February 6.

Fishkin, James. 1995. *The Voice of the People: Public Opinion and Democracy.* New Haven, CT: Yale University Press.

Flagg, Robin. 2016. "Medicaid Expansion: A Tale of Two Governors." *Journal of Health Policy, Politics and Law* 41 (5): 997–1031.

Frakt, Austin. 2011. "How Much Do Hospitals Cost Shift? A Review of the Evidence." *The Milbank Quarterly* 89 (1): 90–130.

Frakt, Austin, Steven Pizer, and Ann Hendricks. 2008. "Controlling Prescription Drug Costs: Regulation and the Role of Interest Groups in Medicare and the Veterans Health Administration." *Journal of Health Politics, Policy and Law* 33 (6): 1079–1106.

Frank, Richard, and Joseph Newhouse. 2008. "Should Drug Prices Be Negotiated under Part D of Medicare? And If So, How?" *Health Affairs* 27 (1): 33–43.

Friedman, Bruce, Peter Veazie, Benjamin Chapman, Willard Manning, and Paul Duberstein. 2013. "Is Personality Associated with Health Care Use by Older Adults." *The Milbank Quarterly* 91 (3): 491–527.

Friedman, Jeffrey. 2006. "Democratic Competence in Normative and Positive Theory: Neglected Implications of 'The Nature of Belief Systems in Mass Publics.'" *Critical Review* 18 (1–3): i–xliii.

Friedman, Milton. 1991. "Gammon's Law Points to Health-Care Solution." *The Wall Street Journal*, November 12, p. A20.

Friendersdorf, Conor. 2012. "Newt Gingrich Supported an Individual Mandate as Recently as May 2009" [Audio clip]. January 30, at http://www.the atlantic.com/politics/archive/2012/01/newt-gingrich-supported-an-individual-mandate-as-recently-as-may-2009/252233/ (accessed January 29, 2017).

Fronstin, Paul. 2010. "What Do We Really Know about Consumer-Driven Health Plans?" August (Issue Brief 345), Employee Benefit Research Institute, Washington, D.C.

Fronstin, Paul, and Christopher Roebuck. 2014. "Quality of Health Care after Adopting a Full-Replacement, High-Deductible Health Savings Account: A Five-Year Study." September (Issue Brief 404), Employee Benefit Research Institute, Washington, D.C.

Fung, Archon. 2003. "Recipes for Public Spheres: Eight Institutional Design Choices and Their Consequences." *The Journal of Political Philosophy* 11 (3): 338–67.

Gantert, Tom. 2013. "Medicaid Expansion Bill Heads to the House," Michigan Capitol Confidential news service from the MacKinac Center for Public Policy. June 13, at www.michigancapitolconfidential.com (accessed July 15, 2015).

Gastil, John, and James Dillard. 1999. "Increasing Political Sophistication through Public Deliberation." *Political Communication* 16: 3–23.

Gavant, Kelli. 2006. "Romney Touts Mass. Health Insurance Plan." *The Patriot Ledger* (Quincy, MA), April 26, p. 17.

Gawande, Atul. 2005. "Piecework: Medicine's Money Problem." *The New Yorker*, April 4, pp. 44–54.

Gawande, Atul. 2009. "The Cost Conundrum." *The New Yorker*, June 1, pp. 36–44.

Gelman, Andrew, Daniel Lee, and Yair Ghitza. 2010. "Public Opinion on Health Care Reform." *The Forum* 8 (1): 1–14.

Gerber, Alan, Eric Patashnik, David Doherty, and Conor Dowling. 2014. "Doctor Knows Best: Physician Endorsements, Public Opinion, and the Politics of Comparative Effectiveness Research." *Journal of Health Politics, Policy and Law* 39 (1): 171–206.

Gigerenzer, Gerd, Peter Todd, and ABC Research Group. 1999. *Simple Heuristics That Make Us Smart*. New York: Oxford University Press.

Goidel, Robert, Craig Freeman, Steven Procopio, and Charles Zewe. 2008. "Who Participates in the 'Public Square' and Does It Matter?" *Public Opinion Quarterly* 72 (4): 792–803.

Goodman, John, and Gerald Musgrave. 1992. *Patient Power: Solving America's Health Care Crisis*. Washington, D.C.: Cato Institute.

Government Accountability Office. 2013. *Medicare: Higher Use of Costly Prostate Cancer Treatment by Providers Who Self-Refer Warrants Scrutiny*, GAO-13–525, July 19. Washington, D.C.: Government Accountability Office.

Gray, Kathleen, and Robin Erb. 2013. "On Medicaid Expansion, Michigan GOP Gov. Snyder Will Need Legislature's Support." *Governing*, February 7.

Gruber, Jonathan. 2008. "Covering the Uninsured in the United States." *Journal of Economic Literature* 46(3): 571–606.

Gruber, Jonathan. 2011. "The Impacts of the Affordable Care Act: How Reasonable Are the Projections?" *National Tax Journal* 64 (3): 893–908.

Hacker, Jacob. 1997. *The Road to Nowhere: The Genesis of President Clinton's Plan for Health Security*. Princeton: Princeton University Press.

Hacker, Jacob. 2010. "The Road to Somewhere: Why Reform Happened." *Perspectives on Politics* 8 (3): 861–76.

Health Affairs. 2012. "Reducing Waste in Health Care," a Health Policy Brief, *Health Affairs*, December 13, at www.healthaffairs.org (accessed February 11, 2017).

Helderman, Rosalind. 2010a. "Cuccinelli Courting Business Leaders." *The Washington Post*, June 28, p. B1.

Helderman, Rosalind. 2010b. "Cuccinelli Sues Federal Government to Stop Health-Care Law." *The Washington Post*, March 24, p. A1.

Henderson, Michael, and D. Sunshine Hillygus. 2011. "The Dynamics of Health Care Opinion, 2008–2010: Partisanship, Self-Interest, and Racial Resentment." *Journal of Health Politics, Policy and Law* 36 (6): 945–60.

Herman, Bob. 2015. "Billing Squeeze: Hospitals in Middle as Insurers and Doctors Battle over Out-of-Network Charges." *Modern Health Care*, September 29.

Herper, Matthew. 2012. "Inside the Secret World of Drug Company Rebates." *Forbes*, May 10.

Herrick, Devon, and John Goodman. 2007. *The Market for Medical Care: Why You Don't Know the Price; Why You Don't Know about Quality; and What Can Be Done about It*, Policy Report 296, February. Dallas, TX: National Center for Policy Analysis.

Hertel-Fernandez, Alexander, Theda Skocpol, and Daniel Lynch. 2016. "Business Associations, Conservative Networks, and the Ongoing Republican War over Medicaid Expansion." *Journal of Health Politics, Policy and Law* 41 (2): 239–86.

Herzlinger, Regina. 1997. *Market-Driven Health Care*. Reading, MA: Addison-Wesley.

Herzlinger, Regina (editor). 2004. *Consumer-Driven Health Care: Implications for Providers, Payers, and Policymakers*. San Francisco: Jossey-Bass.

Hibbard, Judith, Jessica Greene, and Valerie Overton. 2013. "Patients with Lower Activation Associated with Higher Costs: Delivery Systems Should Know Their Patients' 'Scores.'" *Health Affairs* 32 (2): 216–22.

Higgins, Sean. 2006. "Massachusetts Health Care Law May Be Model for the Country." *Investors' Business Daily*, May 3, p. A1.

Holbrook, Allyson, Matthew Berent, Jon Krosnick, Penny Visser, and David Boninger. 2005. "Attitude Importance and the Accumulation of Attitude-Relevant Knowledge in Memory." *Journal of Personality and Social Psychology* 88 (5): 749–69.

House, James. 2015. *Beyond Obamacare: Life, Death, and Social Policy*. New York: Russell Sage Foundation.

House of Representatives, Oversight Committee. 2014. "Behind the Curtain of the HealthCare.gov Rollout," Majority staff report, September 17. Washington, D.C.: House of Representatives, Oversight Committee.

Hunley, Jonathan. 2010. "Cuccinelli: Federalism Itself Is at Stake in Health Care Debate." *Manassa Journal Messenger* (VA), May 19.

Institute of Medicine. 2001. *Crossing the Quality Chasm: A New Health System for the 21st Century*. Washington, D.C.: National Academy Press.

Jacobs, Lawrence, and Timothy Callaghan. 2013. "Why States Expand Medicaid: Party, Resources, and History." *Journal of Health Politics, Policy and Law* 38 (5): 1023–50.

Jacobs, Lawrence, Eric Lawrence, Robert Y. Shapiro, and Steven Smith. 1998. "Congressional Leadership of Public Opinion." *Political Science Quarterly* 113 (1): 21–41.

Jacobs, Lawrence, Theodore Marmor, and Jonathan Oberlander. 1999. "The Oregon Health Plan and the Political Paradox of Rationing: What Advocates and Critics Have Claimed and What Oregon Did." *Journal of Health Politics, Policy and Law* 24 (1): 161–80.

Jacobs, Lawrence, and Suzanne Mettler. 2011. "Why Public Opinion Changes: The Implications for Health and Health Policy." *Journal of Health Politics, Policy and Law* 36 (6): 917–33.

Jacobs, Lawrence, and Robert Y. Shapiro. 2000. *Politicians Don't Pander: Political Manipulation and the Loss of Democratic Responsiveness.* Chicago: University of Chicago Press.

Jacobs, Lawrence, and Theda Skocpol. 2010. *Health Care Reform and American Politics: What Everyone Needs to Know.* New York: Oxford University Press.

James, Julia. 2013. "Health Policy Brief: Patient Engagement." *Health Affairs* 32 (2): 1–6.

Johnson, Glen. 2007a. "Republican Rivals Try to Rough up Romney over Massachusetts' Universal Health Care Mandate." Associated Press, November 15 (available via Lexis-Nexis).

Johnson, Glen. 2007b. "A Year Later, Some Conservatives Question Romney's Health Care Plan." Associated Press, April 12 (available via Lexis-Nexis).

Johnson, Haynes, and David Broder. 1996. *The System: The American Way of Politics at the Breaking Point.* Boston: Little Brown.

Jones, David. 2013. "Do Major Policy Enactments Affect Public Evaluations of Congress? The Case of Health Care Reform." *Legislative Studies Quarterly* 38 (2): 185–204.

Jost, Timothy. 2007. *Health Care at Risk: A Critique of the Consumer-Driven Movement.* Durham, NC: Duke University Press.

Kahneman, Daniel. 2011. *Thinking Fast and Slow.* New York: Farrar, Straus and Giroux.

Kaiser Family Foundation. 2015. "The ACA and Medicaid Expansion Waivers." November, at www.kff.org (accessed December 18, 2015).

Kale, Minal, Tara Bishop, Alex Federman, and Salomeh Keyhani. 2013. "Trends in the Overuse of Ambulatory Health Care Services in the United States." *JAMA Internal Medicine* 173 (2): 142–48.

Kane, Paul. 2013. "House GOP Pushes Vote on Budget to Next Week." *The Washington Post*, September 12, p. A1.

Karlin-Smith, Sarah. 2016. "Drug Lobby Plans Counterattack on Prices." August 4, at www.politico.com (accessed February 11, 2017).

Karsish, Chris. 2015. "More Conservative Than Most, Indiana's Medicaid Alternative Wins Approval." *Governing*, January 27.

Key, Jr., V.O. 1961. *Public Opinion and American Democracy.* New York: Knopf.

Key, Jr., V.O. 1966. *The Responsible Electorate: Rationality in Presidential Voting, 1936–1960.* Cambridge, MA: Belknap/Harvard University Press.

Kim, Eric, Nansook Park, Jennifer Sun, Jacqui Smith, and Christopher Peterson. 2014. "Life Satisfaction and Frequency of Doctor Visits." *Psychosom Med* 76 (1): 86–93.

Kirsch, Richard. 2011. *Fighting for Our Health: The Epic Battle to Make Health Care a Right in the United States.* Albany: The Rockefeller Institute Press.

Klein, Ezra. 2012. "Unpopular Mandate." *The New Yorker,* June 25.

Klein, Philip. 2015. *Overcoming Obamacare: Three Approaches to Reversing the Government Takeover of Health Care.* Washington, D.C.: The Washington Examiner.

Kriner, Douglas, and Andrew Reeves. 2014. "Responsive Partisanship: Public Support for the Clinton and Obama Health Care Plans." *Journal of Health Politics, Policy and Law* 39 (4): 717–49.

Kurtzman, Laura. 2007. "Schwarzenegger Proposes Sweeping Plan to Cover Uninsured Residents of California." Associated Press, January 9 (available via Lexis-Nexis).

Lambrew, Jeanne, and Jonathan Gruber. 2006/2007. "Money and Mandates: Relative Effects of Key Policy Levers in Expanding Health Insurance." *Inquiry* 43 (4): 333–44.

Laugesen, Miriam. 2009. "Siren Song: Physicians, Congress, and Medicare Fees." *Journal of Health Politics, Policy and Law* 34 (2): 157–79.

Lee, Christopher. 2008. "Simple Question Defines Complex Health Debate." *The Washington Post,* February 24, p. A10.

Levendusky, Matthew. 2009. *The Partisan Sort: How Liberals Became Democrats and Conservatives Became Republicans.* Chicago: University of Chicago Press.

Levey, Noam. 2015. "Indiana's Conservative Medicaid Expansion May Catch on." *Governing,* July 7.

Levey, Noam. 2016. "Trump Used to Rail against Drug Prices. Now the Industry's Allies Are Helping Shape His Agenda." *Los Angeles Times,* November 15.

Levine, Deborah, and Jessica Mulligan. 2015. "Overutilization, Overused." *Journal of Health Politics, Policy and Law* 40 (2): 421–37.

Lieberman, Robert, and Greg M. Shaw. 2000. "Looking Inward, Looking Outward: The Politics of State Welfare Innovation under Devolution." *Political Research Quarterly* 53 (2): 215–40.

Lippmann, Walter. 1922. *Public Opinion.* New York: Macmillan.

Lo Sasso, Anthony, Lorens Helmchem, and Robert Kaestner. 2010. "The Effects of Consumer-Directed Health Plans on Health Care Spending." *Journal of Risk and Insurance* 77 (1): 85–103.

Lopert, Ruth, and Marilyn Moon. 2007. "Toward a Rational, Value-Based Drug Benefit for Medicare." *Health Affairs* 26 (6): 1666–73.

Loprest, Pamela. 2012. "How Has the TANF Caseload Changed over Time?" March, Brief 08. Urban Institute, Washington, D.C.

Lupia, Arthur, and Mathew McCubbins. 1998. *The Democratic Dilemma: Can Citizens Learn What They Need to Know?* New York: Cambridge University Press.

Luskin, Robert, James Fishkin, and Roger Jowell. 2002. "Considered Opinions: Deliberative Polling in Britain." *British Journal of Political Science* 3 (23): 455–87.

Lynch, Julia, and Sarah Gollust. 2010. "Playing Fair: Fairness Beliefs and Health Policy Preferences in the United States." *Journal of Health Politics, Policy and Law* 35 (6): 849–87.

Manchester, Joyce, and Jonathan Schwabish. 2010. "The Long-Term Budget Outlook in the United States and the Role of Health Care Entitlements." *National Tax Journal* 63 (2): 285–306.

Mann, Thomas, and Norman Ornstein. 2006. *The Broken Branch: How Congress Is Failing America and How to Get It Back on Track.* New York: Oxford University Press.

Mann, Thomas, and Norman Ornstein. 2012. *It's Even Worse Than It Looks: How the American Constitutional System Collided with the New Politics of Extremism.* New York: Basic Books.

Manning, Willard, Joseph Newhouse, Naihua Duan, Emmitt Keeler, Arleen Leibowitz, and M. Susan Marquis. 1987. "Health Insurance and the Demand for Medicare Care: Evidence from a Randomized Experiment." *American Economic Review* 77 (3): 251–77.

Markham, Annette. 2005. "Go Ugly Early: Fragmented Narrative and Bricolage as Interpretive Method." *Qualitative Inquiry* 11 (6): 1–27.

Marmor, Theodore. 2000. *The Politics of Medicare*, 2nd edition. New York: Aldine de Gruyter.

Martin, Jonathan. 2017. "With Coverage in Peril and Obama Gone, Health Law's Critics Go Quiet." *The New York Times*, February 21.

Martin, Tim. 2013. "Medicaid Expansion: Michigan House Approves Plan, Sending Proposal to Senate." June 14, Michigan Live (mlive.com), at www.blog.mlive.com (accessed July 15, 2015).

McDonough, John. 2011. *Inside National Health Reform.* Berkeley: University of California Press.

McGillivary, Brian. 2013. "Sen. Walker Lashes Out at Vote Critic." *The Record-Eagle* (Traverse City, MI), September 19.

Mettler, Suzanne. 2011. *The Submerged State: How Invisible Government Policies Undermine American Democracy.* Chicago: University of Chicago Press.

"Michigan Panel Rejects Governor's Medicaid Expansion." 2013. *Legal Monitor Worldwide*, April 12.

Mirowski, Philip, and Dieter Plehwe. 2009. *The Road from Mont Pèlerin: The Making of the Neoliberal Thought Collective.* Cambridge, MA: Harvard University Press.

Moffit, Robert. 2008. "Choice and Consequences: Transparent Alternatives to the Individual Insurance Mandate." *Harvard Health Policy Review* 9 (1): 223–33.

Monahan, John. 2005. "Health Care Effort Turns Heads: Romney Concedes Mandatory Coverage Must Be Affordable." *Telegram & Gazette* (MA), June 27, p. A1.

Mondak, Jeffrey, and Belinda Creel Davis. 2001. "Asked and Answered: Knowledge Levels When We Will Not Take 'Don't Know' as an Answer." *Political Behavior* 23 (3): 199–224.

Montgomery, Lori, and Rosalind Helderman. 2013. "Federal Shutdown Ends as Senate, House Vote to Raise Debt Limit." *The Washington Post*, October 17, p. A1.

Morgenson, Gretchen. 2015. "Side Effects of Hijacking Drug Prices." *The New York Times*, October 4.

Morrisey, Michael. 2005. *Price Sensitivity in Health Care: Implications for Health Care Policy*, 2nd edition. Washington, D.C.: National Federation of Independent Businesses Research Foundation.

Mortensen, Karoline. 2010. "Copayments Did Not Reduce Medicaid Enrollees' Nonemergency Use of Emergency Departments." *Health Affairs* 29 (9): 1643–50.

Muirhead, Russell. 2010. "Can Deliberative Democracy Be Partisan?" *Critical Review* 22 (2): 129–57.

Munro, Alice. 1996. *Selected Stories, 1968–94*. New York: Vintage Books.

Murray, Shailagh, and Paul Kane. 2009. "Senators Close to Health Accord." *The Washington Post*, July 29, p. A-1.

Mutz, Diana. 2006. *Hearing the Other Side: Deliberative versus Participatory Democracy*. New York: Cambridge University Press.

Nease, Robert, Sharon Glave Frazee, Larry Zarin, and Steven Miller. 2013. "Choice Architecture Is a Better Strategy Than Engaging Patients to Spur Behavior Change." *Health Affairs* 32 (2): 242–49.

Newhouse, Joseph. 1992. "Medicare Care Costs: How Much Welfare Loss?" *Journal of Economic Perspectives* 6 (3): 3–21.

Newhouse, Joseph, Robert Brook, Naihua Duan, Emmet Keeler, Arleen Leibowitz, Willard Manning, M. Susan Marquis, Carl Morris, Charles Phelps, and John Rolph. 2008. "Attrition in the RAND Health Insurance Experiment: A Response to Nyman." *Journal of Health Politics, Policy and Law* 333 (2): 295–308.

Newhouse, Joseph, and the Insurance Experiment Group. 1993. *Free for All? Lessons from the Rand Health Insurance Experiment*. Cambridge, MA: Harvard University Press.

Newport, Frank. 2004. *Polling Matters: Why Leaders Must Listen to the Wisdom of the People*. New York: Warner Books.

Nyman, John. 2007. "American Health Policy: Cracks in the Foundation." *Journal of Health Politics, Policy and Law* 32 (5): 759–83.

Oakman, Tara Sussman, Robert Blendon, Andrea Campbell, Alan Zaslavsky, and John Benson. 2010. "A Partisan Divide on the Uninsured." *Health Affairs* 29 (4): 706–11.

Oberlander, Jonathan. 2003. *The Political Life of Medicare.* Chicago: University of Chicago Press.

Oberlander, Jonathan, and R. Kent Weaver. 2015. "Unraveling from Within? The Affordable Care Act and Self-Undermining Policy Feedbacks." *The Forum* 13: 37–62.

O'Keefe, Ed. 2013. "Shutdown Looming, Senate Begins Debating Spending Bill." *The Washington Post*, September 24, p. A3.

Oliver, Thomas, Philip Lee, and Helene Lipton. 2004. "A Political History of Medicare and Prescription Drug Coverage." *The Milbank Quarterly* 82 (2): 283–354.

Oosting, Jonathan. 2013. "Michigan Gov. Rick Snyder Signs Historic Medicaid Plan into Law." MLive News Service, September 16, at www.mlive.com/politics/index.ssf/2013/09/michigan_gov_rick_snyder_signs_6.html (accessed October 25, 2016).

Ornstein, Charles. 2014. "An Obscure Drug Rings Up a Growing Medicare Tab." *The New York Times*, August 5.

Orzag, Peter. 2011. "How Health Care Can Save or Sink America: The Case for Reform and Fiscal Accountability." *Foreign Affairs* 90 (4): 42–56.

Owens, Caitlin. 2016. "Medicare's EpiPen Costs Increased 1,151 Percent, Report Says." September 20, at www.morningconsult.com (accessed September 21, 2016).

Page, Benjamin, and Robert Y. Shapiro. 1992. *The Rational Public: Fifty Years of Trends in American's Policy Preferences.* Chicago: University of Chicago Press.

Parente, Stephen, Roger Feldman, and Jon Christianson. 2004. "Evaluation of the Effect of a Consumer-Driven Plan on Medical Care Expenditures and Utilization." *Health Services Research*: 39 (4): 1189–1209.

Parente, Stephen, Roger Feldman, and Jon Christianson. 2008. "The Impact of Health Status and Price on Plan Selection in a Multiple-Choice Health Benefit Program Including HRA and HSA Options." Working Paper, University of Minnesota, May.

Parente, Stephen, Roger Feldman, and Yi Xu. 2010. "Impact of Full Replacement with Consumer Driven Health Plans on Health Care Cost and Use of Preventative Services." *Insurance Markets and Companies: Analyses and Actuarial Computations* 1 (1): 4–14.

Pauly, Mark. 1994. "Making the Case for Employer-Enforced Individual Mandates." *Health Affairs* 13 (2): 21–33.

Pauly, Mark, Patricia Damon, Paul Feldstein, and John Hoff. 1991. "A Plan for 'Responsible National Health Insurance.'" *Health Affairs* 10 (1): 5–25.

Pear, Robert. 2009a. "Health Care Industry in Talks to Shape Policy." *The New York Times*, February 20, p. A16.

Pear, Robert. 2009b. "Insurers Offer to Soften a Key Rate-Setting Policy." *The New York Times*, March 25, p. B1.

Pear, Robert. 2015a. "Obama Administration Seeks Ways to Rein In Pharmaceutical Costs." *The New York Times*, November 21.

Pear, Robert. 2015b. "Obama Proposes That Medicare Be Given the Right to Negotiate the Cost of Drugs." *The New York Times*, April 28.

Pear, Robert. 2016. "Expect Medicaid to Change, but Not Shrivel, under Donald Trump." *The New York Times*, November 15.

Pear, Robert. 2017. "House G.O. P. Leaders Outline Plan to Replace Obama Health Care Act." *The New York Times*, February 16.

Peden, Edgar, and Mark Freeland. 1995. "A Historical Analysis of Medical Spending Growth, 1960–1993." *Health Affairs* 14 (2): 235–47.

Pethokoukis, James. 2008. "How Tom Daschle Might Kill Conservatism." *US News and World Report*, November 21.

Pollack, Andrew. 2015. "Drug Companies Increasingly Pushed to Explain High Prices." *The New York Times*, July 23.

Ponnuru, Ramesh. 2012. "The History of the Individual Mandate." *The National Review Online*, March 27 (accessed March 4, 2015).

Ponnuru, Ramesh. 2013. "A Chronic Disease." *The National Review* 65 (11): 32–35.

Popkin, Samuel. 1991. *The Reasoning Voter: Communication and Persuasion in Presidential Campaigns*. Chicago: University of Chicago Press.

Potter, Wendell. 2010. *Deadly Spin: An Insurance Company Insider Speaks Out on How Corporate PR Is Killing Health Care and Deceiving Americans*. New York: Bloomsbury Press.

Price, Vincent, Clarissa David, Brian Goldthorpe, Macri McCoy Roth, and Joseph Cappella. 2006. "Locating the Issue Public: The Multidimensional Nature of Engagement with Health Care Reform." *Political Behavior* 28 (1): 33–63.

Prior, Marcus, and Arthur Lupia. 2008. "Money, Time, and Political Knowledge: Distinguishing Quick Recall and Political Learning Skills." *American Journal of Political Science* 52 (1): 169–83.

Pugh, Tony. 2006. "Universal Health Care Launched." *St. Paul Pioneer Press* (MN), April 13, p. 4A.

Rampell, Catherine. 2012. "Mr. Health Care Mandate." *The New York Times*, March 29, p. B-1.

Reschovsky, James, Larisa Converse, and Eugene Rich. 2015. "Solving the Sustainable Growth Rate Formula Conundrum Continues Steps toward Cost Savings and Care Improvements." *Health Affairs* 3 (4): 689–96.

Richey, Warren. 2010. "Health Care Law: Why Federal Judge Struck Key Provision Down." *The Christian Science Monitor*, December 13.

Rigby, Elizabeth, and Jake Haselswerdt. 2013. "Hybrid Federalism, Partisan Politics, and Early Implementation of State Insurance Exchanges." *Publius: The Journal of Federalism* 43 (3): 368–91.

Ringel, Jeanne, Susan Hosek, Ben Vollaard, and Sergej Mahnovski. 2005. *The Elasticity of Demand for Health Care: A Review of the Literature and Its Application to the Military Health System*. RAND Corporation, Santa Monica, CA.

Robinson, James. 1999. *The Corporate Practice of Medicine: Competition and Innovation in Health Care*. Berkeley: University of California Press.

Roden, Judith, and Stephen Steinberg. 2003. *Public Discourse in America: Conversation and Community in the Twenty-First Century*. Philadelphia: University of Pennsylvania Press.

Rogers, Everett M. 2003. *Diffusion of Innovations*, 5th edition. New York: Free Press.

Rose, Shanna. 2015. "Opting In, Opting Out: The Politics of State Medicaid Expansion." *The Forum* 13 (1): 63–82.

Rosen, Jay. 1999. *What Are Journalists For?* New Haven, CT: Yale University Press.

Rosen, Jeffrey. 2012. "Obamacare at the Court: Contortions All Around." *The New Republic* 243 (4921): 11.

Rowe, John, Tina Brown-Stevenson, Roberta Downey, and Joseph Newhouse. 2008. "The Effect of Consumer-Directed Health Plans on the Use of Preventative and Chronic Illness Services." *Health Affairs* 27 (1): 113–20.

Roy, Avik. 2014. *Transcending Obamacare: A Patient-Centered Plan for Near-Universal Coverage and Permanent Fiscal Solvency*. Manhattan Institute for Policy Research, New York, NY.

Ryan, Paul. 2016. "A Better Way: Our Vision for a Confident America." Healthcare report, June 22, at www.abetterway.speaker.gov/_assets/pdf/ABetter Way-HealthCare-PolicyPaper.pdf (accessed November 11, 2016).

Sabik, Lindsay, and Sabina Ohri Gandhi. 2015. "Copayments and Emergency Department Use among Adult Medicaid Enrollees." *Health Economics*, February 25.

Samples, John. 2006. *The Fallacy of Campaign Finance Reform*. Chicago: University of Chicago Press.

Sartori, Giovanni. 1987. *The Theory of Democracy Revisited, Part I*. Chatham, NJ: Chatham House.

Savage, Robert. 1985. "Diffusion Research Traditions and the Spread of Policy Innovations in a Federal System." *Publius: The Journal of Federalism* 15: 1–27.

Scalia, Antonin. 1997. *A Matter of Interpretation: Federal Courts and the Law*. Princeton: Princeton University Press.

Schattschneider, Elmer. 1942. *Party Government*. New York: Holt, Rinehart and Winston.

Schattschneider, Elmer. 1960. *The Semi-Sovereign People: A Realist's View of Democracy in America*. Hinsdale, IL: The Dryden Press.

Schneider, Carl, and Mark Hall. 2009. "The Patient Life: Can Consumers Direct Health Care?" *American Journal of Law and Medicine* 35: 7–65.

Schneider, Saundra, and William Jacoby. 2005. "Elite Discourse and American Public Opinion: The Case of Welfare Spending." *Political Research Quarterly* 58 (3): 367–97.

Schumpeter, Joseph. 1942. *Capitalism, Socialism and Democracy.* New York: Harper and Brothers.

Selby, Joe, Bruce Fireman, and Bix Swain. 1996. "Effect of a Copayment on Use of the Emergency Department in a Health Maintenance Organization." *New England Journal of Medicine* 334: 635–42.

Shalit, Ruth. 1994. "The Wimp-Out." *The New Republic*, February 14, pp. 19, 22 (quote at p. 22).

Shapiro, Robert Y., and Sara Arrow. 2009. "Support for Health Care Reform: Is Public Opinion More Favorable for Obama Than It Was for Clinton in 1994?" Working Paper, Department of Political Science, Columbia University.

Shapiro, Robert Y., and Yaeli Bloch-Elkon. 2008. "Do the Facts Speak for Themselves Partisan Disagreement as a Challenge to Democratic Competence." *Critical Review* 20 (1): 115–39.

Shapiro, Robert Y., and Lawrence Jacobs. 2010. "Simulating Representation: Elite Mobilization and Political Power in Health Care," *Forum* 8 (1): 1–15.

Shaw, Greg M. 2007. *The Welfare Debate.* Westport, CT: Greenwood Press.

Shaw, Greg M. 2010. *The Healthcare Debate.* Santa Barbara, CA: ABC-CLIO.

Sherman, Jake, and Jonathan Allen. 2012. "GOP Adjusts Health Care Strategy." June 12, at www.politico.com (accessed March 9, 2015).

Shih, Chuck, Jordan Schwartz, and Allan Coukell. 2016. "How Would Government Negotiation of Medicare Part D Drug Prices Work?" *Health Affairs Blog*, February 1, at www.healthaffairs.org (accessed February 3, 2016).

Silverman, Ed. 2015. "Orkambi's Slick Unveiling Puts Insurers in a Bind." *Managed Care*, August.

Sinozich, Sofi. (forthcoming). "Trends in Public Opinion on the U.S. Supreme Court 1973–2015." *Public Opinion Quarterly.*

Sirianni, Carmen, and Lewis Friedland. 2001. *Civic Innovation in America: Community Empowerment, Public Policy, and the Movement for Civic Renewal.* Berkeley: University of California Press.

Skinner, Jonathan, Doug Staiger, and Elliot Fisher. 2006. "Is Technological Change in Medicine Always Worth It? The Case of Acute Myocardial Infarction." *Health Affairs* 25: 34–47.

Skocpol, Theda. 1996. *Boomerang: Health Care Reform and the Turn against Government.* New York: W.W. Norton.

Slavin, Lauren. 2015. "Pence's HIP 2.0 Medicaid Alternative Approved." *Herald-Times* (Bloomington, IN), January 28, state news section.

Smith, Sheila, Joseph Newhouse, and Mark Freeland. 2009. "Income, Insurance, and Technology: Why Does Health Spending Outpace Economic Growth?" *Health Affairs* 28 (5): 1276–84.

Solomon, Deborah. 2007. "Health Insurance Gap Surges as Political Issue." Associated Press, January 19.

Sommers, Roseanna, Susan Dorr Doold, Elizabeth McGlynn, Steven Pearson, and Marion Danis. 2013. "Focus Groups Highlight That Many Patients Object to Clinicians' Focusing on Costs." *Health Affairs* 32 (2): 338–46.

Soumerai, Stephen, Thomas McLaughlin, and Jerry Avorn. 1989. "Improving Drug Prescribing in Primary Care: A Critical Analysis of the Experimental Literature." *Milbank Quarterly* 67: 268–317.

Starr, Paul. 2011. "The Mandate Miscalculation." *The New Republic*, 242 (4915): 11.

Starr, Paul. 2013. *Remedy and Reaction: The Peculiar American Struggle over Health Care Reform*. New Haven, CT: Yale University Press.

Stein, Howard. 1983. "The Money Taboo in American Medicine." *Medical Anthropology* 7 (4): 1–15.

Steinbrook, Robert. 2015. "The Repeal of Medicare's Sustainable Growth Rate for Physician Payment." *Journal of the American Medical Association* 313 (20): 2025–26.

Stolberg, Sheryl, and Mike McIntire. 2013. "Republicans Long Planned to Use Budget as Weapon." *The International Herald Tribune*, October 7, p. 1.

Stone, Deborah. 1993. "The Struggle for the Soul of Health Insurance." *Journal of Health Care Policy, Politics and Law* 18 (2): 287–317.

Stremikis, Kristof, Stuart Guterman, and Karen Davis. 2008. "Health Care Opinion Leaders' Views on Payment System Reform." November, Publication number 1189, Volume 13, The Commonwealth Fund.

Strine, Tara, Daniel Chapman, Lina Balluz, David Moriarty, and Ali Mokdad. 2008. "The Associations between Life Satisfaction and Health-Related Quality of Life, Chronic Illness, and Health Behaviors among U.S. Community-Dwelling Adults." *Journal of Community Health* 33: 40–50.

Sturgis, Patrick, Caroline Roberts, and Nick Allum. 2005. "A Different Take on the Deliberative Poll." *Public Opinion Quarterly* 69 (1): 30–65.

Sullivan, Peter, and Sarah Ferris. 2015. "Senate Overwhelmingly Approves 'Doc Fix.'" *The Hill*, April 14.

Tamblyn, Robyn, Rejean Laprise, James Hanley, Michael Abrahamowicz, Susan Scott, Nancy Mayo, Jerry Hurley, Roland Grad, Eric Latimer, Robert Perreault, Peter McLeaod, Allen Huang, Pierre Larochelle, and Louise Mallet. 2001. "Adverse Events Associated with Prescription Drug Cost-Sharing among Poor and Elderly Persons." *Journal of the American Medical Association* 285: 421–29.

Tanden, Neera. 2014. "A Short History of Republican Attempts to Repeal Obamacare." *Politico.com*, January 30 (accessed January 11, 2016).

Tang, Ning, John Stein, Renee Hsia, Judith Maselli, and Ralph Gonzales. 2010. "Trends and Characteristics of U.S. Emergency Department Visits, 1997–2007." *Journal of the American Medical Association* 304: 664–70.

Thaler, Richard, and Cass Sunstein. 2008. *Nudge: Improving Decisions about Health, Wealth, and Happiness*. New Haven, CT: Yale University Press.

Trapp, Doug. 2010. "Health Insurance Mandates Face Resistance from States." *American Medical News* 53 (7): 5.

Tumulty, Karen, and Tom Hamburger. 2013. "Some in GOP Ready to Back Down." *The Washington Post*, October 10, p. A1.

Turner, Grace-Marie, James Capretta, Thomas Miller, and Robert Moffit. 2011. *Why Obamacare Is Wrong for America*. New York: HarperCollins.

Unger, Laura, and Chris Kenning. 2015. "Obamacare Takes Root in Appalachia." *USA Today*, April 17, p. 16A.

U.S. House of Representatives, Committee on Oversight and Government Reform. 2014. *Behind the Curtain of the HealthCare.gov Rollout*. Committee report published September 17; available at www.oversight.house.gov/wp-content/uploads/2014/09/Healthcare-gov-Report-Final-9-17-14.pdf; accessed February 11, 2017. Washington, D.C.

Veroff, David, Amy Marr, and David Wennberg. 2013. "Enhanced Support for Shared Decision Making Reduced Costs of Care for Patients with Preference-Sensitive Conditions." *Health Affairs* 32 (2): 285–93.

Volsky, Igor. 2013. "The Complete Guide to the GOP's Three-Year Campaign to Shut Down the Government." September 20, at www.thinkprogress.org (accessed July 7, 2015).

Walker, Joseph. 2015. "For Prescription Drug Makers, Price Increases Drive Revenue." *The Wall Street Journal*, October 5.

Washington Post Staff. 2010. *Landmark: The Inside Story of America's New Health-Care Law and What It Means for Us All*. New York: Public Affairs.

Waters, Teresa, Cyril Chang, William Cecil, Panagiotis Kasteridis, and David Mirvis. 2011. "Impact of High-Deductible Health Plans on Health Care Utilization and Costs." *Health Services Research* 46 (1): 155–72.

Weisman, Jonathan. 2013. "Boehner Seeking Democrats' Help on Fiscal Talks." *The New York Times*, September 12, p. A1.

Wharam, J. Frank, Bruce Landon, Alison Galbraith, Ken Kleinman, Stephen Soumerai, and Dennis Ross-Degnan. 2007. "Emergency Department Use and Subsequent Hospitalizations among Members of a High-Deductible Health Plan." *Journal of the American Medical Association* 297 (10): 1093–1102.

White, Joseph. 1995. "The Horses and the Jumps: Comments on the Health Care Reform Steeplechase." *Journal of Health Politics, Policy and Law* 20 (2): 373–83.

Whoriskey, Peter, and Dan Keating. 2013. "Expensive Drug Costs Medicare Billions." *The Washington Post*, December 8.

Willemé, Peter, and Michel Dumont. 2015. "Machines That Go 'Ping': Medical Technology and Health Expenditures in OECD Countries." *Health Economics* 24: 1027–41.

Yankelovich, Daniel. 1991. *Coming to Public Judgement: Making Democracy Work in a Complex World*. Syracuse, NY: Syracuse University Press.

Zaller, John. 1992. *The Nature and Origins of Mass Opinion*. New York: Cambridge University Press.

Zhang, Yuting, Seo Hyon Baik, Mark Fredrick, and Katherine Baicker. 2012. "Comparing Local and Regional Variation in Health Care Spending." *New England Journal of Medicine* 367: 1724–31.

Index

About the Author

Greg M. Shaw is professor and chair of the Political Science Department at Illinois Wesleyan University. He holds a PhD from Columbia University. His research focuses on health care and welfare politics, and American public opinion. He is the author of two previous books published by ABC-CLIO, *The Welfare Debate* (2007) and *The Healthcare Debate* (2010). Some of his other work on American social policy has appeared in *Political Research Quarterly*, *Political Science Quarterly*, and other venues, including *Public Opinion Quarterly*, where, from 2008 to 2016, he served on the editorial team.